DATE DUE			

A G

PRETEXTS

*Reflections on Literature
and Morality*

by André Gide

Selected, Edited, and Introduced

by Justin O'Brien

Essay Index Reprint Series

BOOKS FOR LIBRARIES PRESS
FREEPORT, NEW YORK

The essays in this volume were translated from the
original French texts by Angelo P. Bertocci, Jeffrey J.
Carre, Justin O'Brien, and Blanche A. Price.

*The essays in this volume are translations from the follow-
ing French works:* PRÉTEXTES *and* NOUVEAUX PRÉTEXTES, *published by Mercure de France, and* DIVERS *and* INCIDENCES,
published by Gallimard.

INTERNATIONAL STANDARD BOOK NUMBER:
0-8369-2396-0

LIBRARY OF CONGRESS CATALOG CARD NUMBER:
75-156648

PRINTED IN THE UNITED STATES OF AMERICA

Contents

Introduction by Justin O'Brien

The ancient opposition between creator and critic no longer prevails in tutored minds. The examples of Goethe, Coleridge, Poe, Baudelaire, and more recently, of Valéry and Eliot have shown conclusively that the creative and critical faculties can cohabit harmoniously. Today no one contests the justice of Baudelaire's statement in his *Art romantique* that "It would be an unheard-of event in the history of the arts for a critic to become a poet, a reversal of all psychic laws, a monstrosity. On the other hand, through a natural development, all great poets eventually become critics. . . . It would be stupendous for a critic to become a poet, and it is impossible for a poet not to contain a critic. Hence the reader will not be shocked that I look upon the poet as the best of all critics." As Baudelaire's application of the term "poet" to Wagner and Delacroix makes clear, he called any maker, any creator in whatever art, a poet, always careful to spell the name with a dieresis rather than a grave accent to indicate its particular nobility.

In the same spirit, André Gide—who quoted part of Baudelaire's statement as an epigraph to his essay on Paul Valéry—could confidently state elsewhere: "Criticism is at the base of all art." Partly because Gide himself produced so much critical work and partly because, like every great artist, he never failed to temper his lyricism with an almost infallible critical sense, Gide belongs in the tradition of the Goethes, Baudelaires, and Eliots—in the tradition of the creator-critics.

Indeed, Gide's voluminous work—and why shouldn't it be voluminous, for he lived beyond his eighty-first birthday while devoting himself all life long to letters? —counts no fewer than fifteen volumes of criticism. Besides, his *Journals* and the eight published collections of his letters are brimming with additional critical comments. His second published book, which appeared before he was twenty-two, was already a work of literary and artistic criticism, for the *Traité du Narcisse* of 1891 with its "theory of the Symbol" stated better than had Gide's elders the theoretical bases of symbolism. Six years later, when his own volumes of poetry and imagination already numbered six, he brought out discreetly in an anonymous edition of a hundred and twelve copies his first *Réflexions sur quelques points de littérature et de morale* and began contributing his incisive literary criticism to periodicals with the brilliant review of Barrès's novel *Les Déracinés* in *L'Ermitage*. The controversy which that single review called forth from the best established (Emile Faguet) and the most thoughtful (Charles Maurras) of French critics led Gide to reply in 1903 with "The Poplar Tree Quarrel," which established him as one of the keenest polemicists in a nation of keen polemicists. But in the meantime he had written his series of ironic "Letters to Angèle" for the *Ermitage* between 1898 and 1900, followed up the question of nationalism in his lyrical "Normandy and Bas-Languedoc" in *L'Occident* for 1902, and brought out three major essays on aesthetics in *L'Ermitage* between 1900 and 1903. In addition, he had succeeded his friend Léon Blum in 1901 as regular reviewer for *La Revue Blanche* and held the post for several months. And somehow he had found time—while issuing his first plays and his first novel—to write for still other periodicals in Paris and Brussels.

In 1903, then, as a thirty-four-year-old writer who already had to his credit an impressive list of titles representing the different genres of poetry, satire, fiction, drama, aesthetic theory, and travel impressions, André Gide brought out his first volume of collected essays, *Prétextes,* with the subtitle that he had used before and was to use again: "Reflections on Some Points of Literature and Morality." When the volume reached the poet Paul Claudel in distant China, where he occupied a diplomatic post, he wrote Gide enthusiastically: "Why don't you write criticism deliberately and out of preference? It seems to me that you have to a very high degree the critical sense, which is as rare as the poetic sense and perhaps rarer. Not everyone knows what a man or a tree means. At least I know of only two critics who really deserved the name: Baudelaire and Poe."

Obviously Gide liked the title *Prétextes,* sufficiently vague so that it suited equally the literary, moral, and social problems that he treated with the same urgency. Eight years later he brought out his *Nouveaux Prétextes* and still later a third collection of essays, which he called in his *Journals* "a third volume of *Prétextes"* until he hit upon the title *Incidences (Angles of Incidence).*

Most of the essays in those collections of 1911 and 1924 had first appeared in the *Nouvelle Revue Française,* or *N.R.F.,* which Gide had founded in 1908-9 with a group of friends and disciples. For he had eventually tired of writing for others' journals, in which he could never feel altogether at home. To be sure, he shared many ideals with Adrien Mithouard, the editor of *L'Occident,* and with the young groups in Brussels that had launched *La Vie Nouvelle* and *Antée.* In Edouard Ducoté's *Ermitage,* to which he had begun contributing at the age of twenty-five, he had his greatest chance to influence editorial policy, but even there he had to get along with his fellow editor Remy de Gourmont, whose theories and attitudes were often at variance with Gide's. The moment he could set the policy for his own monthly review, he revealed, as St.-John Perse wrote of Gide the editor, "a sense of values that has never failed; an innate sense of the mainsprings and, as it were, the very essence of French genius; a predilection for the human in the written word and for the universal in the individual work; the perception, in everything, of its quality, urgency, veracity." From 1909 until 1940 the *N.R.F.* illustrated, in its choice of authors as in its rigorous standards, the Gidian critical spirit through which it influenced several generations of French writers.

Like Baudelaire, Gide had early "resolved to inquire into the *why,* and to transform into knowledge the pleasure he took in art." It is in this way that the creator who questions his art and that of his predecessors and contemporaries inevitably becomes a critic. When the young novelist Jean Prévost wrote: "André Gide could have been the greatest of French critics; he probably knew this, and yet he preferred to be a creator," Prévost subscribed to the outmoded distinction between creation and criticism. More recently, Albert Camus implied the necessary fusion of the two activities by stating: "When Gide criticizes, he creates."

Gide himself, who never tired of quoting Oscar Wilde to the effect that "the imagination imitates, whereas the critical spirit creates," would have liked Camus's remark. Commenting on Wilde's paradox and thinking more of self-criticism than of the criticism of others, he once pointed out that "among the multiple phantasms that the imagination offers us in disorder, the critical spirit must choose. Any drawing implies a choice—and it is a school of draftsmanship that I admire most in France.' But the exercise of that choice in one's own work leads inevitably to judging the work of others, and that Gide considered his critical essays no less important than his "works of imagination" there can be no doubt. The critical spirit persisted in him to the very end. Late in life he took pride in the fact that many of his "judgments of still unclassified works were premonitory." During his last ten years he brought out no fewer than seven volumes of literary and art criticism, and his *Ainsi soit-il* (*So Be It*), which he left in manuscript, abounds in literary judgments.

The qualities that made André Gide a good critic are simply those that are doubtless essential to any good critic. From early in life, to begin with, he was a voracious reader in many domains, and a critical reader. From the first part of his *Journals* we have some indication of this, but we shall know far more if ever anyone publishes the *Cahier de lectures* that he kept between the ages of twenty and twenty-three and that Dr. Jean Delay has drawn upon so effectively in his *Jeunesse d'André Gide*. There he not only listed his readings but also commented on them at length; for instance, this is what he noted with adolescent punctuation at twenty about Turgenev's *Virgin Soil*: "Infinite charm—one of the most beautiful books read—mysterious psychology, quite intimate though without analysis—monochrome poetry—odd feeling of life, personal vision of things, even at times somewhat upsetting just because of his great personality. . . . How I should like to have said all that; I should have said it at less length, with, if I could, less mystery in the external life and more (but I should have been wrong) in the inner life."

Secondly, Gide always read with an open mind, free of prejudices. Some of his keenest critical remarks are found in a little volume he entitled *Un Esprit non prévenu* (*An Unprejudiced Mind*), which opened with the statement that there is nothing rarer than such a mind ("or one that has managed to get rid of its prejudices"). It was this quality that allowed Gide to note the flaws of his close friends Jammes, Ghéon, Claudel, and Rivière, and the virtues of those he did not in general admire. It was this that kept the *N.R.F.* from

ever becoming the organ of a school, because it chose
its contents according to their quality rather than according to the tendencies they manifested. Claudel
could fulminate periodically when he found *his* contribution beside one that he considered shockingly revolutionary by Proust or Valéry or Léautaud, but the
review continued to maintain its eclecticism by just
such juxtapositions.

Thirdly, and this is perhaps but an illustration of
the same independence, Gide commonly looked upon
the past and the present with the same eye. No *laudatur
temporis acti,* he never revered the past merely because
of its venerability. Rather, he sought occasions to reread and to revise his scale of values. "Originality,"
he said, "is perhaps never so rare as in matters of judgment; and never less noticeable, for an opinion, though
it is original, does not necessarily differ from the accepted opinion; the important thing is that it does not
try to conform to it. I can admire Bossuet, La Fontaine,
or Voltaire for the same reasons as the most banal
literary handbook and not suffer at all from this. But I
can perceive later that some of my admirations were
not altogether sincere and that my judgment on that
point was merely conforming." He knew as well as anyone that, to the classics as to mythology, each generation
brings a different thirst.

Surely it was that same independence of judgment,
free from the shackles of fashion, that gave Gide such
an extraordinary ability to judge his contemporaries.
At the height of their popularity he saw the shallowness
of Catulle Mendès and Edmond Rostand and was willing to risk his reputation on his apparently untimely
condemnation of such dramatists as Bataille and Bernstein. On the other hand, he stood among the first to
applaud the genius of Claudel and Valéry, of Perse and
Proust, of Larbaud and Giraudoux and Romains, of
Malraux and Camus. Instead of being shocked by such

manifestations as Dada and Surrealism, he hailed them as healthy signs of youth in revolt and helped them to express themselves fully.

When the poet Heredia died, whom he had known and frequented, Gide refused to force his voice and exaggerate his grief as is the custom. Keeping his usual intonation, he dared to say: "Conservative minds scarcely like innovators, who are inclined to look upon the conservatives as useless and tedious tardigrades and profess a scorn for them. It is essential, however, that neither that right nor that left should cease to be represented in our literature. I shall even go so far as to say that the innovating element owes its strength to the excellence of the conservative element, and the soundness of its forward thrust is in direct ratio to the solidity of its purchase. Many an error of the Romantic drama is due perhaps to the lack of firmness of Ponsard, and I do not think it really paradoxical to assert that those who owe the most to Heredia today are not his imitators but, on the contrary, the practitioners of free verse and Symbolists, those, it so happens, who, repulsing him, find in his work a smooth, hard, vibrant surface from which to spring forward."

In this case Gide sacrificed the conventional, ceremonial praise of the famous poet who had died to a truthful evaluation of his place in modern letters. And this is doubtless why we can still read today with profit his few pages on Heredia written in 1905.

Gide's attitude toward Heredia might suggest that he was always on the side of the innovators. To be sure, he did consistently show a particular understanding for the artists "who ever fight [as Apollinaire says] on the limitless frontiers of the future."

But, on the other hand, for those who do not see classicism as he did, Gide's lifelong preoccupation with classicism might belie a view of him as a champion of the *avant-garde*. Probably no other question, not even that of nationalism or the glorification of individualism, returns more insistently in his critical writings than the question of classicism. Indeed, that concept subsumed for Gide the idea of individualism and that of universality, which he opposed to the doctrine of such nationalists as Barrès, Maurras, and their followers. Whether he is composing a lecture on "The Limits of Art" in 1901, writing his answer to Faguet's criticism of Baudelaire in 1910, prefacing the *Fleurs du mal* in 1917, jotting down his fragmentary "Thoughts on Greek Mythology" of 1919, indulging in one of his ironic "Notes to Angèle" in 1921, or compressing into a few lines his reply to a periodical's inquiry in 1923, André Gide constantly returns to the concept of classicism, ever refining and sharpening his definition, as if it provided the solution to all critical problems.

First of all, he sees classicism as "the demonstration of a hierarchy" in which the word is subordinated to the sentence, the sentence to the page, the page to the work, and the writer's individuality to the work he is writing. In other words, individuality must be sacrificed to achieve true individualism. The really classical writer becomes human to the point of banality (what Baudelaire called *"la forme banale de l'originalité"*), thus achieving a truly personal form by dominating his inner romanticism. Just as Valéry spoke of a prior romanticism that all classicism presupposes, so Gide stated that "the classical work will be strong and beautiful only by virtue of a romanticism brought under control." As late as 1940 Gide summed up this whole argument in his *Journals* by saying: "The sole art that suits me is that which, rising from unrest, tends toward serenity."

Even though, France being the last refuge of true classicism, the terms "classical" and "French" are almost equivalent to Gide, he refuses to reject romanticism—which such great writers as Ronsard, Corneille, and Hugo manifest in their writings. Upon reading

Pierre Lasserre's attack on romanticism, Gide applauds because he has always had a horror of romanticism and artistic anarchy—not so much, as he ironically notes, because they are un-French as because their inaesthetic character shocks his French sensitivity. But Hugo, Michelet, and so many others have enriched French literature, and he would not reject them. In another essay he loyally points out that Pascal, Rabelais, and Villon are often as far as possible from classicism, that Shakespeare, Michelangelo, Beethoven, Dostoevsky, Rembrandt, Dante, and Cervantes (all of whom he admires) are not by any stretch of the imagination classical.

The classicism that Gide admires—an art of delicate understatement which consistently expresses the general through the particular—embodies a whole ensemble of moral qualities, the first of which are modesty and reserve. Here Gide's strict Protestant upbringing and his refined aestheticism combine to harmonize an artistic ideal with a way of life. Hence the struggle between classicism and romanticism takes place in every individual mind and "the greater the initial revolt of the object brought under subjection, the more beautiful is the work of art," as he says. And one might add: the more beautiful is the personality. This is the sense in which true classicism is not conservative, but creative.

By constantly returning to the consideration of classicism, which he frequently discovers in the most unlikely men and works, André Gide takes the concept out of the musty atmosphere of the classroom and revivifies it as a perenially young and robust force operating upon art. His own deep interest in such non-French writers as Shakespeare and Dostoevsky, Blake and Browning and Nietzsche (to mention but a few of those on whom he wrote), made him keenly conscious of French classicism's narrowness, its distrust of the foreign. In the same comprehensive and basically optimistic spirit, he never ceased to combat La Bruyère's

idea that we are born too late, when everything has
been said by our predecessors. On the contrary, alert
to the present and curious about the future, he could
never have taken the side of the ancients in any new
quarrel of the ancients and the moderns. Once he called
on his readers to try to imagine a Balzac, a Walt Whit-
man, or a Dostoevsky among the Greeks, and then
proposed a new definition of genius: "Genius is an
awareness of hidden resources."

Delacroix alluded ironically to "that immutable concept of the beautiful, which changes every twenty or
thirty years." It might be said that at the basis of Gide's
thought also lies the belief that beauty is not one but
many, not stable but changing. This it was that allowed
him, while entertaining standards and an intimate set
of criteria, to keep an open mind before new manifestations in the arts. In his last piece of writing, at the age
of eighty, Gide wonders whether he would be capable
of recognizing at once an utterly new form of beauty
at variance with all tradition. He shudders to think
that a new Rimbaud or Lautréamont might strike him
as a madman. Aesthetic judgments continued to be
important to him until the day he died, and he longed
for the elasticity of mind and eye that he had known
in youth. Despite such regrets, however, he had remained throughout life, as St.-John Perse said of him,
"more—and how much more!—than a man of culture
or a man of taste. A writer of the noble French type
well known to old Europe, who according to his needs
extended the uses of every literary form, freely tran-
scending the implications of the occasion." Indeed, the
moment we go beyond his provocative and highly personal study of Dostoevsky (the one purely critical work
by Gide that has hitherto been available in English)
to his occasional literary and moral essays, we find that
he was equal to every passing pretext—a lecture before
a literary society, a preface, an imaginary interview, a

memorial tribute, an open letter, a book review, or a mere answer to a periodical in need of copy—because he had simply to refer to a whole background of serious thought on the subject.

February 1959

Four Lectures

Because of his fundamental modesty and his horror of
rhetoric, André Gide gave but few lectures throughout
his long life. Yet when it came to collecting his critical
essays in *1903* under the title of Prétextes *and again in
1911 under that of* Nouveaux Prétextes, *he set two lectures at the head of each volume. He did this doubtless
because, although they were not his earliest critical
writings, they represented his most general and sustained literary essays of the early years.*

*Gide was just a few months over thirty on 29 March
1900, when he delivered "Concerning Influence in
Literature" before a Brussels literary society named La
Libre Esthétique. In accepting an invitation to Brussels
he was not so much following the example of Baudelaire's Belgian lecture tour of the sixties as yielding to
his friendship for Maeterlinck, Verhaeren, and the Belgian painter Théo Van Rysselberghe (1862-1926) to
whom he dedicated this essay.*

*In the summer of 1901 he wrote "The Limits of Art,"
which he was to give as a lecture in connection with the
Independent Artists' Show of that year. But, as he stated
in a note appended to the printed essay, "a mishap prevented me, to my extreme regret, from delivering it. I
offer here merely the outline." In a letter of July 1901,
however, to the poet Paul Valéry, he had already admitted having polished the text as a favor to* L'Ermitage,
*the periodical that was publishing it. He appropriately
dedicated the published essay to his close friend Mau-*

rice Denis (1870-1943), a painter of the neoimpressionist school.

"The Importance of the Public" was delivered at the court of Weimar on 5 August 1903, in conjunction with an exhibit of French paintings. The invitation to Gide had been instigated by Count Harry von Kessler (1868-1937), the German diplomat and essayist.

Gide gave ("very badly" according to him) "The Evolution of the Theater" before La Libre Esthétique of Brussels on 25 March 1904, after others had talked of the evolution of poetry, of painting, and of music. He dedicated his essay to the Belgian poet Emile Verhaeren (1855-1916), an active member of the group he was addressing.

The first three lectures were originally published in the monthly literary review L'Ermitage in 1900, 1901, and 1903, respectively. The fourth first appeared in 1904 in a volume containing Gide's first two plays, Saül *and* Le Roi Candaule.

CONCERNING INFLUENCE IN LITERATURE

To Théo Van Rysselberghe

Ladies and Gentlemen:
    I come before you to defend influence.
    It is usually agreed that there are good and bad influences. I shall not take it upon myself to distinguish between them. It is my intent to make an apologia for all influence.

I am of the opinion that there are very good influences which do not seem so in the eyes of all.

I am of the opinion that an influence is neither good nor bad in an absolute manner, but only ·ı) relation to the one who experiences it.

I am of the opinion especially that there are bad natures for whom everything is bad luck and for whom everything turns out wrong. On the other hand, there are those for whom everything is positive nourishment, who change stones into bread; Goethe said: "I devoured *everything* that Herder was willing to teach me."

First an apologia for influence; then an apologia for him who influences: these will be the two points of our talk.

In his memoirs, Goethe speaks with feeling of that period in his youth when he yielded to the outer world and allowed each creature to act upon him indiscriminately in its own way. "The result was a marvelous relationship with each object," he wrote, "such perfect harmony with all of nature that every change of place, hour or season affected me intimately." With delight he submitted to the most fleeting influence.

There are many kinds of influences—and I have reminded you of this passage from Goethe because I should like to have the opportunity to speak of *all* kinds of influence, each important in its own way, beginning with the most vague, the most natural, and saving for the end the influence of men and their works. These I put last because they are the most difficult to discuss; they are the ones people try to resist, or claim they try to resist, the most. As I intend to defend these influences as well, I should like to prepare my apologia to the best of my ability—that is, slowly.

It is impossible for man to avoid influences; the most

carefully protected, the most sheltered man still feels them. The fewer they are, the stronger they may be. If we had nothing to entertain us during bad weather, the slightest shower would make us disconsolate.

So impossible is it to imagine a man completely free of all natural and human influences that when heroes have appeared who seemed to owe nothing to outside influences, whose development would not be explained, whose actions, sudden and incomprehensible to the outsider, were such that no human motive seemed to inspire them, people have preferred to attribute their success to the influence of the planets, so impossible is it to imagine anything human completely, profoundly, and basically spontaneous.

In general it can be said, I think, that those who had the glorious reputation of obeying only their star were individuals on whom personal influences, chosen influences, acted more powerfully than general influences—I mean those influences that act upon a whole nation, at least upon all the inhabitants of a single city at one and the same time.

There are, therefore, two groups of influences: common influences and particular influences: those that a whole family, a group, a country, experience at one and the same time; those that a single being is the only one in his family, his city, or his country to experience (whether this be voluntary or not, conscious or not, deliberately chosen or imposed). The first group tend to reduce the individual to the common type; the second to contrast the individual with the community. Taine was concerned almost exclusively with the former; they flattered his determinism better than the other type.

But as we alone can invent nothing new for ourselves, those influences that I call personal—because in some way they will set the individual who experiences them apart from his family, his society—will, moreover, be the influences that bring him into fellowship with a stranger who also undergoes them or has undergone them. Thus new groups are formed, a kind of new family created with members sometimes widely dispersed; bonds are forged, relationships founded. Some unknown man in Moscow and myself can be impelled toward the same idea, and despite the intervening centuries Jammes can link to Virgil—and to that Chinese poet whose charming, modest, and ridiculous poem he read to you last Thursday.

The common influences are necessarily more *gross*— it is not by chance that the word "gross" has become synonymous with "common"—and I should be almost ashamed to speak of the influence of food if Nietzsche, for example (speaking in paradox, I feel certain), did not claim that drink has a considerable influence on the manners and thought of a people in general: that the Germans, for example, by drinking beer, deny themselves forever any claim to that lightness, that keenness of spirit which Nietzsche attributes to the French drinkers of wine. But let us not tarry.

However, I repeat: the less gross the influence, the more it acts in a particular manner. And even the influence of the weather, the seasons, although it acts upon crowds at the same time, acts upon them in a more delicate and sensitive way, provoking very different reactions. Heat exhausts one person but animates another. Keats could work well only in summer, Shelley only in autumn. And Diderot said: "When the wind is high, I feel madness in my spirit." Many other statements could be quoted—but let us not tarry.

The influence of climate ceases to be general and therefore becomes perceptible to the one who experiences it as a foreigner. Now we come to particular influences, the only ones in truth which rightly concern us here.

When Goethe, arriving in Rome, exclaimed: *"Nun bin ich endlich geboren!"* At last I am born!—when he tells us in his correspondence that upon entering Italy he seemed to become aware of himself and to *exist* for the first time—he certainly gives us reason to consider the influence of a foreign country as most important. Moreover, it is a *chosen influence:* I mean that excluding unfortunate exceptions, forced trips or exiles, we usually choose the country in which we want to travel: the choice in itself is proof that the country has already exercised some influence on us. In fact we choose a certain country for the very reason that we know it will have an influence upon us, because we hope for, wish for that influence. We choose those very places we think capable of influencing us the most. When Delacroix set out for Morocco, it was not to become an Orientalist, but rather, through the understanding he was to gain of more lively, more delicate, more subtle harmonies, to become more "perfectly aware" of himself, of the colorist that he was.

I am almost ashamed to quote the words of Lessing, repeated by Goethe in his *Elective Affinities,* words so well-known that they bring a smile to the lips: *"Es wandelt niemand unbestraft unter Palmen,"* words that can be translated only by the fairly trite sentence: "No one walks with impunity under palm trees." What is meant but this: Though we leave their shade, we are never the same again.

I have read a certain book; when I finished it, I closed it, put it back on the shelf in my library—but there were certain words in that book which I cannot forget. They have penetrated so deeply into me that I cannot separate them from myself. Henceforth I am no longer the one I was before I met them. Though I may forget the book in which I read them, though I may even forget that I read them, though I remember them only imperfectly—this is of little importance; no longer will I be the person I was before I read them. How can their power be explained?

Their power comes from the fact that they have merely revealed to me some part of myself of which I was still in ignorance; for me they were only an explanation—yes, but an explanation of myself. It has already been said that influences act through resemblances. They have been compared to mirrors of a kind that might show us not what we already are in actual fact, but what we are in terms of our latent characteristics.

"This inner brother which you have not yet become," said Henri de Régnier. I shall compare them more exactly to that prince in Maeterlinck's play who came to awaken princesses! How many sleeping princesses we carry about inside ourselves, unknown, awaiting only a touch, a sound, a word to awaken them!

In comparison, what matters all I learn through my brain, all that I succeed in retaining only by a great effort of memory? Thus through learning I can accumulate within me weighty treasures, a great encumbering wealth, a fortune, a precious instrument, to be sure, but forever, to the end of time, *different* from me. The miser puts his gold pieces into a coffer; but as soon as the coffer is closed, it is as if it were empty.

This type of knowledge bears no similarity to that intimate cognition which can be termed rather recognition mixed with love—true recognition, like a feeling of kinship rediscovered.

When in Rome I read the wonderful poetry of Keats beside his solitary little tomb, how naïvely I allowed his gentle influence to penetrate me, touch me tenderly, recognize me, ally itself to my most undefined, uncertain thoughts. So much so that when, ill, he exclaims in the "Ode to a Nightingale":

> O for a draught of vintage! that hath been
>   Cool'd a long age in the deep-delved earth,
> Tasting of Flora and the country-green,
>   Dance, and Provençal song, and sunburnt mirth!
> O for a beaker full of the warm South! . . .

I seemed to hear this marvelous plaint spring from my own lips.

To grow in learning, to open up to the world, seems truly to be finding those to whom we are akin.

I can sense that we have now come to a sensitive and dangerous point and that it is going to become more difficult and delicate to speak. Now it is no longer a question of—shall I say, natural influences—but rather of human influences. How can it be explained that whereas *influences* seemed up to this point to be a fortunate means of personal enrichment—or at least a divining rod that allowed us to discover our inner wealth—how can it be explained that we suddenly are on the defensive, that we are afraid (especially nowadays, may we stress), that we are distrustful? Now influence is looked upon as a baneful thing, a sort of attack upon the self, a crime of *lèse*-personality!

The reason is that just now, even though we do not profess individualism, we each claim to have our personality. As soon as this personality is no longer very robust, as soon as it seems to be a little vague, shaky, feeble to ourselves or to others, we are haunted by the fear of losing it, and our truest joys may be spoiled.

The fear of losing our personality!

In this blissful literary world of ours, we have been in a position to know of and to encounter many fears: the fear of the new, the fear of the old—recently the fear of foreign languages, etc.—but the most sordid, the most stupid, the most ridiculous of all these fears is indeed the fear of losing one's personality.

"I don't want to read Goethe," a young man of letters said to me (do not be afraid, I mention names only when I praise), "I don't want to read Goethe because he might make an impression on me."

Does it not seem that one must have reached a point of unusual perfection to think that one can change only for the worse?

The personality of a writer—that delicate, coddled personality which people are afraid of losing, not so much because they consider it precious, but because they always think it is about to be lost—consists too often in never having done one thing or another. It might be called a privative personality. To lose it is to want to do what one has promised himself not to do. Some ten years ago a volume of stories appeared which the author had entitled *Stories without Who or Whom*. The author had created for himself a kind of originality, a special style, a personality that consisted in never using a relative pronoun. (As if the "who's" and "whom's" did not continue to exist all the same!) How many authors, how many artists have no further personality than just that! If the day were to come when they consented to use "who" and "whom" like everybody else, they would quite simply melt into the common, infinitely varied mass of humanity.

It must be admitted, however, that the personality of the greatest men is made up partly of their lack of comprehension. The very accentuation of their characteristics requires a violent limitation. No great man leaves us a vague image of himself, but rather a precise, well-defined one. It can even be said that a great man's failures to understand define him.

Does not the fact that Voltaire understood neither Homer nor the Bible, that he burst out laughing when he encountered Pindar, trace the visage of Voltaire just as much so as if a painter, tracing the contour of a face were to say to it: You shall remain within these limits.

Does not the fact that Goethe, the most intelligent of beings, did not understand Beethoven—who played for him the Sonata in C-sharp minor (commonly called the "Moonlight Sonata") and then cried out to him in anguish as Goethe remained coldly silent: "But Master, if *you* say nothing to me—then who will understand me?"—does not this define both Goethe—and Beethoven—at the same time?

These cases of lack of comprehension can be explained in this way: they most certainly are not stupidity; they are dazzlement. Thus, every great love is exclusive and the admiration of a lover for his mistress makes him blind to all beauty that is different—Voltaire's love of wit made him insensitive to lyricism. Goethe's adoration of Greece, of the pure and smiling tenderness of Mozart, made him fear the passionate outburst of Beethoven—and made him say to Mendelssohn, who played the beginning of the Symphony in C minor to him: "I feel only astonishment."

It can perhaps be said that every great producer, every creator, is accustomed to projecting such an abundance of spiritual light, such a cluster of rays upon the point he wants to operate upon—that all the rest around about appears dark. Is not the opposite of this the dilettante: he who understands everything precisely because he loves nothing passionately, that is, exclusively?

But when I consider a man not endowed by fate with a personality composed exclusively of shadow and dazzling light, who tries to create for himself a restrained, composite individuality by depriving himself of certain influences, by putting his mind on a diet, like a sick person whose weak stomach can take only a small choice of similar foods (but then he digests these so well!)—when I consider such a man, how much I love the dilettante, who is incapable of producing and speaking, but who makes the charming decision of being attentive and truly creates a career for himself by learning how to listen admirably. (We lack listeners today just as we lack schools—one of the results of this need for originality at any cost.)

The fear of resembling everyone else makes such a

man seek out henceforth what characteristics, strange and unique (thus, often incomprehensible), he can display. Immediately he finds them to be of such primary importance that he thinks he must exaggerate them even though it be at the expense of all the rest. I know one man who will not read Ibsen because he says he "is afraid of understanding him too well." Another has sworn never to read foreign poets, for fear of losing "his pure feeling for his own language."

Those who fear influences and shy away from them are tacitly confessing the poverty of their souls. There is nothing very new to be discovered in them since they do not want to co-operate with anything that might lead to such a discovery. And if they are so little concerned about finding relationships, I think it is because they sense ahead of time that they are very badly connected.

A great man has but one concern: to become as human as possible—or, to put it better, to become *commonplace*. To become commonplace, Shakespeare commonplace, Goethe, Molière, Balzac, Tolstoy. . . . The wonderful thing is that he thus becomes more personal. But he who flees humanity for himself alone, succeeds only in becoming special, bizarre, incomplete. It is perhaps appropriate to recall the words of the Gospel here —I do not think I am distorting the sense: "Whosoever shall seek to save his life [his personal life] shall lose it; and whosoever shall lose his life shall preserve it." (Or, to translate more faithfully the Greek text: ". . . shall make it truly alive.")

This is why we see great minds never fearing influences, but on the contrary seeking them with a sort of eagerness like the eagerness of *being*.

What wealth a man like Goethe must have felt in himself for having refused himself nothing—or, according to Nietzsche, "for having *said no*"—to nothing! The life of Goethe seems to be the history of the influences that touched it: national with *Götz*; medieval with *Faust*;

Greek with *Iphigenie;* Italian with *Tasso;* and finally
even toward the end of his life, Oriental with the *Divan*
of Hafiz, whom Hammer had just translated—an influence so powerful that at more than seventy years of age
he learned Persian and wrote, in turn, his *Divan.*

The same frenzy of eagerness which urged Goethe
toward Italy urged Dante toward France. Because he no
longer found sufficient influences in Italy, he hastened
up to Paris to subject himself to the influence of our
University.

However, we must be convinced that the fear I speak
of is a very modern fear, the final result of the anarchy
of letters and the arts; before our time this fear was
unknown. In every great period, people were content
with being an individual without seeking to be one,
so that the artists of the great periods seem to be united
by an admirable common background, and through the
assembly of their faces, involuntarily diverse, they form
a sort of society, almost as admirable in itself as is each
isolated face. Was a Racine preoccupied with the question of not resembling any other? Is his *Phèdre* diminished because it was born, so they say, of a Jansenist
influence? Is the seventeenth century in France less
great for having been dominated by Descartes? Did
Shakespeare blush when he put the heroes of Plutarch
on the stage, when he revived the plays of his predecessors or his contemporaries?

One day I suggested a subject to a young man of letters which in my opinion seemed so right for him that
I was almost astonished that he had not yet thought of
using it. A week later when I saw him again, he was
heartbroken. What was the matter with him? I was worried. "Well," he said to me bitterly, "I don't want to
blame you in any way, because I think you had a good
motive in giving me advice—but for heaven's sake, dear
friend, no more advice! On my own I have just come
upon the subject that you mentioned to me the other

day. What in heaven's name do you expect me to do with it now? You suggested it to me. Never shall I be able to believe that I found it on my own." Truly I am not inventing this. I confess that it took me some time to understand—the poor fellow feared that he would not be personal.

They say that Pushkin said to Gogol one day: "My young friend, a subject came into my head the other day —to my mind a wonderful idea—but I feel that I myself can do nothing with it. You ought to take it; judging from what I know about you, it seems to me that you would make something of it." Something! Indeed, out of this little subject, this germ that Pushkin placed in his mind one day, Gogol merely made *Dead Souls,* the book that established his fame.

We must go further and say: The great periods of artistic creation, the fecund periods, have always been those most profoundly influenced. Such was the period of Augustus, influenced by Greek letters; the Renaissance in England, Italy, and France, influenced by the invasion of antiquity; and so on.

Today we can be filled with regret and sadness by the contemplation of those great periods during which, as the result of a series of fortunate conjunctions, all that had been sowed and planted long before, all that was germinating and ready to burgeon, suddenly grew, flowered, and burst forth. In our period, which I admire and love, it is good, I think, to seek out the source of this reigning anarchy that can excite us momentarily by making us mistake the fever it gives us for a superabundance of light—it is useful to understand that in a great period what creates unity in all its luxuriant diversity, in spite of everything, is the fact that all the minds composing the period come and drink of the same waters.

Today we no longer know at what spring we should

drink—we think that too many waters are salutary, and off we go to drink, one here, another there.

Also no single great spring leaps forth, but the waters that flow in sluggishly from all sides just barely seep up and then lie stagnant over the soil—and the appearance of the literary soil of today is quite appropriately that of a marsh.

There is no longer any powerful current, any channel, any great general influence that groups and unites minds by subjecting them to some great common belief, to some great dominant idea—no longer a *school*, in short —but through fear of resembling one another, through horror at having to submit, through uncertainty as well, through skepticism and complexity, there is a multitude of individual little beliefs for the triumph of strange little individuals.

If great minds then avidly seek influences, it is because, certain of their own wealth, filled with intuitive feelings, ingenuous with the inherent abundance of their being, they live in the joyous expectation of their new flowering. On the other hand, those who do not have any great inner resources seem always to be possessed by the fear of seeing the tragic words of the Gospel confirmed in their case: "Unto him who hath shall be given, but from him who hath not shall be taken away even that which he hath." Here again life it pitiless for the weak. Is this any reason for fleeing from influences? No. But in doing so, the feeble will lose the little originality that they claim as their own. Gentlemen: *all the better!* This is what allows a school to exist.

A school is always composed of a few great leading spirits—and of a whole succession of other subordinate minds, which form the neutral terrain, as it were, upon which the several great minds can rise. In a school we first note a subordination, a sort of tacit, unconscious submission to several great ideas that several great minds propose and lesser minds accept as Truths. Whether they *follow* these great minds or not matters little to me! For the great minds will lead them further than they would have been able to go by themselves. We cannot know what Jordaens would have been without Rubens. Thanks to Rubens, Jordaens sometimes rose to such heights that my example seems to be badly chosen, and on the contrary, it seems that I must place Jordaens among the great leading spirits. And what if I were to speak of Vandyke who, in turn, creates and dominates the English school?

Another thing: often a great idea cannot be expressed, completely amplified, by one great man; a single great man is not enough; several must work on it, take up the raw idea, restate it, refract it, bring out a final bit of beauty in it. Though it is no longer true today, the greatness of Shakespeare, which seemed immeasurable, long prevented us from seeing, from admiring the admirable pleiad of dramatists who surrounded him. Was the idea that the Dutch school extols satisfied by a Terborch, a Metsu, a Pieter de Hooch? No, no, each of these was necessary, and how many others as well!

Finally, let us say that if a whole series of great minds devote themselves to extolling a great idea, others also are needed to devote themselves to exhausting it, compromising it, destroying it. I do not mean those who oppose it—no—they usually are of service to the idea that they fight; they strengthen it by their hostility. But I speak of those who think they are serving it, of that unfortunate progeny in whom the idea finally runs its course. And since humanity consumes and must consume a fearful number of ideas, we must be grateful to the latter who, by finally exhausting what fertility still remained in the idea, by transforming it from the Truth it seemed to be, back into Idea, finally empty it of all essence and force those who come later to seek a new idea—an idea that, in turn, assumes for a time the appearance of Truth.

Blessed be the Mieris and the Philip van Dycks for having completed the ruin of the dying Dutch school and for breaking down its last attempts at domination.

In literature you may be certain that it is not the partisans of free verse, not even the greatest, the Vielé-Griffins, the Verhaerens, who will probably conquer the Parnassian school, it is the Parnassian school itself that is destroying itself, compromising itself through its last pitiable representatives.

Furthermore, let us add that those who fear influences and refuse to undergo them are punished in this admirable manner: as soon as an imitator is spotted, he will be found among these men. They do not behave well in the presence of others' works of art. Their fear makes them stop at the surface of the work; they taste it with the tip of their tongues. What they are looking for is the very outer secret (they think) of the material, the craft —precisely what exists only in an intimate, profound relationship with the very personality of the artist, what remains the most inalienable of his gifts. They have a total lack of understanding of the reason for the existence of the work of art. They seem to think they can take the skin of a statue, blow air into it, and get a new work of art.

The true artist, eager for deep influences, will pore over the work of art attentively, trying to forget it and to penetrate more and more deeply into it. He will think of the finished work of art as a stopping point, a frontier; in order to go further or to go elsewhere, we must change our cloak. The true artist will seek the man behind the work and will learn something from him.

Open imitation has nothing to do with pastiche, which always remains an underhanded, hidden labor. It would take too long to discuss by what aberration we no longer dare imitate today—besides, all this is interdependent, and if you have followed me up to this point, you will have no trouble in understanding me. Great artists have never feared to imitate.

Michelangelo first imitated the ancients with such determination that he amused himself by passing off certain of his statues—among others a sleeping Cupid—as statues found in excavations. Another statue of love was, so they say, buried by him and then exhumed as a Greek marble.

In his frequentation of the ancients, Montaigne compares himself to the bees, which "pillage the flowers here and there" but afterward turn them into honey, "completely their own"—it is no longer, he says, "thyme or marjoram."

No: it is Montaigne, and so much the better.

Ladies and Gentlemen:

I had promised myself that after I had defended the person influenced, I would defend the one who influences. At present it no longer seems to me very useful to do so. The defense of the one who influences—would it not be the defense of the "great man"? Every great man has an influence. As an artist, his writings, his pictures are only a part of his work; his influence explains the work, carries it further. Descartes is not just the author of the *Discourse on Method,* the *Dioptrics,* and the *Meditations;* he is also the author of Cartesianism. Sometimes even, the influence of the man is more important than his work; sometimes it breaks loose from the work and seems to follow after it only at a great distance; of such a nature was the influence of the *Poetics* of Aristotle on seventeenth-century France, after centuries of inaction. Finally, sometimes the influence is the only work, as it happens to be in the case of those two unique figures whom I scarcely dare mention: Socrates and Christ.

The responsibility of great men has often been discussed. Christ has not been blamed as much for all the martyrs of Christianity (for the idea of salvation is mingled with that of martyrdom) as certain writers are still blamed for the sometimes tragic repercussions of their ideas. They say that after *Werther* there was an epidemic of suicides. The same was true in Russia after a poem of Lermontov. "After this book," said Mme de Sévigné speaking of the *Maximes* of La Rochefoucauld, "there is nothing left to do but to kill oneself or to become a Christian." (She said this certainly thinking that there would be no one who would not prefer a conversion to death.) I think that those who have been killed by literature already bore death within themselves; those who have become Christians were already admirably ready to do so; influence, I have said, creates nothing: it awakens.

I shall be careful, moreover, not to try to diminish the responsibility of great men; for their greater glory we must even imagine it as heavy and as terrifying as possible. I do not know that it has made any one of them draw back. On the contrary they seek to take on even greater responsibility. Whether we suspect it or not, they consume a tremendous amount of life round about them.

But they are not always led on by the need for domination: often in the artist, the submission of others which he achieves has very different causes. They might be summed up, I think, in a few words; *he is not sufficient unto himself.* His consciousness of the importance of the idea that he bears torments him. He is *responsible* for it. He feels this. This responsibility seems the most important to him; the other will come only later. What can he do? Alone! He is overwhelmed! His five senses are not sufficient to seize the world; his twenty-four hours a day are not enough in which to live, to think, to express himself. He is not sufficient for his idea, this he feels. He needs surrogates, substitutes, secretaries. "A great man," says Nietzsche, "does not have only *his own* mind, but also those of all his friends." Each friend will lend him his senses; much more: will live for him. He becomes a center (in spite of himself), he looks at everything and takes advantage of it. He influences: others will live and act out his ideas for him; they will risk the danger of testing them out in his stead.

It is sometimes difficult to defend great men. So at this point I do not want to say that I approve of this; I merely say that without it the great man is hardly possible. If he wanted to produce works without influencing, he would first of all be poorly informed, not having been able to see his ideas in operation; then he would be of no interest to us, for only what influences us is important to us. That is why I was careful first to make an apologia for those who are influenced—in order to be able to have the courage to say now that they are indispensable to great men.

Ladies and Gentlemen:

Now I have said to you just about what I wanted to say. Perhaps the several ideas that I have tried to examine here will appear to you either paradoxical or false. However, I shall consider myself satisfied if, though it may be only to protest against them, I have caused to be born in you—I mean awakened in you—certain ideas that you will find accurate and beautiful. This is what we may call influence through reaction.

TRANSLATED BY BLANCHE A. PRICE

THE LIMITS OF ART

To Maurice Denis

Ladies and Gentlemen:

If I come before you to speak of the limits of art, it is not, you may be assured from the outset, that I have any pretensions to extend them or contract them, even if only for the duration of this talk; and if the title I have allowed myself seems somewhat general, my boldness, I assure you, lies not in choosing this title but in speaking before painters.

The time is past when fugitives from the Rouault atelier could repeat with Gautier the *ut pictura poesis* of Horace; but if today's writers have understood the danger, at the very least the peril, of attempting to use a pen like a brush, painters have for their part understood equally well that *ut poesis pictura* would be a yet more disastrous theory for them. Literature and painting have fortunately split ranks, and I do not come here to complain of that; quite the contrary. It is admitted in advance that I have no special knowledge of your craft and that you have no special knowledge of mine. You cultivate your garden; we cultivate ours; sometimes, briefly, we exchange views; that is all.

And yet, if you have been kind enough to ask me to address you today, and if I do so gladly, it is not just because we are neighbors. There are some among us who think that it is not good that artists of the same country, each absorbed in his art, fail to recognize that, above the questions peculiar to literature and those peculiar to painting, there are certain questions of a more general aesthetic—which, resolved, make Poussin brother to Racine, for example—and before which we can forget for a moment, you, gentlemen, that you are painters, I, that I am a writer, the better to remember that we are, whatever the differences of craft, alike artists.

Accordingly, if I enter upon such generalities today before you, I say that it indicates not boldness but, on the contrary, a modest fear that I do not possess, for any more specialized theme, the necessary competence.

A few days ago, leafing through, rather than reading, one of the thick volumes of the *Cours de philosophie positive,* I was struck by a curious passage. It concerned the praise of science; Auguste Comte knows what he is about in these matters and praises well—a little the past, more the present, almost unreservedly the future— I say "almost," for at the same moment, inspired by a healthy horror of hyperbole and a concern for precision, Comte, after having vaguely outlined what the future could hope for and expect from science, adds that expectations and hopes cannot be boundless. It is, he writes (in these general terms, for I quote from memory) almost easy to forecast now the limits of science and indicate what areas will remain forever closed to it; we know, for example, that science will never penetrate (do you know what example he cites?) the chemical composition of the stars. A generation passed by, and then simply, without fanfare, spectrum analysis seized upon those same stars, and science crossed the boundaries assigned to it.

From this page by the positivist, in which, despite everything, I find more to admire than to ridicule, is born, together with the title and theme of this talk, a heightened diffidence about myself, like the strange warning that it was folly to claim to fix in advance lim-

its to the power of human intelligence—a folly as pre-
sumptuous as to claim to foresee and outline beforehand
the future manifestations of this power and believe them
limitless.

Doubtless new means make possible to the scientist
new investigations and findings, each new discovery
serving in its turn as means; but just for that reason, and
because in this way each new effort is added in, each
preceding effort is absorbed and loses identity, so that
the only thing seen in each part is the most recent victory. It can thus be said (and it is almost tautological)
that the limits of science retreat always in the direction
of its progress. The question is: How far will it go?

In art, the question is posed in a quite different way.
There the word "progress" loses all meaning, and as
Ingres has written, it is impossible to hear or read calmly
the statement: "Observing the immense progress that
painting has made from the Renaissance to our days, the
present generation profits accordingly." So the question
ceases to be: How far will painting, music, and literature go? But still more vaguely: *Where* will they go?
And still less can we hazard an answer.

For the true artist it is no longer a matter of finding
support in the art that preceded him in order to go
further, but rather of changing the aim of art, of inventing a new direction for his effort. And if, on the one
hand, the work of past artists retains its value intact, to
the extent that each seems always to have almost invented afresh and as though defined his art, each new
genius seems first to wander, so resolutely does he turn
his back on the others; each new genius seems again to
raise the problem of the art itself. After a Johann Sebastian Bach, it is thought: This is what music is. A Mozart
appears, and a Beethoven; after them, it can again be
said: So this is what music is—unless, already alerted,
the thought comes: What is music? And one understands
finally that music is neither Bach, nor Mozart, nor

Beethoven; that each of them could delimit only himself; and that music, in order to continue to be, must be
continually something other than what it was through
them alone.

Nevertheless, in failing to comprehend that there is
nothing more to attempt along *his* path, that the artist
of genius indicates only the direction to him, seems to
guide, but guides only toward himself, and impedes the
drive of his follower as a backdrop impedes the actor's
progress on stage, some think they will discover in following him a secret of beauty, a recipe, or rather, that
the success of the master will relieve them of effort. They
think that since the master finds, it is no longer important to seek; it is not precisely that they imitate him (at
least they deny it stoutly), but they follow his direction;
it is a powerful eddy which draws them in its wake; and,
still better, since the master has fallen silent first, they
hope to go beyond him, to go further than he, interpreting as boldness their folly and the inhibition that keeps
them from striking out on another course. It is through
them that the form of a master becomes a formula, since
no inner necessity continues to motivate it. It is through
them and upon them that night falls suddenly, because
their eyes, dazzled by the sun already set, see always the
star rather than the darkened west—while behind them,
at the other pole of art, a rejuvenated sun, radiant, is
rising.

Truth (that is, the wellspring) is always found this
side of the genius, never beyond him.

What is this territory the genius leaves behind him as
he advances to his frontiers—the territory from which
each artist must start forth? What is the common ground
of masterpieces? What is the element always at hand?

Must I here excuse myself, gentlemen, because I propose to say to you only what is banal and simple? How
could things so deliberately general be other than very
simple and familiar? And if I, nevertheless, dare repeat

them, it is because in art it is good, I believe, that each
new generation set itself the problem anew; that it never
accept ready-made the solution handed down by those
of the recent past and their predecessors; it must not
forget that all those of the past whom it admires are precisely those who have themselves initially and laboriously
sought their answer. Every thirty years it is good to repeat or to contradict Lessing's *Laokoon*. A great perspicacity existed always in the great periods; we still often
seem devoid of it; too enamored often of what we already possess, we lose the sharp sense of what we do not
have, of what our defects are; and I see, alas, more artists
today than *works of art*, for the taste for the latter is lost,
and the artist too often assumes he has done enough
when, in his painting or his verses, he has shown that he
is an artist, esteeming the role of reason, intelligence,
and will, in a word, composition, as negligible and vul-
garizing. The abominable discredit into which the mediocrity of the great charlatans has cast what used to be
called (what we no longer dare call without a smile) "the
great genres" is the reason that painters no longer dare
paint "scenes" and writers are no longer capable of
carrying a subject more than a year in their heads, that
in literature, in painting, and in music, impressionism
and topical poetry dominate.

The neutral ground to which, swinging about, we
must always return, you understand, of course, gentlemen, is simply nature. Shall I, too, speak of this famous
return to nature, which some deem the one key to all
art, so that once it is mentioned, everything has been
said?

The return to nature!—but what does it mean? To
what else can we return? What can be found outside
ourselves save nature, everywhere and everlasting? And
what can we find within ourselves except nature, too?

The true return to nature is the definitive return
to the elements—death. But so long as there persists in

man some will to live, some being, is it not in order to combat death, and is it not proper for the artist to oppose nature and affirm himself?

How and why not understand that these two natural states—the external and the intimate—are opposed, and that it is according to the second that the first is shaped and informed? Has this inward nature therefore less value than the other? Is the right to be refused it or the power denied it without which there can be no work of art? Or is it claimed that all of art is confined to realism?

I trust that this opinion, formulated in all its excessiveness, has no defenders, but is this not the point made when it is said that the artist must be absent from his work, that objectivism is one of the conditions of art? So that if it were possible to attain the goal set, all personality withdrawing before the thing represented, one work would no longer differ from another save by the subject recorded, and the artist would really satisfy himself by assuring permanence for some vain contingency —unless, reluctant to immortalize any chance object, he chooses . . . but by what right even choose? And what is "interpretation" if not choice, too, more subtle and more detailed, which, like the choice of "subject," comes always to indicate, if not my will, at least my preference?

And do you not think precisely that it is fitting to make of this very choice, of this originally instinctive and later voluntary preference, the very affirmation of art, of art which is not in nature, of art which is not natural, art which the artist alone forces upon nature, and with difficulty?

But here again let us be precise:

For then it is not sufficient to say (as you know has been said) that the work of art is a part of nature seen through a temperament. In this specious formula, neither intelligence nor the will of the artist is accounted for. Therefore the formula could not satisfy me.

The work of art is a work of the will. The work of art is a work of reason. For it must find in itself its sufficiency, its end, and its complete justification; forming a whole, it must be able to isolate itself and rest, as though out of space and time, in a satisfied and satisfying harmony. If a painting stops at the frame, it is not because the frame is there, but, quite the contrary, the frame is there because there the painting stops. And the frame is there, marking this stop, only to make that isolation more evident.

In nature, nothing can isolate itself or come to a stop; everything continues. Man can try it out, can propose beauty; nature immediately takes possession of it and disposes of it as she wills. And here is demonstrated the opposition of which I spoke: here man is submissive to nature. In the work of art, on the other hand, he submits nature to himself. "Man proposes and God disposes," we have been told; this is true in nature; but I shall sum up the opposition I indicate by saying that, in the work of art, on the contrary, *God proposes and man disposes.* And every self-styled producer of works of art who is not conscious of this may be anything you wish; but not an artist.

Cut the sentence in two, take for credo only one of the two elements of the formula, and you will have the two great artistic heresies continually locked in battle through refusal to understand that it is from their union and compromise alone that art can be born.

God proposes: this is naturalism, objectivism, call it what you will.

Man disposes: this is apriorism, idealism . . .

God proposes and man disposes: this is the work of art.

Why must it be that for each new false "school" the absurd intransigence of sects comes to see salvation in the exclusive adoration of one of the two parts of the formula? Yesterday it was: *man disposes;* today it is *God proposes.* And at one moment they seem not to know that the artist has full rights to *dispose;* at another they seem not to know *that he must dispose only what nature proposes to him.*

For if I was speaking a moment ago of the artist as standing in opposition to nature, and seemed to see in the work of art first an affirmation—would it be in order now to extol individualism, and shall we have torn ourselves from one excess only to hurl ourselves toward another? What is an individualistic artist? What is an anti-individualistic artist? Let him leave "convictions" to others. They cost him too dear and they deform him too greatly. The artist is neither of one camp nor of the other; he is at every point of conflict.

Art is a moderate thing. And surely I do not mean by that either that the most accomplished work of art would be that which should maintain itself equidistant from idealism and realism; certainly not! and the artist can indeed come as near as he dares to one of the two poles, but on condition that his heel not leave the other; one leap further, and he loses his footing.

"One does not show his greatness," as Pascal said, "by being at one extremity, but by touching the two at the same time and filling the space between."

And the limits of art, the search for which we quickly abandoned as long as we demanded that they be external, these limits, gentlemen, which are neither obstacles nor challenge, we find them wholly within: they are limits of extension.

There is a point of extreme tension, beyond which the work suddenly gives way and loses form—or has never been formed. The limits are in the artist alone; fortunate is he who widens them within himself, pushes them back, and who, just as each should will to do, submits the maximum possible to himself, the maximum possible of nature.

Ladies and Gentlemen:

Though all this was known to you, if I permitted myself to repeat it, it is because you who think thus are
but a very small group and the number of false artists
and heretics is very great.

TRANSLATED BY JEFFREY J. CARRE

THE IMPORTANCE OF THE PUBLIC

To Count Harry von Kessler

When it was proposed—with a courtesy and kindness
for which I have, and shall always have, the liveliest
gratitude—that I come to speak at Weimar, my first impulse was a feeling of great joy. Weimar, where I have
dwelt so often in my imagination, Weimar, into which
I strove to deserve an entree by the cult I have for
Goethe! It seemed that, in calling me to her, the old city
had felt my love from afar and was accepting my homage.

But as the time approached for my journey, joy gave
way to fear. My anticipations, so ardent and delightful
at the beginning, soon turned to fear and apprehension.
I speak at Weimar! Speak! I who love silence best.
Speak to you, whose language I do not know very well;
to let you judge, through me, what a Frenchman may
have to say at Weimar . . . I wondered at my audacity.
It seemed to me that Goethe, the Grand Duke Charles

Augustus, the Duchess Amalia, and Mme von Stein would come secretly to prevent me.

The welcome that Weimar has proffered nevertheless overcame my misgivings, and if I still feel somewhat ill at ease as I speak before auditors with whom, for all their kindness, I am not very well acquainted, and if my talk should bear some trace of this, at least I can already appreciate on my own account the enormous importance for the artist, no matter who he is, of one factor: to feel in the presence of a public; to feel toward it certain precise duties. That is exactly what I propose to discuss today—and perhaps also, if you will permit, that other side of the question, much more difficult to envisage here: the duties (pardon the word, I use it only because I find none to replace it), the duties of the audience toward the artist. It is furthermore quite difficult to approach the question from one side only; these duties (and once more I use the word "duty" only to indicate a kind of obligation freely accepted), these duties are practically reciprocal, more or less consciously agreed upon, and imply each other. Action and reaction collaborate. And the time when the voice of the artist wins its way to the public ear is also the time when the attention of the public knows how to attract the voice of the artist. The artist who makes himself heard is the artist that the public allows to speak.

What is meant by the public?

I should not like to give the name "public" to just any group, but to a chosen society, capable of enjoying artistic emotions, just as I keep the name "artist" only for those capable of evoking these emotions in such a public.

A public—it has become so rare a thing that nowadays we hardly know what it is. We must look too often into the past if we are to find it. A public—the artist, alas! has had to learn, for better or for worse, to do without it; and we often lose the very consciousness of its absence; or we even go so far as to claim that the artist *should* do without it. That is a dangerous mistake, and I should like to tell you why.

"They behave just as if there were nobody in the theater," Goethe writes to Schiller, speaking of the actors in Leipzig. "Nobody in the theater"—what freedom for the actor! His personality can triumph without obstacle. A year later, still speaking of the Leipzig theater, Goethe again writes to Schiller: "These actors comport themselves just as if there were nobody in the theater. They recite, they declaim without the slightest concern for being understood, turning their backs to the spectators, etc., etc.—and this so-called naturalness (or as we should put it today, this sincerity) is always on the increase." Elsewhere, on the same subject: "Naturalism and a spirit of do-just-as-you-please could go no further; not a trace of art, nor even of a sense of the fitting!" And Goethe adds: "These are symptoms of a public not inattentive or spoiled—but completely uncultivated." And how could Goethe not have been thrice shocked, he who at the court of Weimar had been given such a lesson in what a public was and could be!

"It is a strange enterprise," said Molière, "to make *les honnêtes gens* laugh." A strange enterprise, and no doubt arduous, but to it we owe his masterpieces. And if Molière had aimed only at getting a laugh out of his cook, as they allege he did also, we should have had other *Fourberies de Scapin,* and other *Monsieur de Pourceaugnac*—but I doubt that he would have given us the *Misanthrope.* These *"honnètes gens,"* as Molière called them, equally distant from a court a little too rigid in its ways and a pit a little too free, were precisely what Molière looked upon as *his public;* and this was the public to which he addressed himself. The court of Louis XIV represented formalism; the pit represented naturalism; they represented *good taste.* Without the court such a social set, I think, would not have been possible. This is the set that maintained for so long the admirable French tradition.

This set of *honnêtes gens* may have made mistakes, but it permitted, demanded, and maintained in its day that inestimable thing: style. Style everywhere; in writing, in furniture, in the plastic arts, in music, in morals —the style that the invasion of the best seats by the pit often makes impossible in our day.

The artist cannot get along without a public; and when the public is absent, what does he do? He invents it, and turning his back on his age, he looks toward the future for what the present denies. Other artists (if I still dare to use the name) who want a public at all costs, buy one at cut rates from among the mob. But let us begin with the first group of artists.

It was a dangerous thing for art to separate itself from life, dangerous for both art and life. When the artist no longer felt his public close to him, when art could no longer justify its existence or find its meaning and its normal use in society, in manners and morals, it did not pine away, as might have been expected—it did not die, for the laurel of Apollo is tenacious and dies only with the race itself that once nourished its deep roots; no, art did not die: it lost its head. The history of modern art is inexplicable otherwise; the artist who has lost a sense of his public is not fated to stop producing but rather to produce works with no destination. As painter, he paints without knowing what wall his canvases will adorn; as sculptor, he does not know the source of the light that will bathe his statues; as poet, he sings and is the only one who listens to his song.

I am not going to assert that the great artists of the
Renaissance or of antiquity would have blamed the doctrines of so-called "art for art's sake"—what I do assert
is that they would not even have understood them. For
these doctrines are evidently born of a period when art,
having lost its place, unable to take an active part in and
to find its true role in the common life, proudly isolates
itself, becomes conceited, and scorns to appreciate those
who had failed in appreciation. And while the artist,
with no external check left upon the excellence of his
work, is inevitably driven to seeking only his own ap-
proval, a new kind of criticism is born and thrives—
what is called a "subjective criticism"—which, finding
no support in a society without taste, judges works
nevertheless (for the need to judge never dies) in the
name of a personal taste and the amount of pleasure
they provide.

Our hatred today for all dogmatic criticism (it seems
dogmatic to us today when there is no dogma to hold us
together) is something worth noticing. It is something
very significant. All the great periods of lofty artistic
production relied on an extremely dogmatic criticism,
a criticism whose strength of conviction came of the
consciousness of cultivated society, which backed it up.
The critic spoke in the name of that society; it provided
the reasons for applauding or hissing, even though the
dictates of a spontaneous good taste would have been
enough.

For the important thing was to create, with as little
artificiality as possible, a certain idea of the beautiful—
let us say rather, a certain *ideal*—to establish certain

rules, to call attention to certain limits, short of which or beyond which art could not go and still be true to itself or avoid losing caste.

Art manifests itself in many forms; its schools are legion, but I doubt that any civilization, at a given moment of its history, is capable of producing and supporting more than one. When Louis XIV, in the presence of some paintings by Teniers, cries: "Get those grotesques out of my sight," he is displaying a very intelligent narrowness. Had Teniers been three times as great, there still would have been good reason for such language, and even if applied to Rubens or Velázquez. Nor was it at all necessary for Louis XIV to be a connoisseur of painting. The art of a given society comes of its need—and not of a greater or lesser degree of understanding. It was in order to produce a Poussin that French society refused to understand Teniers, and reciprocally, a society capable of producing Teniers—or Rubens—was bound to misunderstand Poussin.

Our time lays claim to a greater intelligence, especially to a greater eclecticism. In the galleries of our museums, those great cemeteries of art, we have learned how to make Poussin, Velázquez, and Rubens cohabitate. We enjoy Cranach and Dürer; but we also enjoy Delacroix and Goya. That goes without saying, and it is as it should be. Indeed, not to enjoy them, in our day, would be silly: we can't learn all over again how to be ignorant. Likewise, who can blame us for enjoying at a concert, and for applauding, after a Mozart quartet, the "Ride of the Valkyries." But we must admit that such intelligent eclecticism, which is our pride and joy, proves, alas! that art is no longer a natural product, that it no longer responds to some specific need of the public, and that a society formless in itself, without any distinct ideal to express in any particular style, is likely to accept, just as they come, all the ideals of the past and every ideal that every one of the new artists proposes. And the artistic tradition, which so many successive generations had built up so high, seems like a tree whose powerful trunk is finally beginning to die, society no longer being there to prune and to cut off at the base the multitude of suckers that shoot up (for the root is still alive). Those suckers are often admirable, taken singly, but the sap finally becomes exhausted—and they lead nowhere.

An artist can do very little by himself. Who can say what persistent effort, what effort continuously the same through successive generations of a society alert in its concentration was needed to inform, for instance, Greek beauty in both art and life? To give form to one's ideal—that is to say, to draw its portrait—remained a kind of moral and civic duty in the eyes of that admirable people for whom morals, civilization, and art all concurred.

We are astonished today at the polychrome architecture of the Greeks, and it offends our "good taste." It is the abstract needs to which our temples and public monuments have been responding for some time that makes their color white. We no longer understand that the Greek temple, born of the soil, was not far from the earth, and that the gods, in order to live there, took on the colors of life.

Art, in spite of the expanse of heaven it reflects, is thoroughly human. Since it exists in a constant relation with the beliefs of men, nothing can be more deadly to it than religion in a state of overrefinement. A people without art means that the gods live far from men, whom they dominate without loving them. Likewise, as soon as man's abstract reason dares see in form's varied cloak nothing but a lie and a disguise, that divine hypocrisy, religion, returns to a heaven which is itself receding into the distance; divinity abandons the earth; the color of the temple itself begins to grow pale.

The birth of art is possible in our world only where heaven touches earth, I mean when gods become men or men gods. No art has ever been the offspring of monotheism—be it Jewish or Arab—and in order for Christianity once more to image forth the earth, the formless God of the prophets had to descend into man and become flesh. Even that was not enough. Art, not subject to Christianity but subjecting Christianity to itself, appropriated everything it could lay its hands on, everything that deigned to accept a human form: apostles, prophets, saintly men and saintly women, a whole multitude of demigods. Could the Holy Ghost or the theological virtues be painted? Christian art, insofar as it is Christian art, hardly exists, and is perhaps a contradiction in terms. But society (for we must come back to it) asked art to be Christian; art immediately pretended it was, and the artist served up what people ordered.

A singular misunderstanding in our day leads us to extol above everything else in a work of art the virtue of sincerity. Above all, we say, an artist must be sincere. What that means everyone finds it hard to say. The artists of the Renaissance bothered very little about such questions. Nor need we think that the myth of a common religion, to which the society of that day required artists to submit, hurt their personalities. On the contrary. The cloak of Catholic hypocrisy with which they were forced to clothe their naturally pagan sensuality served the ends of art; and we have seen the greatest among them cloak themselves in the greatest hypocrisy. In the most hypocritical ages art has ever shone at its brightest. Hypocrisy is a condition of art. It is the public's duty to force the artist into hypocrisy.

The important thing was that there should be a society and that it should voice its demands. What it asked for was glorification, exaltation, intoxication. It had the good taste to require all this to be artistic, for it was a cultivated society. And the artist, that cupbearer, kept pouring it out. But if there is to be this thirst for art, society must no longer be hungry. Material hunger was indeed quite satisfied, and as for hunger of soul and spirit, the Church attended to that. For only satiated societies have an art, when their spirit is ready for rest in the acceptance of a religion or dogma. Skepticism is perhaps the beginning of wisdom; but where wisdom has its beginning, art reaches its end.

"Panem et circenses," cried the Roman mob; bread first, games next. The free play of art cannot be enjoyed on an empty stomach. Only after the dinner do we bring the artist onto the stage. His function is not to nourish but to intoxicate.

I like to think that Plato who, out of love for truth presents, in the *Gorgias,* a Socrates indignant at flattery —that is, at seductiveness, at intoxication of spirit— is the same who likewise closes his Republic to artists, and who, speaking of Orpheus, calls him "cowardly," adding, "like the musician that he was."

The work of art is a form of flattery. The artist errs not when he flatters, but when he flatters indiscriminately. The value of flattery depends upon the personal worth of the flattered. The public should insist upon its being exquisite and should refuse to be flattered by less than the best. The public does not make the artist, but it can make demands upon him, at least, and refuse to be easily satisfied. It can be hard on the mediocre and exalt only the best; its culture will give it the right to be exacting.

Such a public, I repeat, must no longer be hungry; it must be cultivated; in addition it must be restricted in numbers. They were small in number, the Greeks of Pericles, the *"honnêtes gens"* of Louis XIV, the high-born Italians of the Renaissance, and the nobles of the court of Weimar. So small in number that each of them could feel personally flattered by the work of art.

The danger of the crowd, of this "completely uncul-tivated" public of which Goethe spoke, is due not only to its lack of culture, so that it can be too easily flattered, but also to its very bigness. A heterogeneous public coming from anywhere and everywhere, having in com-mon neither culture nor taste, ideals nor duties—where can flattery take hold? It can be flattered as a whole only in spots common to all men—in the most common spots. This is felt especially in the theater. Praised be Weimar society for its susceptibility to flattery in *Iphigenie* and *Tasso*! How good it is for the artist to know whom he is addressing! No longer knowing this, in our own day, the artist either breaks with his age and seals himself off, as has happened to the best; counting on posterity to compensate for the present, he flatters ideally an un-known public, vaguely dispersed in the future, or else (but does he still deserve the name of artist?) flatters a crowd hit or miss. The resulting works I will not name, but you know them.

The danger of the crowd, alas! is this: that it is also hungry. It demands that it be fed. Old dogmas no longer suffice. Today the mind rejects them like food without savor. The oldest questions raised all over again, with regard to which the elect of another day had a quiet and sensitive understanding, now wait for new answers.

Moral questions, social questions especially. (May heaven preserve Weimar from them!) Consequently no disinterestedness in the work. The thesis play is invented—rather hollow fare. But what does it matter if the crowd is satisfied?

As for the work of pure art of which they are themselves incapable, these providers of substitutes hold it in disdain, and the crowd, following them, disdains in the name of a utilitarian art the work of art which has not been utilized.

When Joseph was in prison, two men, likewise in prison, two servants of Pharaoh, addressed him, as the story goes in the Bible. Each of them had had a dream, and each was worried about it. Now, Joseph was an interpreter of dreams. When the first man had spoken:

"Your dream," Joseph explained, "means that in a few days, or in a few years, Pharaoh, remembering you, will recall you to his court, where once more you will have as many joys as in prison you had sorrows."

And when the second man had spoken:

"As for you," Joseph said, "in a few days, the King, remembering you, will have you hanged."

The first was the chief butler, he who pours out what men shall drink. Pharaoh, remembering him, had him recalled to court. He is the one who, as Ganymede, intoxicates the gods at their banquet table.

The second, the chief baker, who gave men what they should eat, was hanged. He it was who, as Prometheus, was chained upon Mount Caucasus.•

Present-day providers of substitutes, you need not feel

• To speak of the true providers, alone worthy of the hatred of men and of gods, would have been to exceed the limits of this short lecture. Such men can and must know how to do without the public, be unaware of it, at the worst wait for it, as they repeat with Stendhal, Nietzsche, and many others: "The men who will one day understand me are not yet born."

any anxiety! No one has a thought of hanging you, for you cannot be said to bring us anything to eat. But you do not intoxicate us either, and therefore you are hateful. In a cultivated society you would have no place, nor even exist. May Weimar never know you!

Ladies and Gentlemen:

In the *Festzüge* that Goethe used to organize at the court, order, harmony, and the joy of all were achieved only through a kind of subordination (I almost said renunciation) on the part of the individual for the sake of the whole. Every man had his role; Goethe excelled in assigning it. I have spoken of the role of the public; I have spoken of the role of the artist. The role of the lecturer seems less clear—unless it be to present, in the name of French artists, thanks for our gracious reception at Weimar.• Be so kind as to accept them through me —and may your Highness not be dissatisfied with their respectful expression.

TRANSLATED BY ANGELO P. BERTOCCI

THE EVOLUTION OF THE THEATER

To Emile Verhaeren

Ladies and Gentlemen:

The evolution of the art of drama is a topic of peculiar difficulty. I should like to begin by telling you why. Then perhaps you will permit me, afterward, to talk

• An exhibit of French painters opened at Weimar a few days before this lecture.

around the subject in an informal fashion rather than to discourse upon it.

Since a work of dramatic art, I should say, is not and does not mean to be an end in itself—and this is one of the worst difficulties of the subject—but is situated by the dramatist, as it were, between spectators and actor, I propose to adopt the standpoint of the author, then of the actor, and then of the spectator, as I seek to envisage this same evolution in each of its three aspects.

Another difficulty, and by no means the slightest, is owing to the many factors that may enter into the success of a play, or even of a type of play, and which have nothing to do with literature. I do not refer merely to the many accessories to which the dramatic work must have recourse if it is to be staged, and be a success: the sumptuousness of its scenery, the splendor of its costumes, the beauty of its women, the talent and reputation of its actors. I refer especially to the extraliterary interests—social, patriotic, pornographic, or pseudo artistic—of the author himself.

The dramatic hits of our day are often contrived of just such extraliterary interests: were these to be dropped one by one, practically nothing would be left of the play.•

• Such interests exist, to be sure, in the novel also; but, apart from the lesser damage they do because the novel as a literary genre lacks clear outline and is multiform and omnivorous, the novelist who allows himself to be led by them finds himself more obviously out of bounds in literature. And no matter how outrageous the advertising that precedes or follows publication, a bad book, written only for profit, is not introduced, after all, to the public with a much greater degree of impertinence than a good book. Better still, exaggerated advertising itself puts the reader on his guard; when a Champsaur advertises that his *Arriviste*, even before public sale, has reached its thirtieth thousand copy sold, the public knows what to think, both about the book and its author. The novel can never put up the kind of front a play can; the playwright, furthermore, is never the sole party

Yet it must be recognized that, most of the time, it is to these very extraliterary interests that the play owes its vogue; the author who does not submit to them, and who writes only with the work of art in view, runs a real risk of never having it staged.

Now, since the work of dramatic art lives only potentially in the book, living completely only on the boards, the critic who in our day aims to deal with the evolution of the theater would find himself obliged, in order not to neglect the parallel evolution of author and public, to speak of works that have only a very distant relationship to literature, and to neglect, on the other hand, works of purely literary merit. I mean not only such as the *Phocas* of Francis Vielé-Griffin, *La Gardienne* of Henri de Régnier, or *Un Jour* of Francis Jammes— which quite understandably are considered no more than poems—but works like the first plays of Maeterlinck, like the dramas of Claudel, like *Le Pain* of Henri Ghéon, like others still. I almost said: like *Le Cloître* of Verhaeren, except that I remembered the success it had in Brussels.● If the critic does speak of them, it can only be as of purely bookish manifestations alien to boards or theater, their evolution remaining not only distinct—quite distinct—from that of the other type of play, but even in sharp contrast to it.

"Among animals living in society," Darwin writes, "natural selection transforms the nature of each individual so as to make it useful to the community—*upon condition, nevertheless,*" he adds, *"that the community profit from the change."* In this instance the community

---

concerned. There are also the actors, and the producer with his costs. A serious literary critic would not talk about or even read books of the mediocrity of those plays to which our critics of drama feel in duty bound to devote several columns.

● Elsewhere also, since this lecture.

does not profit; it has no desire to profit. The artist who fails of performance withdraws into his work, falls out of line in the general evolution, and ends by opposing it. All the works I have mentioned are works of reaction.

Reaction against what? I am tempted to say: against realism; but the word "realism," already overburdened with imputed meanings, would soon get me into serious trouble. Even the most ingenious misuse of language could not make the term "realism" stick for the works of M. Rostand, for instance, nor antirealism for the comedies of Molière or the dramas of Ibsen.

The reaction, let us say then, is against "episodicism." Yes, in the absence of a better term, "episodicism" seems the right word. For art does not consist in the use of heroic figures, historical or legendary; no more than it is necessarily inartistic to populate the stage with our contemporaries from the middle class. Yet there is a truth in Racine's works as I read them in the preface to *Bajazet:* "Characters in tragedy must be envisaged in rather a different way from that in which we ordinarily look upon characters whom we have seen close up. It may be said," he adds, "that the respect we have for heroes increases with their distance from us." It may be said, however, if I may be permitted to add my word, that such respect for the characters represented may not be indispensable. The artist's choice of figures at a distance from us is due to the fact that time, or any kind of distance, allows only that image to supervene from which everything episodic, bizarre, and transitory has been refined away, so that what subsists is only that portion of deep truth with which art can do its work. And that sense of estrangement from the habitual that the artist seeks to create in us by presenting his characters at a remove from us indicates precisely his intention: to present his work of art as a work of art, his play simply as a play—and not pursue an illusion of reality which, even if effected, would only make for a redundance of reality. Was it not this same desire that, almost unawares, led our classical writers to restrict themselves to the three unities: the desire to make of a dramatic work a work deliberately and manifestly artistic?

Every time that art languishes, we send it back to nature, just as the sick are sent to the waters for a cure. Nature, alas, cannot help: here there is room for serious confusion. I agree that it may be good for art now and then to rusticate, and if it grows pale from exhaustion, to seek in the fields and in everyday life some renewal of vigor. But the Greeks, our masters, knew very well that Aphrodite is born of no natural fecundation. Beauty will never be a natural product; it is obtained by the artifice of constraint. Art and nature are rivals on earth. Yes, art embraces nature, it embraces the whole of nature, and clasps it to itself; but in the words of a celebrated line it might say: *"J'embrasse mon rival, mais c'est pour l'étouffer"* ("I embrace my rival, the better to smother him").

Art is always the result of some kind of constraint. To believe that the freer it is, the higher it rises, is the same as believing that what keeps the kite from flying is its string. Kant's dove, which thinks that it would fly better were it not for the air, which bothers its wing, forgets that it needs, in order to fly, that very resistance of air upon which it can support that wing. Likewise, it is upon resistance that art must be able to lean if it is to mount. I was speaking of the three unities of drama, but what I am saying now is equally true for painting, sculpture, music, and poetry. Art aspires to liberty only in periods of sickness; it would like an easy life. Every time it feels vigorous, it looks for a struggle and an obstacle. It loves to burst its sheaths, and so it chooses them tight. Is it not in periods when life is full to overflowing that the need of the strictest forms torments the great heroic geniuses? Hence the use of the sonnet during the luxuriant Renaissance by Shakespeare, Ronsard, Petrarch, and even Michelangelo; the use of the *terza rima* by Dante; the love of the fugue in Bach; that restless need of the constraint of fugue in the last works of Beethoven. How many more examples could be quoted! And is it any wonder that the expansive power of the lyrical afflatus is directly proportional to its compression; or that it is the weight to be overcome that permits of architecture?

The great artist is one whom constraint exalts, for whom the obstacle is a springboard. It was to a defect in the marble, they tell us, that Michelangelo owed the massed tension in the gestures of his Moses. It was to the limited number of speakers at his disposal on the stage simultaneously that Aeschylus, under constraint, was led to invent the silence of Prometheus as they enchained him to Mount Caucasus. Greece proscribed the man who added a new string to the lyre. Art is born of constraint, lives on struggle, dies of freedom.

The artist, congratulating himself at first upon his success in adding to expression in the drama what the drama correspondingly lost in beauty, diminished little by little the distance between the stage and the auditorium. An inevitable evolution, it seems; the "distance" that Racine demanded between the spectator and the *dramatis persona,* the actor saw fit to diminish as much as he could in order to humanize the hero. He rejected one by one mask, cothurnus, everything that made for strangeness and which was to be envisaged, to repeat Racine's phrase, in "rather a different way from that in which we ordinarily look upon characters whom we have seen close up." He suppressed even the conventional costume that, withdrawing the dramatic figure from the day and age represented, and abstracting it, as it were, allowed to subsist in it only the general and the human. If that was progress, it was at any rate a very dangerous progress. With truth as the excuse they strove for exactitude. Costumes, accessories, backgrounds, sought to give an exact idea of the time and place of the action, caring little for what had been, in a Racine, an opposite concern. In *Über Kunst und Alterthum* Goethe writes: "Properly speaking, there are no historical characters in poetry; only, when the poet wants to represent the world that he has conceived, he does certain individuals whom he encountered in history the honor of borrowing their names in order to attach them to the beings he has created." I take these lines just as they were quoted by Victor Hugo in one of the notes of his *Cromwell:* "One is astonished," he says, "to come upon such lines in M. Goethe." Today we are perhaps not quite so astonished.

But the author, in this instance, has the actor against him. Talma, assigned the title role in the *Mahomet* of Voltaire, thought it well to study the character in history for a whole month. He tells us himself how, "having found too great a disparity between his conception of the man and Voltaire's representation of him, he had immediately given up a role that it would have been impossible for him to play." I quote the exact words of Guiraud's memoirs: I could not improve upon them if I made them up. That may all be very well because the *Mahomet* of Voltaire is not a good play; but at a rehearsal of *Britannicus,* one of the greatest actors of our day was reproached for not interpreting his role in such fashion as might have pleased Racine: "Racine? Who is that?" he cried; "I know none but Nero." •

• We sometimes grow quite indignant at the pride of actors. It seems quite natural to me, and artists, I think, should be the last to talk about it: they whose works lay claim to an eternity of duration. The player can create only ephemeral figures like those snow statues that Pietro de' Medici forced Michelangelo to model in his gardens all through one winter. We are reminded of the words of a great actor

The indispensable collaboration of the actor particu-larizes, then, where the author generalized. I do not mean to blame the actor; the work of dramatic art is not an abstract work of art: the characters are an excuse for generalization, but have always their particular truth; and the theater, like the novel, is a place for characters.

Ladies and Gentlemen:

The theater is really an extraordinary thing. People like you and me assemble at night in a hall to see others pretend to passions that we have no right to have —for our laws and our morals forbid. I propose for your meditation a phrase of Balzac's; it can be found in his *Physiologie du mariage:* "Morals are the hypocrisy of nations." Does he mean, perhaps, that the passions that the actor represents are not suppressed in us by morals, but only hidden? That our carefully calculated gestures are meant to deceive; that it is we, in reality, who are the actors (*hypokrites* in Greek, you know, means "actor"); that our politeness is only a pretense, and that our virtue, that "politeness of the soul," as Balzac calls it, that our virtue is most of the time no more than a façade?

Could that be partly the reason for our pleasure in the theater: to hear those voices ring out which conven-tional morals are apt to muffle? Sometimes. Yet even more often man looks upon passions on the stage as if they were so many monsters overcome. He has an ad-mirable faculty for becoming quickly what he claims

who one night went into a box to slap the illustrious critic whose column had that very morning treated him roughly—or so he thought: "Milords the writers, your work has time ahead of it; but we actors, if you writers fail to do us justice on the very day of the performance, to what tribunal shall we appeal? And what will the future think of us?"

Is it any wonder, then, if the actor seeks first and last to exist, were it occasionally at the writer's expense?

to be, and that is what made Condorcet (I am glad to be able to hide behind so august a name) write in his biography of Voltaire: "The hypocrisy of morals, a vice peculiar to the modern nations of Europe, has contributed more than we think to destroying the energy of character that distinguished the people of antiquity." Hypocrisy of morals, then, has not always existed.

Yes, man becomes what he claims to be; but to claim to be what one is not is a very modern kind of pretension: to be exact, it is the peculiarly Christian form of pretension. I do not mean that the will intervenes to no purpose in the formation or deformation of one's being; but the pagan did not believe he had to be any different from what he was. Personality did not grow banal under pressure of constraint, but strained to fulfill itself in a virtuous impulse; everyone demanded of himself nothing but himself, and without deforming himself, brought out the god within. Hence the great number of gods, as numerous as the instincts of men. It was not by free choice that a man consecrated himself to a god; it was the god who recognized in the individual his own image. Sometimes it could happen that the man refused to see it; and the god, denied in the man, would revenge himself, as happens so horribly in the case of Pentheus, in the *Bacchae* of Euripides.

The pagans very seldom looked upon qualities of soul as advantages that could be acquired, but rather, like those of the body, as natural properties.

Agathocles was good, Charicles courageous, just as naturally as if one had blue eyes and the other brown. Religion for them did not set up, at the head of a cross or on the earth below, a certain group of virtues, a kind of moral phantom that one must resemble if he were not to be held impious; the ideal type of man was not one but legion—or rather, there was no ideal type of man. The mask, not needed under these conditions in life itself, was reserved for the actor.

The important thing in discussing the history of
drama, the all-important question to ask oneself is:
Where is the mask? In the auditorium? or on the stage?
In the theater? or in life? It can only be in one or the
other. The most splendid ages of the theater, those in
which the mask wins its triumph on the stage, are those
in which hypocrisy ceases to cover life with its pall. On
the other hand, those periods where what Condorcet
calls the "hypocrisy of morals" prevails are the ones in
which the actor's mask is snatched away and he is asked
not so much to be beautiful, but to be natural; that is to
say, if I am correct, to take as his model the realities or,
at least, appearances of reality, that the spectator holds
before him—and that amounts to the models of a humanity in all its monotony or already masked. The author himself, who also takes pride in his naturalness,
will readily undertake to furnish a drama of this kind:
a monotonous and masked drama where the tragedy of
situations (for of course they still want the tragic) will
little by little replace the tragedy of characters. Here is
something worth considering: how in the naturalistic
novel, which is supposed to copy reality, there can be
such a distressing poverty of real characters. Is it any
wonder? Our modern society and our Christian morality
do their utmost to prevent them. "The religion of the
ancients," as Machiavelli saw, "beatified only men whose
glory was of the earth—such as military leaders and
founders of states—while ours has glorified men of
humble and contemplative cast rather than men of action. It has placed supreme value upon humility, renunciation, the disdain of earthly things, whereas the
other placed it upon greatness of soul, strength of body,
and whatever encourages audacity. Ours wants them
strong in endurance, and not strong in action." With
such characters—if they may still be called characters—

what dramatic *actions* remain possible? To say drama is to say character, and Christianity will have nothing to do with characters, proposing for every man a common ideal.

Thus a purely Christian drama, to tell the truth, does not exist. Plays like *Saint-Genest* and *Polyeucte* may be called, if you wish, Christian drama. They are indeed Christian by virtue of the Christian element involved, but they are not dramatic except by reason of the non-Christian element that the Christian element combats.

Another reason why a Christian drama is not possible is that the last act must of necessity always take place in the wings—I mean in the other life. Goethe felt this: *Faust,* Part Two, is concluded in heaven; in the heaven where, I suppose, the sixth act of *Polyeucte* is played out, or the sixth act of *Saint-Genest.* For if neither Corneille nor Rotrou wrote such an act it was not merely out of respect for the three unities but also because Polyeucte, Pauline, and Saint-Genest, letting go on the threshold of paradise the passion by which drama is sustained, having become perfect Christians, and without a trace of character left, really have nothing more to say.

Ladies and Gentlemen:

I am not proposing a return to paganism. I am simply calling attention to the obvious: our tragedy is dying of a dearth of characters. Christianity, alas, is not solely responsible for a leveling process of which Kierkegaard said: "The leveling process is not of God, and every good man must want to weep at times over this labor of desolation." For men whose desires are conquerors it is not hard to believe in the gods.

They are real gods as long as they govern; if they are to be convicted of falsity, it can be only through the unity of a despotic reason that takes their place. It was

the invention of a moral code that made Olympus a
desert. Monotheism lies within the man before it becomes externally his god. Before he projects his faith
into the heavens, it is within himself that man serves one
or several gods. Paganism or Christianity are psychology
first and then become metaphysics. Paganism was both
the triumph of individualism and the belief that man
cannot become what he is not. It was the school of the
theater.

But to repeat: it is not an impossible return to
paganism that I mean to propose; nor am I here to confirm dispassionately the death of the theater; but rather
by a diagnosis of what is killing it in our day to suggest
what might keep it alive—for it is not the decay of
dramatic art that matters to me, but its rebirth, in which
I believe and of which I catch a glimpse.

The way to deliver the theater from "episodicism" is
to provide it with new constraints. The way to make
characters live on the stage once more is to withdraw it
from life once more.

I should be almost ready to say: give us back freedom
of morals and the constraint of art will follow; suppress
the hypocrisy of life and the mask will return to the
stage. But since our morals are not as yet inclined to give
heed, then let the artist begin. I have some hope that
morals will follow; let me tell you why.

It is evident that new forms of society, changes in the
distribution of wealth, unforeseen external influences,
have a great deal to do with the formation of characters;
but I think that it is very easy to exaggerate their effect
and importance: I think they are simply revelatory.
Everything has always been in man, but more or less
apparent or hidden, and what a new age discovers may
unfold under our eyes but slumbered there since the
beginning of time. Just as I believe that a Princesse de
Clèves still lives in our day—an Onuphre, a Céladon—
so do I find it easy to believe that—much before their

appearance in books—an Adolphe existed, a Rastignac, and even a Julien Sorel. Furthermore, since humanity, after all, counts for more than race, I believe that even outside of St. Petersburg—in Brussels, for instance, or in Paris—one can find Nezhdanovs, Myshkins, and Prince Andrés. But as long as their voices have not resounded either in a book or on the stage, they languish or toss about under the cloak of conventional morals, watching and waiting for their hour. We do not hear them because the world hears only those whose voices it recognizes; also because their voices are too new not to be muffled. We gaze upon the black cloak of conventional morals and we do not see them; worse still, these new forms of humanity are not even aware of themselves. How many unknown Werthers waited all unconscious for the bullet of Goethe's Werther to kill themselves! How many heroes lie hidden, waiting only for an example in the hero of a book, for the spark escaping from his life in order to live, for the sound of his speech in order to speak. Isn't that, Ladies and Gentlemen, what we hope for in our theater? That it shall set before humanity new forms of heroism, new figures of heroes?

The soul cries out for heroism; but our society allows but one form of heroism in our day (if it be heroism at all): the heroism of resignation, of acceptance. When a powerful creator of characters like Ibsen cloaks his figures in the dark hues of our morals, he is inevitably condemning his most heroic heroes to bankruptcy. Yes, his admirable theater presents from beginning to end—and necessarily—bankruptcies of heroism. How could he have done otherwise without drawing too far away from reality, since if such heroism appeared in reality—I mean the heroism the theater can display— we should know it; and since, if such real heroes existed, we should recognize them?

That is why the bold enterprise of a Pygmalion or a Prometheus is reserved, I think, for those who deliberately place the footlights on the other side of a moat, and draw the stage back once more from the auditorium, fiction back from reality, actor back from the spectator, and the hero back from the proffered cloak of conventional morals.

That is why my eyes turn, full of joy and expectation, toward that unperformed theater of which I spoke, toward those plays—more and more numerous from year to year—which I hope will soon find a hospitable stage. Every turn of the wheel of history brings to light what was hidden in the shadow of night. "Slow time in its infinity," said the Ajax of Sophocles, "reveals in the light all things hidden, and what is manifest it hides, and there is nothing but what may come to be." We expect from humanity novel manifestations. Sometimes those who take it upon themselves to speak for us keep the floor for themselves an awfully long time; the generations that have not yet spoken meanwhile grow impatient in silence. It is as though the speakers knew, despite their claims to represent all mankind in their day, that others are waiting and that, once these have been given the floor, they themselves will not have it back—for a long time. The floor today belongs to those who have not yet spoken. Who are they?

That is what the theater will tell us.

I am thinking of the "open sea" that Nietzsche tells about, of those regions as yet unexplored, full of novel dangers, of surprises for the heroic navigator. I am thinking of what voyages were when men had no maps and no catalogue of the known, exact but limited. I reread these words of Sindbad: "We saw the captain then cast his turban down, smite himself on the face, tear his beard, and collapse right in the middle of the deck, a prey to unspeakable anguish. Then all the passengers and merchants gathered around him and asked: 'O

Captain! What evil tidings can you have for us?' The captain answered: 'Know, my good folk, that we and our ship have gone astray, that we have come out of the sea we were in to enter into a sea where we have but little knowledge of our course.' " I am thinking of Sindbad's vessel and that, as it leaves realism behind, the theater of our day is weighing anchor.

TRANSLATED BY ANGELO P. BERTOCCI

The Barrès Problem

In his famous thesis novel of 1897, Les Déracinés *(The Uprooted),* Maurice Barrès *advocated federalism by showing the harm done to seven youths who had been uprooted from their native Lorraine and transplanted to Paris. Earlier the same year, André Gide had extolled in his* Nourritures terrestres *(The Fruits of the Earth) the necessity of uprooting and of a permanently cultivated unrest. It was inevitable that his views should clash with those of the popular and slightly older Barrès (1862-1923) and that on the question of nationalism Barrès and Gide should carry on a debate for many years.*

Gide's review of Les Déracinés, *which appeared in* L'Ermitage *for December 1897, first clearly marked the opposition between the two minds. In the same periodical for November 1903 Gide's article entitled "The Poplar Tree Quarrel" answered an article in defense of Barrès's position by another nationalist, Charles Maurras (1868-1952) who later founded the movement known as Action Française and eventually became an apologist of the Vichy government during the Second World War.*

"Normandy and Bas-Languedoc," which Gide grouped with the Barrès articles in his Prétextes, *appeared in July 1902 in the monthly* L'Occident *as the first of a series of articles by various hands devoted to the French provinces. It emphasizes the author's conflicting heredity already stated in the opening of the review of* Les Déracinés *and shows more clearly why Gide*

rather relished the observation that his father was from Uzès in ancient Languedoc and his mother from Rouen, the old capital of Normandy. Some thirty years later he noted in his Journals: *"I have discovered quite by chance and without much believing in astrology that it just happens that on the 21st of November, my birthday, our earth leaves the influence of Scorpio to enter that of Sagittarius. Is it my fault if your God took such great care to have me born between two stars, the fruit of two races, of two provinces, and of two faiths?"*

APROPOS OF "LES DÉRACINÉS"

Born in Paris, of a father from Uzès and a mother from Normandy, where, Mr. Barrès, do you expect me to take root?

So I chose to travel.

Having enjoyed its amenities (to use one of your exquisite expressions from the past) and especially, I make bold to believe, profited thereby, I permitted myself to recommend travel to others. I did even more: I urged, I constrained others to travel; some who had never traveled came to join me in quite distant lands; some I saw off on the train; some I accompanied. I did even more: I wrote a whole book, of a deeply reasoned madness, to exalt the beauties of travel, striving, perhaps through a mania for proselytizing, to teach the joy there would be in feeling free of ties, or "roots" if you prefer (to be sure, you have written *L'Homme libre*—but "free" in a somewhat different sense). And it was while traveling that I read your book. It is not surprising, then, if to my great admiration I am impelled to join some criticism: forgive me this preamble; it exists only to show how obviously I am designated to be your critic, for those designated to praise you are legion.

Yet I should like to begin by saying how much I admire your book. It is true that your earlier works gave us reason to expect from you the most exquisite subtleties, and many pages dated from Spain or Italy were hardly inferior to the marvelous narrative of Mme Aravian; we knew the sharpness of your eye, the clarity of your judgments, your valor, your prudence, the excellence of your advice. Despite all that, *Les Déracinés* surprised even your warmest admirers; there is maintained untroubled within it (if perhaps not sufficiently concentrated) so serious a work, so authoritative an assertion, that respect for you follows as a matter of course, and even your most stubborn opponents are now compelled to esteem you. Under names as frightful as those of *L'Education sentimentale,* you have created types; they are painful, but they are unforgettable. You have done more; you have grouped them, graded them, established their hierarchy, or, even better, you have shown the inevitability of this hierarchy, as a professor of physics demonstrates the "vase of the four elements." The establishment of the newspaper, its harsh existence, the manner in which Sturel makes his way, all that, weighty, is of a remarkable consistency, a complete absence of fantasy. Why did you feel the need of swelling inartistically this fine plan with an electoral thesis, certainly interesting in itself (quite apart from its rightness or wrongness), but which stiffens almost all the pages and drags upon the slightest action? If you haggle over every point, and by dint of argument, attach it to your general thesis, can it be that these events were not sufficiently eloquent in themselves? Can it be that you feared others might not think of them all that you think; can it be, perhaps, that had you left the reader's mind free, he would have reached a different conclusion? And the result of your oratorical skill is that the events you recount, after you have spoken about them, seem, taken outside the book, less eloquent than you yourself were, or are less persuasive than you would wish them. For after all, Suret-Lefort, Renaudin, Sturel, Romerspacher are successful; if he had more money, it is likely that Racadot would succeed, too. Besides I grant that, *if* Racadot had never left Lorraine, he would never have killed; but then he would no longer interest me at all. While, thanks to the strange circumstances which force him into a corner, it is upon him, you know, that the dramatic interest of the book is focused; so that your book, concerned also with psychological truth, as though despite you, seems to prove nothing so much as this: "In a situation in which it often finds itself and which for many is the same, the organism acts in a banal way; in a situation which is presented to it for the first time, it will give proof of originality, if it cannot avoid doing so." • *Uprooting constraining Racadot to originality:* it might be said, half-seriously, that this is the subject of your book.

For your insistent assertion inspires in us the desire to contradict, the desire to assert this: uprooting can be a school of virtue. It is only after a significant increase in external novelty that an organism, in order to lessen its suffering, is provoked into discovering an appropriate modification permitting a more assured assimilation.•• For lack of stimulation by what is *strange,* the rarest virtues may remain latent; undetected by the very being that possesses them, they may be for him but the source of a vague uneasiness, the seed of anarchy.

On the other hand, the weaker the being, the more it is repelled by strangeness, by change; for the slightest new idea, the least modification of routine, necessitates

• The formulation is Max Nordau's.
•• "Ease engenders only inertia; discomfort is the principle of movement." Renan (*Dialogues*); or "One rarely acquires the qualities one can do without." Laclos (*Les Liaisons dangereuses*).

a virtue, an effort at adaptation that it will perhaps fail
to supply. But what can be said other than that it is too
weak? All right, it cannot be helped! Let it take root and
may it profit thereby.

But do not seek to educate it either. All education is
a process of uprooting by way of the mind. The weaker
the being the less education it can stand. Is it not on that
account that you say: "Many women and children are
made for a single landscape"? This might be rendered:
"Education is good only for the strong." Take care of
the weak; protect him, but out of pity for us, do not
establish our rule on his example.

Education, that is, the presentation of unfamiliar
elements, can be beneficial only to the degree that the
being to whom it is directed will find within himself the
capacity to face up to it; what he does not master may
well overpower him. Education overpowers the weak.

True enough, but the strong man is strengthened
thereby.

If we must have in view only the comfort of the greatest number, I admit that it is obtained with the least
effort by not stirring from home, since usually one needs
only to follow along an inherited drive. But might it not
also please us to see a man demand of himself the greatest possible merit? In comfort every virtue is vitiated;
new, arduous paths necessitate virtue. I like (forgive me)
everything that calls on man to perish or become great.
The historical events that have forced men out of their
element are assuredly those that have made the most vic-
tims; they have also excited and enlightened the greatest number of heroes. It is a process of sifting; in the
calm of habit, wings unextended, with no need of being
widespread, forget how to be so; the higher the wind
rises from abroad the more a powerful wing-span is
necessary.

Yes, but the weak will perish in it.

Need we console ourselves by saying that they were

weaklings? Let us say rather: true education is for the strong alone. Taking root is for the weak, sinking into the hereditary habit that will keep them from cold. But for those who are not weak, who do not put comfort above all else, uprooting is called for in proportion to their strength, to their virtue—the pursuit of the unfamiliar setting that will require of them the maximum of virtue. And perhaps we could measure the worth of a man by the degree of displacement (physical or intellectual) to which he can adjust. Yes, displacement; that which requires of a man a gymnastic of adaptation, pulling himself upright in his new setting—this is the education that the strong man demands. Dangerous, to be sure, trying; it is a struggle against the unfamiliar. But there can be education only when teaching effects modifications. As for the weak: take root, take root!

Education, displacement, uprooting•—they should be

• Herewith a note from M. Charles Maurras:

"M. Doumic, in the *Revue des Deux Mondes*, admits the thesis of *Les Déracinés*, but with the following reservation: 'The characteristic of education is to tear man from his formative milieu. Education must uproot him. Such is the etymological sense of the word "elevate." But the professor is pulling our leg. M. Barrès has only to ask him at what moment a poplar tree, of whatever elevation, can be subjected to uprooting. . . .'"

No, M. Maurras. I deeply regret it, but you are the one pulling our leg and not M. Doumic; and unless M. Doumic is as ignorant of arboriculture as you appear to be, he has already explained to you, I suppose, that the poplar of which you speak, as it is beautiful and well-formed, doubtless did not first sprout on the ground it now shades, but in all probability came from a nursery—such as the one from whose catalogue I copy this sentence for your edification:

"Our trees have been *transplanted* [the word is emphasized in the text] two, three, four, and more times, according to their strength [which here means according to their age], an operation that favors their growth; *they are correctly spaced, in order to obtain well-formed tops* [here the emphasis is mine, for this is one of the aspects of the question which you do not mention but which is important]." *Catalogue of the Croux Nurseries.*

Are you also ignorant of the operation that in culture is called *setting out?* Allow me to copy these few instructive sentences for you:

"As soon as the plants have a few leaves, one must, according to utilized according to the strength of the individual. There is danger as soon as there is no longer benefit; and *Les Déracinés* shows us that the weak succumb in the process. But to preserve the weak from harm, are we to close our eyes to the gain for the strong? And it is not shown in *Les Déracinés* that the strong are strengthened by uprooting, or at least it is shown only involuntarily.

For this dilemma confronted you then: either to favor your thesis and show the danger of uprooting, to depict characters so weak and mediocre that we should have exclaimed: good riddance; or to favor the novel, to depict characters strong enough not to suffer from a new situation, characters important enough to invalidate your thesis.

There are many of these points, I am well aware, upon which we could endlessly contradict each other; indeed, I should not have been so assertive had you not so strongly asserted the contrary.

What is certain is that if the seven Lorrainers whose story you tell had not come to Paris you would not have written *Les Déracinés;* you would not have written this book if you yourself had not come to Paris. And that would have been most regrettable, for because of its very preoccupations, this weighty book of an excessive but admirable tension restores to their mediocre place very many unimportant novels with which, for lack of

---

the species and the particular care they require, either *thin them out* or *set them out.*

"Setting out is of the highest importance for the great majority of plants." And in a note: "All plants could if necessary be set out." Vilmorin-Andrieux, *Les Fleurs de pleine terre,* p. 3.

Either *set out or thin out.* That is the frightful dilemma that your learned fellow supporters MM. Croux and Vilmorin-Andrieux propose. Abandon your search for examples from their field. And if that does not suffice to invalidate M. Barrès's thesis, you will at least agree that it does not fortify it either.

(The passage from M. Maurras that I quote is cited by M. Barrès in *Scènes et doctrines du nationalisme.*)

anything better, we were in danger of concerning ourselves.

TRANSLATED BY JEFFREY J. CARRE

THE POPLAR TREE QUARREL

(*In Answer to M. Maurras*)

When, in 1897, my article on *Les Déracinés* appeared in
L'Ermitage, it did not attract much attention. Last year,
having to gather into one volume a few pages of criticism, I reread this forgotten article; finding it passable
I added it to the others unchanged—but with the addition of a note, and for the following reason:

Between 1897 and 1902, an article by M. Doumic had
appeared to which M. Maurras had replied immediately. I learned of the article and the reply by a note in
M. Barrès's *Scènes et doctrines.* This note has since been
so often quoted that I am ashamed to quote it once
more; people will get to know it by heart. But that cannot be helped:

"M. Doumic, in the *Revue des deux mondes,* admits
the thesis of *Les Déracinés,* but with the following reservation: 'The characteristic of education is to tear man
from his formative milieu. Education must uproot him.
Such is the etymological sense of the word "elevate." '
But the professor is pulling our leg. M. Barrès has only
to ask him at what moment a poplar tree, of whatever
elevation, can be subjected to uprooting. . . ."

Oceans of ink were flowing at that moment on the

subject of uprooting; I found M. Maurras's contribution singularly pale. I permitted myself to point out to him the rashness of his question; it was in fact more than easy to answer that these exemplary poplars came in all probability from a nursery—like the one, I added, from the catalogue of which I copy this sentence:

"Our trees have been *transplanted* [the word is emphasized in the text] two, three, four, and more times, according to their strength, an operation which favors their growth; *they are correctly spaced, in order to obtain well-formed tops* [here the emphasis is mine]."

M. Maurras having once written: "I declare publicly that M. Gide does not deserve criticism," prepared to make no reply. "His mind, his talent, the bent of his imagination," he affirms further, "are those of a perfect flirt. Such qualities would lose by being generally known. They can be tolerated only thanks to an obliging half-light or a propitious chiaroscuro." Therefore, out of consideration for me, he should have left me in shadow.

But MM. Faguet, Blum, and Remy de Gourmont did not have the delicacy to understand this. To the impertinence of reading me, they added that of mentioning my book and mentioning it with approbation; even more, they quoted my note.

M. Maurras then held back no longer and suppressed me in eighteen columns of *La Gazette*.

My articles on M. Barrès, whom I still heed, whom I often admire, and for whom I should retain the liveliest affection if he did not sometimes make it difficult for me to do so—my articles are most moderate in opposition to a thesis of which I criticize only the excessiveness and which I blame for spoiling many a page of one of our best writers.

This doctrine of taking root which he advocates, I think it, in fact, good for the weak, for the mass; I grant that it is with them that we must concern ourselves, for the individuals who escape the mass look out for themselves sufficiently well and one cannot reckon on them. But I maintain that they do find profit in being uprooted and that taking root, on the contrary, limits them. They too are necessary to the country. "Education, displacement, uprooting," I wrote in the conclusion of my first article, "they should be utilized according to the strength of the individual. There is danger as soon as there is no longer benefit; and *Les Déracinés* shows us that the weak succumb in the process. But to preserve the weak from harm, are we to close our eyes to the gain for the strong?• And it is not shown in *Les Déracinés* that the strong are strengthened by uprooting, or at least it is shown only involuntarily."

"Because the seven Lorrainers of M. Barrès's novel were wrong in coming to Paris, since they were all more or less submerged there, it does not follow that an eighth Lorrainer will be wrong to follow their example; for this eighth Lorrainer will perhaps be a Barrès," writes M. de Gourmont, summarizing my conclusion. "Thus the dispute ends with a compliment," he concludes in his turn.

M. Maurras does not see it that way. He has a horror of reconciliations. The oil brought for his wounds is spilled by him into the fire. I doubt that he has read our articles. At least he does not answer them, but merely the note in which his name is mentioned. And the argument that he revives is not on the heart of the matter: it is he who baptizes it "the poplar tree quarrel." It is essential that he not have been wrong in choosing the poplar tree as an illustration. The proof is not an easy

---

• "Education," I said above, "that is, the presentation of unfamiliar elements, can be beneficial only to the degree that the being to whom it is directed will find within himself the capacity to face up to it; what he does not master may well overpower him. . . ." But I cannot quote my entire article! If M. Maurras has not read it, there is nothing I can do about it. But then why does he speak about it?

one to make. He is going to talk loud and long. Eighteen columns against twenty lines. I am beaten.

"This lesson in aboriculture delighted me," we read in *La Gazette de France* of 14 September 1903, after quotation of my note. "M. André Gide has discovered setting out in Vilmorin-Andrieux's treatise and transplanting in the Croux Nurseries' catalogue."

Let it pass. M. Maurras could not be expected to know, and his readers still less, that I live nine months out of twelve in the country, where I look more often at my garden than at my books—nor even that the Society of Agriculturists of Normandy awarded my nursery a first-prize medal a few years ago. It really requires an opportunity like this one to make possible such a declaration.

"The naïve surprise that M. Gide betrays," continues M. Maurras, "in revealing to us setting out and transplanting is unquestionably foreign to those among us who . . . etc. . . . but if they have not experienced this wondrous emotion they are also protected from introducing into the vocabularies of honorable men like MM. Emile Faguet and Remy de Gourmont . . . a ridiculous confusion between *transplanting* and *uprooting*. Were we in the position in which M. André Gide —a subtle writer and exigent critic—has placed himself, we should not reconcile ourselves to this misadventure." Many thanks for the compliments—but decidely, M. Maurras, you are far too confident that your readers are not ours. Here is the beginning of M. de Gourmont's article:

"To the word found by M. Barrès, 'the uprooted,' it would be necessary, I think, to contrast another that would express the same material idea and a very different psychological idea: 'the transplanted.' One or the other would be used according to whether one spoke of a man for whom the change of milieu was unfortunate, or of a man who found new vigor through the very fact of being transplanted on a new soil.

"This proposal is suggested to me by the reading of a few pages of M. Gide's new book. . . . Having a thoroughly logical mind, he was shocked by M. Barrès's thesis presented as an absolute. He recognizes that uprooting is unfavorable to weak natures, that it is good that most men live and die where they are born; but he believes that transplanting is beneficial for the strong and that it further strengthens them." Then follow illustrations in support of this thesis. I cannot quote the entire article;• it is perfect.

But let us get back to our poplar tree. M. Maurras, not having at hand his "old gardener Marius" calls to his aid one of those great gardening fanciers who combine a wide culture with the pleasures of their art.

"When these (poplar) cuttings have leaves and seem to be furnished with roots—" says the great fancier.

"You uproot them?" interrupts M. Maurras.

"Not at all. *You thin out the plot, that is, you remove, as you see fit, the strongest to make of them select trees* [italics are mine], or the most numerous and the most delicate to set out in less crowded rows, thus permitting a good development of the roots."

"And what if they are shipped away?"

"The roots are wrapped very carefully so that they will not dry out during the journey."

Well, is that not just what I have maintained?

But further, this enlightens us:

"In sum," continues M. Maurras, "to take up, to transplant, to set out, to replant, even to tear out are operations which have nothing in common with uprooting. Only dead trees or those that are sacrificed are uprooted." And further:

"I explained then to my gardener friend what is now

• *Weekly Critical Review,* 30 July 1903.

called, according to the powerful and precise expression of Barrès, an *uprooted* man. . . . I explained how a faulty education had *cut the roots* which joined these young men to Lorraine." Now we have it! "Uprooted" means for M. Maurras *"the roots of which have been cut."* Why did he not say so earlier? I should have left his poplar tree in peace.•

We should then understand without any difficulty M. Barrès's metaphor, and his writings would shed a clear light upon it; but however eloquent the metaphor may be, it is most unfortunate that in arboriculture, the one field where the word "uprooted" has *a precise meaning,* the meaning is unlike that which M. Barrès is forced to attribute to it, under penalty of seeing almost all the examples he would seek in it contradict outright his theory. The great fault of M. Maurras today, in this absurd quarrel over words, is to make evident an error that had not hitherto been clearly noted, by undertaking to transfer this new meaning for "uprooted"—"the roots of which have been cut"—to arboriculture, where the word "uprooted" has never meant and will never mean anything but "the roots of which have been torn from the ground." It is the only meaning Littré gives— the only meaning there is to give.

But what does the word matter, it will be said, if the thing . . .

The word may not matter, but behind the erroneous word the erroneous thought hastens to hide. And if M. Maurras did not feel it to be a grave error he would not devote to it such keen attention, nor would he encounter so many difficulties in defending it.

TRANSLATED BY JEFFREY J. CARRE

• With all deference to M. Maurras it even happens often that these roots, at the moment of replanting, are cut by a stroke of the pruning hook, *in order to better assure their growth;* for new roots form immediately and the tree takes hold all the better because the old roots have been cut. The catalogues of nursery men and the treatises of arboriculture inform us that it is especially important to cut the central root, the taproot (precisely that of "the soil and the dead").

NORMANDY AND BAS-LANGUEDOC

There are regions that are more beautiful and I believe that I should have preferred them. But I am born of these regions. Had I been able, I should have set my birthplace in Brittany, in Locmariaquer the pious, or near Brest, in Camaret or Morgat, but we do not choose our parents. And even this desire I inherited, I think, with the Norman and Catholic blood of my mother's family and the Protestant and Languedocian blood of my father. Between Normandy and the South I would not nor could I choose, and I feel myself the more French because I am not of a single parcel of France, because I cannot think and feel especially as a Norman or a Southerner, as a Catholic or a Protestant, but as a Frenchman, and because, born in Paris, I understand alike the *langue d'oc* and the *langue d'oïl,* the thick Norman jargon and the singsong speech of the South, because I have a taste for wine and a taste for cider, a love for deep woods and *garrigue,* for the whiteness of the apple blossom and the white flowering almond.

And in these pages, too, I make no choice; not to speak of the two regions would be ingratitude, and since you urge me to speak, allow me to speak of both.

I

From the edge of the Norman woods I evoke a burning rock—an air all perfumed, eddying with sun, and rolling commingled the scent of thyme, lavender, and the shrill cry of the cicadas. I evoke at my feet, for the rock is steep in the narrow valley which falls away, a mill, washerwomen, water all the cooler for being the more desired. A little farther on I evoke the rock once again, but now less steep and milder, enclosures, gardens, then roofs, a charming little town—Uzès; it is there that my father was born and there that I came as a very young child.

We would come from Nîmes by carriage; we would cross the Gardon at the Saint-Nicholas bridge. In the month of May its banks are covered with asphodels like the banks of the Anapos. There live the gods of Greece. The Pont du Gard is very near.

Later I came to know Arles, Avignon, Vaucluse. A land almost Latin, of grave banks, clear poetry, and beautiful in its severity. No softness here. The city is born of the rock and retains its warm tones. In the hardness of the rock, the antique soul is set; inscribed in the hard, living flesh of the race, it makes the beauty of the women, the flash of their laughter, the gravity of their walk, the severity of their eyes; it makes the pride of the men, the somewhat easy assurance of those who, once having declared themselves in times past, have now only to repeat themselves without effort and no longer find anything particularly new to seek; I hear this sound again in the micaceous cry of the cicadas, I breathe it with the aromatics, I see it in the sharp foliage of the ilex, in the slender boughs of the olive trees.

From the edge of the flaming *garrigue,* I evoke a thick grass ever damp with rains, boughs down-bent, deep shaded paths; I evoke a wood into which they plunge— but others have already sung of the verdant land of Calvados. There, no buzz of cicadas; all is softness and lushness; under the plant, the naked rock never breaks through. There live other gods and other men; the gods are beautiful, I believe, the men are ugly. The race, heavy with material comfort, and yet concerned only with augmenting it, has deformed itself. Incapable of song, of music, it passes in drinking its finest idle hours. Here love of gain alone overcomes sloth. The indolent man lets slip from his hands the most precious goods, the rarest of all.

But perhaps the qualities of the Norman race, less evident than those of the Southerners, receive added strength from the heavier flesh enveloping them and gain in gravity and depth what they lose in brilliance and surface.

Everything changes with the Caux region; there vast fields replace the meadows; the men are more laborious and the women less misshapen. And on this fifteenth of July, where I am writing this, near Etretat, now sitting, now walking under the full noonday sun, never has this country appeared more beautiful to me. There is still flax in bloom. They are cutting the colza; the rye has been mowed. In the last few days the wheat has turned yellow. The harvest gives promise of being superb. Here and there, in spots, everywhere, great poppies accent the ground in red.

II

The few places of which I speak are no more all of Normandy and all of the South, than the South and Normandy are all of France.

I think sadly that if some chance brought them together, the Norman peasant whom I know and the Southerner whom I know, not only would they not love each other, but they could not even understand each other. Yet both are Frenchmen.

In the eyes of a German, an Italian, a Russian, what represents "a French city"? I do not know. I do not have enough perspective to understand it. I see a Brittany, a Normandy, a Basque country, a Lorraine, and of their sum I make my France. In Savoy I know that I am in France; I know too that a little farther on I am no longer there. I know it and I want to feel it. But will a mere annexation make a country French? No; no more than a wretched treaty would succeed in making a German land of Alsace-Lorraine; Germany has fully realized that. In order that the sentiment of unity of a country be formed and strengthened it is necessary that the different elements that compose it mingle, cross, and blend. The doctrine of taking root, too rigorously applied, would run the risk, by protecting and accentuating the heterogeneity of the diverse French elements, of making them forever misunderstand one another, of forming Bretons, Normans, Lorrainers, Basques, who are more Breton, Norman, Lorrainer, and Basque than French. Nothing is more local than the provincial temper; nothing less local than the French genius. It is good that Frenchmen like Hugo are born *"d'un sang breton et lorrain à la fois"* ("of Breton and Lorrainer blood together"), who bearing in themselves at one and the same time the most dissimilar riches of France, organize them and press them into unity.

It should be added that there are heaths more harsh than those of Brittany; pasturelands greener than those of Normandy; rocks that burn more than those of the Arles countryside; beaches more sea-green than our Channel beaches, bluer than those of our South Coast—but France has all that at once. And the French genius is, for that very reason, not all heaths, nor cultivated lands, nor forests, nor all shade, nor all light—but it organizes and holds in harmonious balance the diverse elements offered to it. That is what makes France the most classic of countries; just as such diverse elements —Ionian, Dorian, Boeotian, and Attic—formed the classic land of Greece.

TRANSLATED BY JEFFREY J. CARRE

Imaginary Interviews from
"L'Ermitage"

The dialogue form was a favorite with Gide, who called himself "a creature of dialogue." In order to maintain an informal tone in the exposition of serious ideas, he needed a correspondent or interlocutor to interrupt, raise objections, and ask questions. For his literary criticism between *1898* and *1900* in L'Ermitage *he had borrowed the naïve Angèle he had created in* Paludes (Marshlands) *and written "Letters to Angèle," a form he was to resurrect in 1921 in the* Nouvelle Revue Française *with his "Notes to Angèle."*

When Edouard Ducoté (1870-1929), the editor of L'Ermitage, asked Gide to create a regular column in his pages which would not be limited to the novel or poetry or the theater as the other columns were, Gide invented an even more anonymous, less clearly defined "interviewer," and for three months in early 1905 couched his critical remarks on a variety of subjects in a series of talks with an interviewer. This device, a particularly happy one for Gide, reappeared in 1943 in the Interviews imaginaires.

LETTER TO M. EDOUARD DUCOTÉ

My dear Ducoté:

Yes, I think your plan will work out quite well. Thank you for being so considerate of my leisure time. The *"chronique générale"* ("general intelligence") would have confiscated the little that was left.

I understand, then, that the gentleman who just came over to see me need only return once a month to try to extract from my conversation my opinions concerning the things that remain and those that pass away. That's what is meant by "being interviewed," isn't it? I'm not quite accustomed to it yet; but that will come, I am sure. As a matter of fact, your man need not be very clever, I think, to get me to tell him much more than I should have managed to write down.

I must give you an account of the interview:

At the hour we had set, then, the man came over.

"I'm not disturbing you?"

"No. I was expecting you."

"But you seemed to be busy."

"You don't want me to remain idle, to show that I'm expecting you?"

"If I am too early . . ."

"Not at all. Not at all."

"Perhaps, having figured out my questions in advance, you were already preparing your answers?"

"Oh, not at all, sir; you will always catch me empty-handed, you may be sure of that. I mean to show myself to you without disguise and to say anything that comes into my head. This is not the place, I suppose, to strive

for artistic effect; permit me to save that for my works.
I shall hardly let you have my best thought, which finds
nothing quite so disconcerting as to have to offer opinions about people. It's bad enough to speak of the dead
—*molliter ossa quiescant*—but to speak of the living,
sir! When they press upon you on all sides, what can a
man do but get out some lopsided judgments? If you
would only be satisfied with general truths! But I know
why you come; you want particular truths about particular individuals. You won't often get what you want from
me; or you will have to be very clever . . . Well, aren't
you going to ask any questions?"

"You have been talking away without questions well
enough."

"No more of that, then. I'm waiting for your questions. Come on."

At these words the man took a little notebook out of
his pocket.

"Question One," said he after having opened it.
"What do you think of . . ."

"Ah! permit me," I interrupted. "If I'm not going to
prepare my answers, I will ask you not to prepare your
questions. You will begin by putting that notebook back.
Ask your questions more or less at random."

"But, sir, in order to be logical . . ."

"Put it back, put it back, I say. You want to be logical;
and that means I won't be able to be. I don't believe in
abstract logic; at least this is not the place for it. Nothing
can be more personal than the rhythm of one's thoughts.
If your notebook holds mine back, I'll leave them on
account. Now then, go ahead."

He puts his notebook into his pocket, then begins just
the same as before:

"What, then, do you think of . . ."

"One more word, sir. My position in the *Ermitage* is
a difficult one. The hunting is restricted; all the depart-
ments are taken; I can't shoot anywhere without poach-

ing on a colleague. Let me tell you, if you didn't know it already, that our friend Francis Viele-Griffin has reserved poetry for himself; our friend Jacques-Emile Blanche, music; our friend Henri Ghéon, novels; our friend Michel Arnauld, philosophy and anything else he may want to add; our friend Jacques Copeau, the theater; and our friend Maurice Denis, painting. What do you think is left for me?"

"Sir," said the man, smiling, "if those gentlemen are your friends, as you say, no doubt every one of them will give you leave to take a few shots in his domain. There is no lack of game."

"That's true."

"And even if you should fire on the same . . ."

"No more of that metaphor: you are going to make it look like a massacre. Why not say, rather, that none of us makes any claim to exhausting the subject—only fools make such a claim—and that any man of intelligence knows that, on any topic, the mere fact that a more intelligent man has spoken only leaves the more to be said. A clever mind makes everything it touches increase and multiply . . ."

"Fortunately, now and then, some fools come along; otherwise there would be no reason to stop."

"No reason to stop. . . . And that's why the artist never really likes to practice criticism; discussion broadens the subject beyond all limits. What makes a picture possible for the painter is the fixed limit of the frame. But the moment you begin to talk about it . . ."

"I promise to do as you do. Before going any further, excuse me, but have you named all your reporters?"

"I hope I'm not forgetting any. Twice a year each of the six I have named will try to hold the reader's attention a moment by a well-considered account of anything new in his field the past six months. Properly speaking, they won't be *chroniques;* that's the .greatest advantage of the scheme. To keep up a chronicle day by day, or even once a month, you are forced to pay attention to too many things not worth the trouble. This other way, the sifting will be automatic; at the end of only a few months, what is bad will seem even worse, and the good will look even better; meanwhile the worse we pass over in silence leaves all the more time to speak of the better. I must confess that I am expecting studies rather than *chroniques,* in the journalistic sense of the word. But, frankly, I see nothing in that to . . ."

"Astonish me? . . . That's because you start right off without waiting for my questions."

"Go ahead and ask them. I'm waiting."

"Here they are: Who will handle columns on politics?"

"Nobody."

"Do tell me the truth, who will be in charge of them?"

"Nobody, I tell you; nobody."

"And you really mean to make *L'Ermitage* a serious journal?"

"Pardon me, sir. We have no idea of doing that."

"That's just what amazes me. I've come to the point where I wonder what I've come here for anyway."

"Oh, my dear fellow, don't expect me to tell you! But please let's not quibble about words. Unless it is boring, people very rarely are willing to call serious any activity that represents no material interest. When I say that *L'Ermitage* does not pretend to be a serious journal, I am talking like the majority of people, whom I believe you represent. But you must admit that for me as, I think, for every one of our writers, the things *L'Ermitage* is concerned with are serious, very serious. So far as I am concerned, my dear sir, I will add that if I knew anything else more serious, I . . . Don't let me go on; I'm afraid I would talk too long."

"Allow me another question, nevertheless: Do you really mean that you consider politics and the rest, that is, social and economic questions, etc., matters of no

serious interest and not worth the attention of a cultivated mind? . . ."

"I will consent to give you an answer on that point,
sir, since this is a first interview; but we shan't return
to the question any more, shall we? It would not do any
good. Furthermore, anything I could say would be the
commonplace thing everybody works to death. Politics,
sir! How could you pay no attention to it, even if you
wanted to? No matter what we do it has its eyes on us,
and insists on an answer. Without meaning to or being
aware of it, we engage in politics. Our very thoughts,
according to the form they take, spontaneously assume
a red or white tinge; you can't get away from it; everyone is forced to sit with the "whites" or the "reds." And
you do have to sit down, or everybody and everything
looks at you with an air of reproach. You do sit down
rather hesitantly. But once you are seated, the trouble
begins. It's not long before your seat dictates your opinions, instead of the opinions choosing a seat. Soon after
that you are judging other people's ideas, and even your
own, by their color. You begin to say, in the presence
of a work of art: it is red, therefore it must be bad; it is
white, therefore it must be good; or the other way
around. That may be serving a party, but it certainly
does warp the judgment."

"Yet that is the very question that has come up of
late: once you have recognized that your party is an
excellent one, isn't it worth serving, even with warped
judgments?"

"If that is so, how can one tell that the original judgment, by which the party was found excellent, was not
warped, too? Let me repeat, you don't *choose* your party;
you sit down where the color of your thoughts forces you
to sit."

"Along that line permit me an indiscreet question:
Have you taken a seat?"

"I don't think so, I hope not. Once seated, I shouldn't feel comfortable; however comfortable the chair, I should be worried; I never feel quite alive except in motion."

"That's what your enemies, even your friends, will quickly call indecisiveness, inability to make up your mind. . . . Can it be that you are a dilettante, sir?"

"Shame on you!"

"By your wavering and indecision you do nobody any good. Since no party can claim you, you are no use to any party."

"That's where I think you are wrong, sir. Disinterested thought, I believe, is really more useful than the kind where one knows beforehand what the person will think and that it will already have been dictated by a party. Anyway, it doesn't matter. The important thing, for me, is to give free play to my thoughts."

"Didn't you say a minute ago that our thoughts, by their natural tinge, forced us on the side of a color like them? Do you mean to imply, perhaps, that your thoughts are only of the colorless kind?"

"Colorless thoughts are sickly things, badly put together. I like to feel that mine have plenty of color. But . . . I have some of every color."

"That must be a nuisance."

"Thank you; but not always. In a discussion with others, yes, it is inconvenient; and that is why I don't like discussions very much. At the very first turn of the argument, I find myself abandoning my own side; whether the other fellow is red or white, there I am serving him up his color. But, when I'm all by myself, my dear fellow, that's when the inner debate goes on; there is no stopping it, the dialogue commences. And just as naturally, it shapes itself into a novel, into something dramatic . . . Isn't that the way it should be?"

"The way it should be! Why? What's the use of all that?"

"Pardon me . . . I'm afraid I don't understand the question."

"I can hardly put it more clearly: What is the use, in your opinion, of the novel, or of drama, in short, of belles-lettres?"

"Do you mean from the point of view of the individual?"

"Certainly not; but from the point of view of the majority, the people, the country, or of civilization in general."

"It's somewhat as if you were asking me what the use is, for the tree, of the fruits it bears. I find it very difficult to think of a work of art as anything but an end-product. It seems to me, furthermore, that the critic should consider it in that light. It is by its fruits that you judge the tree."

"The prime resource of the critic should be, then, in your opinion . . . ?"

"Taste."

"I must admit, sir, that I find your ideas bewildering. I am afraid that, in our day, they will meet with little response."

"So am I; but what can be done about it? For the same principle applies here, too: must I, as I speak, think of the echo my voice will raise?"

"Suppose you did think of it? . . ."

"Nothing is so sure to distort the sound of one's words, nor more sure to compromise freedom of thought. 'In order to think freely,' Renan wrote somewhere, 'one must be sure that what one writes will have no practical consequences.' "

"Do you admire that pronouncement?"

"Profoundly."

"As for me, it's a paradox, that's all. Renan was the first to know that what he wrote would have 'practical consequences,' we may be sure of that."

"But it wasn't *for the sake of the consequences* that he made it up. That's the whole point."

"You will grant me at least, that the work of art—and more precisely the written work—can have repercussions . . ."

"The most prolonged, of the utmost concern to all, very serious; I even agree that the artist may have some idea of this; but, to give a twist to thought for their sake, that is the great sin against the spirit, the unforgivable sin."

"In short, you refuse to consider a work of art as more than a natural end-product?"

"Like a fruit, and from which the future must be born. Enough for today, sir. Such introductory considerations are, I daresay, indispensable, but should really be taken for granted. It seems a shame to have to spell them out. But you are the one who is forcing them upon me. For today people want to impose upon us an Apollo made in *your* image, with a yielding look, full of pity, a domestic's voice plus his deferential bow. But Apollo is the proudest of the gods—and that is why he gives light. Good-by for now, sir; I shall speak to you later about the questions of the day. Today, I have done no more than to establish my point of view, to tell the truth."

The gentleman gets up; on his way out, he suddenly turns around.

"I saw," he said, "I admired the exhibition of Maurice Denis; weren't you the one who wrote the preface to the catalogue?"

"Yes."

"At the end of it, you speak of the moral qualities of a work of art or of the artist. Can it be, after what you have just been telling me, that such qualities exist for you? Can moral questions be of any interest to you?"

"Why not? The stuff of which our books are made!"

"But what are morals, in your view?"

"An appendage of aesthetics. Good-by, sir, until our next."

TRANSLATED BY ANGELO P. BERTOCCI

SECOND INTERVIEW

"Yes, an important age," I was quick to agree with my interviewer, "an admirable age . . . and how could I ever find the age in which I live less than admirable; most interesting of ages also because it is the most recent, the latest, but for that very reason less admirable nevertheless and perhaps less interesting than the one which is to follow . . . of which I can catch a glimpse.

"Don't interrupt me; I know what you are going to say, but I'm not going to let your smile prevent me from saying it. Yes, I demand the right to love my age just as Barrès loves Lorraine, his fatherland, and to defend my love by as specious a chain of reasoning as his. I can't do a thing about it: here and now is when I am alive. I belong to my time and I am the child of my country; not being able to avoid that, I am not so foolish as not to know how to love and admire them both."

"Do you mean to say that, no matter in what times you might have lived, and, in his case, no matter in what country he might have been born, both of you would have talked in the same way?"

"In no other age could I even imagine myself possible; nor, any more than Barrès, in any other country whatsoever. Let us not get oversubtle. Simply understand this, sir, that since neither Age nor Fatherland exists apart from the individuals that enter into them, the greatness of the former is measured by the fervor they can inspire in the latter. Now I happen to think that our age offers us rich sources of fervor."

"These sources, sir . . ."

"Please don't smile. These sources, sir, are poisonous for you because they are brand-new sources of nourishment, and because it takes new stomachs to digest them. As for me, I can't help making them my form of nourishment. I am hungry; what our fathers ate is no longer adequate for me. But old gentlemen like you, alas! as well as certain young men born with old stomachs, can't stand the new foods and prefer to complain bitterly if their favorite words, chewed over so many times, no longer have the nutritive qualities people found in them in their prime. So much the worse for them! Woe to these people who have no appetite for the very dish that their age serves up."

"I cannot be expected, nevertheless, to call anything good simply because it is new, nor to guarantee that the last course will have the best taste."

"No one is going to prevent you, sir, from remaining behind with your reason and your logic. The best of reasons will not prevent the man who falls behind from perishing. Taking a chance on the logic, those of us who want to live, we just press on."

"Why insult me? It won't help you to press on. I don't believe in your novelties. Unceasingly, the world begins all over again. Like Solomon I think that there is nothing new under the sun, and I repeat with La Bruyère: 'We are born too late,' and 'Everything worth saying has been said.' "

"La Bruyère, sir, came at a time when culture was localized within narrow limits. They thought they had found the recipe for right living and right thinking. We had inherited from the Latins an image of man harmonious and beautiful, a model that we had used for our own development, without realizing, at first, that it did not, perhaps, express the whole essence of our humanity.

It seemed somehow that we ought to hold fast to it; and
since, in our country, the mind's activity is unresting, we
went to the very limits of self-expression: we began to
refine upon it. From abroad we would accept nothing
but reflections of the same image. We knew Spain, Italy.
We felt we were members of the same race. We visited
within the family circle. Everything else, all around us,
was dark. Just to look around might mean to besmirch
the mind with the works of night.

"Yes, that's it! Everything had been said in the seven
thousand years since there have been men, 'indulging in
thought'—but far back in the abyss of time, ever since
there had been savages *not indulging in thought*—who
had not yet thought, how many things there remained
to say! For we had other cousins: the Barbarians—who
were finally ready to speak, who were just beginning to
speak. When we got over our fear of soiling ourselves,
we stretched out our hands to those first cousins of ours.
One would dare to do it, perhaps, only if one's own
hands were not too clean. Those blackguards of the
eighteenth century knew how to do that only too well.
Thus began our 'traveling in bad company . . .' since
then we have gone far in the same company!"

"Which, slowly, made us lose what we had so patiently
and wisely developed, that sense of dignity, of distinct-
ness, of specialty that characterizes our breed. That is
what certain farseeing minds deplore in our day."

"I can't join them in deploring it. Where you insist
on seeing only a loss, I insist on seeing a gain. I need
not point out that what you call 'our breed' is something
of a mixture. That, I think, is what gave the French
spirit its suppleness, adventurousness, and curiosity.
Here we catch a glimpse of what France was: a meeting-
place, a crossways. Small wonder, then, that, of the
various elements entering into us, the Latin element,
which had already expressed itself before, should be

the first to recognize itself, identify itself, attain to full
consciousness, and with the help of what it had already
said in another time and place, should soon and almost
without effort take over again the role of spokesman.
The only really difficult things to say are those we have
not already said. But, for her sake, do not limit France
to what she has already said; because it is less Latin, do
not assume that what she still has to say is less French.

"To tell the truth, sir, I believe the fundamental
genius of our race to be very different from what certain
superficial critics usually call the 'French spirit,' which,
so much of the time, is but a certain gloss upon the com-
monplaces of thought. At best the term applies to the
spirit of the general public. However little Laforgue,
Rimbaud, Mallarmé, may have been attuned to such a
public, I consider them as perfectly French as Lavedan,
Donnay, or Rostand are said to be today. Their apriorism, their disinterestedness, or if you prefer, a certain
gratuitous quality in their motivation, seem to me more
essentially French than all the other qualities; more
unimaginable in any other country whatsoever. Shall we
say that Maurice Barrès is less French because he presents qualities apparently so Spanish? Perfumes and the
feel of flesh, the love of death which borders on love
itself, the broken rhythms, the hint of a swagger in the
over-all movement, that fine tension suddenly grown
slack, that smile where the lips alone smile, the shadows
à la Zurbaran, the languors à la Murillo. . . . Are we
going to like him less when he sings at his most melo-
dious of Toledo, Venice, or Vladikavkaz? Shall he suddenly seem to us more French when he speaks of Lorraine? It is not difficult to recognize as French a Boylesve,
a Régnier, an Anatole France; but we must agree that
Claudel is just as much so, in a more important way,
too, because so novel a way. No, the French genius develops and thrives and defines itself with greater precision

every day. If we could say right now: This is what it is, and all that it is, alas! we would be saying: It has had its day.

"For the moment, good-by, sir. Trying to keep up with the absence of questions today has simply worn me out. If you don't ask me better questions, and if you allow me to go on the way you do, we shall never get past general considerations. And yet there are several good books on my table that I would have liked to talk about."

"I shall press you more closely with my questions another time."

TRANSLATED BY ANGELO P. BERTOCCI

[THIRD INTERVIEW]

My interviewer has the grippe. I am using the time his visit would have taken to write down my random thoughts. Certainly the fellow was a disappointment. He came to me without any interest in anything I might say, and with no real curiosity. He is one of those people who, before they even reach thirty, come to a stop; what they happened to know before that time is considered enough. They stick by their positions; if you are to make progress, you can do so only by pulling further and further ahead of them.

One thing my interviewer does know: my words are those of an enemy. It is my fault, I admit. He is discreet, courteous, not too unintelligent; but it's no use. The moment I open my mouth, out comes my irritation against him. I cannot forgive him for not having read Claudel, for not liking Dostoevsky. And I even sense that if he should speak of Shakespeare or Racine, we could not agree. Great authors are admirable in this respect: in every generation they make for disagreement. Through them we become aware of our differences. A sudden unanimity in praise is no guarantee of survival; those who please universally at the outset are the ones who are drained at a draught. I should like to feel sure that we shan't quickly drain Anatole France. No trace of half-lights in him, and that's what worries me. I should like to think that in a hundred years they will accuse us of not really having understood him; and that his first word will not turn out to have been his last! His *Pierre Blanche* is on my table, but I have not read it yet; my mind is occupied with another book, the *Promenades littéraires* of Gourmont. A perfect example of a book by which a reader becomes conscious of his age, about which one can agree—or disagree; one of those books, in short, that every man of some literary culture should read. It has taken me two weeks, and I haven't wasted my time. I read him as I should like to be read, that is, very slowly; to read a writer is for me not merely to get an idea of what he says, but to go off with him, and travel in his company. With Gourmont, you accept the invitation in his title, you take a walk, chatting as you go. With him there seems to be no monologue; he invites a conversation.

Can I have read them less carefully, those first books of his which I didn't like so well? They seemed to shock more, yet have less real power; he was violent without effect. Few affirmations in this book, but he insinuates himself; without ever discussing, he persuades. He slips into the reader's mind on the oblique; I don't know quite how he manages it, but he wins our thought over to himself.

How clever what he says of Lemaître! How nicely he handles Mirbeau! Could anyone present Barrès any better, give a better explanation of Huysmans, and mock Rostand more subtly? Each chapter has only a few pages;

I like him for not exhausting his subject. I like him for
taking his leave after walking along with us a while, for
not accompanying us too far. We are grateful to books
only for the initial impulse. We don't like to have people watch over our steps to the end.

Where I drop Remy de Gourmont's arm very suddenly is when he speaks of Barbey d'Aurevilly. No,
there I certainly cannot follow him. To write: *"Les
Diaboliques,* if it were Balzac's, would be Balzac's masterpiece"; to look upon this stuffed shirt as "one of those
singular and as it were subterranean classics who are the
life of French literature" •—this kind of thing makes
me wonder if it is Gourmont I am reading and if he can
really be speaking of Barbey d'Aurevilly. Very much
disturbed, I go back to *Les Diaboliques*—I would take
another look at *Le Prêtre marié, L'Amour impossible,
La Vieille Maîtresse, Le Traité du Dandysme,* if I
didn't have them so well in mind, for I must acknowledge the witchery with which, as writer, he drives his dry
barbs, without any discretion, deep into you. But no, in
that pretentious style I can see nothing but bluff, in
that dazzling display of language and in the impertinence of tone nothing but dissimulation of a defect of
thought, in the showy excesses of a cavalier wit nothing
but essential poverty of mind. In the bold line of the
posture I feel the busk of the corset.

It is nevertheless evident that we shall have to take
account of Barbey d'Aurevilly in the history of literature. He has his deplorable retinue. I should really like
to know if M. Paul Hervieu did not come upon it somewhere along the road. It would give me great satisfaction
to be able to blame D'Aurevilly here, too, make him
somewhat responsible for "so very individual a style," as
the newspapers put it, by which Hervieu nowadays
strains toward affectation. Is it no more than a natural
evolution that leads the incisive and quiet-spoken author

• Didn't D'Aurevilly speaks of "that big booby of a Goethe"?

of *Diogène* to write sentences like those we read in his address to the Académie Française: "You have resolutely ventured an entrance into the soil of the peninsula through the darkened corridor of the year one thousand." "Inversely, with reference to education for girls, his hopes and expectations stopped at a milestone less extended in space than yours." "And now that the brain of the mother is to receive so much less illumination, they inflict the most dismal extinction of light upon that greater number of hearths which are those of children bereft of a father." "We sojourn in a haven, and the great billows of the deep never enter here to disturb a calm to your portion of which, if I may repeat, you are, sir, most welcome." "The smile upon the lips already retracts, in advance, the bitter words still being ground between the teeth." "And besides, do not the finer minds almost all retain in their thought some prejudice at whose feet they bow in penitence for the intelligence they have?"

This last sentence is from Barbey d'Aurevilly; already it holds a promise of the others to come.

TRANSLATED BY ANGELO P. BERTOCCI

*André Gide never ceased exploring the relationship
between literature and nationalism. The question lies
at the basis of his early quarrel with Barrès and Maurras, rises to the surface in his "Reflections on Germany"
and "The Future of Europe," constantly preoccupies
him in his* Journals, *and even enters prominently into
his numerous considerations of the nature of classicism.
But he never became more explicit on the subject than
in the following two essays, first published between
June and November 1909 in the then recently founded*
Nouvelle Revue Française.

*His ingenious application of Carey's economic theory
to the domain of art, in the second essay, answers in advance those critics who later accused him of delving un-
healthily into the romantic* terrae incognitae *of the
soul and expressing his explorations in a rigorously
classical form.*

CONCERNING AN INQUIRY OF "LA PHALANGE"

The inquiry that *La Phalange* has just terminated after
several months was bound to degenerate into a quarrel.
To be sure, the questionnaire appeared quite harmless,

but the word "national" had been enunciated, and everybody knows the exclusivism that goes with that word. The way in which the investigation was conducted aroused some dissatisfaction; the way in which that dissatisfaction mounted up aroused the dissatisfaction of the editor of the journal. Now that politics is suspected of entering into the affair, I don't know whether it will ever be cleared up.

The object of the inquiry was to know whether "serious literature" could avoid being national or not.

The question struck me, even then, as irrelevant.

A people can be imagined without literature, a kind of deaf-mute people, but how is it possible to imagine a word that is not expression for somebody, or a literature that does not express a people?

Would it not have been more interesting, more intelligent, to ask if anyone dared to give the name "serious literature" to a literature which, besides inevitably representing a nation, did not also present a universal, that is, a broadly human, interest? It would then have been easy to observe what I do not offer as a discovery: the most broadly human works, those that retain the most general interest, are also the most individual and concrete, those in which the genius of a race manifests itself in a special way through the genius of an individual. What is more national than the work of Aeschylus, Dante, Shakespeare, Cervantes, Molière, Goethe, Ibsen, Dostoevsky? What is more broadly human? And also more individual? For it should be clear by now that the three terms can be superposed and that no work of art has a universal significance if it does not have first of all a national significance; nor a national significance if it does not have first of all a personal significance.

"Individuality," Hebbel said, "is not so much a goal as it is a route. It is not the best; it is the only way."

Viewed externally, nevertheless, our literature was never quite so French as in the days when it was under

great constraint and regulation. For this reason—not
realizing sufficiently, perhaps, that this constraint, far
from suppressing the individual, actually stimulated
him—some people have tried to set up as opposites a
"specifically French" literature and an emancipated or
romantic literature, have tended to see in the masterpieces of our literature a triumph of the general over the
particular, and to acknowledge in a work qualities more
or less French according as that work seemed more or
less effectively disciplined.

For the first question in the inquiry served as bait
and immediately raised the second one. It was not
enough to observe that a "serious literature" must necessarily be national; immediately its most common characteristics had to be determined in order to know whether
that national literature was still alive or whether it was
dead or on the point of death.

It is easy to determine those most common characteristics.● You pick throughout the course of the centuries
the handful of works which seem to you the best, that
is to say, in the case in point, those most pleasing to your
temperament●● and taste. When this taste is good (and
it is understood in advance that it is very good if it is
very French), it will be discovered that those works are

● "I believe it is quite possible to characterize, throughout the course
of our aesthetic history, a literature that is specifically French: Do we
need to do more than come to an agreement concerning the essential qualities of our race and to seek out the works where they are
best expressed?" M. de Bersaucourt writes with a charming ingenuous-
ness.
●● Racine, Marivaux, Barrès, Moréas, Mme de la Fayette, Gérard de
Nerval, and Fromentin are the authors and the sole authors that M.
Clouard names and acknowledges as "our center," promising "some day
to seek a common denominator." He will find it, we may be sure. As
for a few eccentrics, such as Pascal, Molière, Saint-Simon, Corneille,
etc., since they might stand in the way of the theory, somebody will
no doubt discover, as has just happened in the case of Montaigne, an
unmentionable origin, and that will get them out of the way. As for the
pen-pushers of the eighteenth century, Marivaux excepted, what an
assortment of hacks!

masterpieces which have in common such characteristics
as well-balanced structure, passionate feeling tempered
by reason, etc., etc., in short: beauty.

For my part, I like to think that these conditions of
beauty are the same for all countries, and that what may
make them seem more especially or specifically French
is the fact that in no other country besides France have
they happened to be so often or so fully realized, nor by
an apparently more natural impulse. Similarly, in other
times, the most accomplished work of art also seemed
the most Greek. It was also the most individual, and at
the same time, the most generally human kind of art,
and therefore the most universal. "You know that
France is today for Letters what Greece was in another
day"; I find this remark in Fontenelle and could find it
elsewhere, for it is a common opinion.

To what does France owe this extraordinary favor?
Doubtless, as in the case of Greece, to a happy con-
fluence of racial stocks, to the very kind of mixture
which the nationalists deplore today. For we must recognize that our greatest artists are often the products of
hybridization and the result of uprooting, or better, of
transplantation. M. Maurras once called them, rather
wittily, "seals"—that is, amphibians—setting them off
against writers of purely Celtic, Norman, or Latin
blood, creatures limited to a single element and incapable, therefore, of associating fully and classically in
the multiple intellectual life of France. Shall I quote a
passage from the reply of M. Ghéon, which M. Clouard
seems particularly to relish? "Truly ours is a very special
case. We French do not form a race, but a nation, and
precisely the nation where western racial stocks make
contact, fuse together, and set up an equilibrium. And
France becomes fully herself only through that equilibrium, only through that fusion."

But, if France becomes fully herself only in the harmonious balance of the very different elements that go

into its make-up, by what right do we call any particular
element French or less French? Certainly I applaud
M. Lasserre's book; but it is because I have personally
always had a horror of romanticism and artistic anarchy.
Is it because they are not very French? I need go no further than their inaesthetic character, which my brain,
that of a particular Frenchman, finds repugnant. But
are Hugo, Michelet, etc., for all that, less a part of our
literature? And if, by virtue of my culture and taste, I
prefer to French turbulence what represents French
culture and the elite, shall I condemn France as a whole
to reduce itself to that particular elite? Shall I recognize
as French only the manifestations of that culutre?

Many people today, in order to admire anything, seem
to want to ask not whether it be beautiful, but only
whether it be French!

I hope they won't mind if I refuse to feel anything of
the intruder in Montaigne. Nor do I consent to cede
Calvin and Rousseau to Switzerland. However great my
love for Ronsard, so receptive to everything Italian, I
do not consent, event when he pours his invective on the
Huguenots, to consider him more French than the
Huguenot D'Aubigné. And, in our own day, I have no
illusions concerning the ruinously antisocial nature of
the Jewish theater that has been invading the French
stage for the last ten years; but for all the nationalists
may do, can it prevent the theater of Porto-Riche from
being written and thought in French, and *Amoureuse*
from being a masterpiece?

It was evident, from the very first number of the inquiry, that M. Clouard, who was directing it, aimed less
at his own enlightenment through the opinions of his
contemporaries than to enlighten the latter through his
own. To each of the men questioned he seemed to consider it his function to give a mark of "satisfactory" or a

rap on the knuckles—discreetly, politely, in the French fashion.• And he didn't hide his surprise when his superior air got on some people's nerves so that they answered him in a fashion not the less French for its tartness, while others did not deign to reply at all.

Not that M. Clouard is necessarily weak in logic; but in their intense desire to appear French, some people lose a natural grace that goes with it—for the pleasure of being French diminishes with constraint. If you are French, it is in spite of everything; to be conscious of it, or at least to aim at it deliberately, may very easily spoil certain delicate and secret qualities. Nor does one become more French by aping the manners of old France; and the best way to be French is to be French naturally.

TRANSLATED BY ANGELO P. BERTOCCI

SECOND ARTICLE

I

First came the inquiry by M. Clouard. Then, apropos of that inquiry, came the article I wrote four months ago; after that, the article of M. Henri Ghéon. To these two articles, as well as to M. Francis Vielé-Griffin's on Swinburne, which also appeared in the *Nouvelle Revue Française*, M. Jean-Marc Bernard writes a rejoinder in *Les Guêpes*.

This piquant little review brings together some young

• I say this because I know it will please M. Clouard, who seems to be a well-meaning fellow; but, to tell the truth, I find something horribly Germanic in the boredom his inquiry exudes, while his notes are Teutonic and his conclusions positively outlandish.

men of definitely conservative and reactionary tendencies. It is not the whole of French youth, but is by no
means a negligible portion. I cannot as yet distinguish
these young "wasps" very clearly from one another; besides, every one of them seems to make a point of reduc-
ing himself to a given type, out of a praiseworthy concern
for preserving the rule against the individual. For that
reason, doubtless, the whole swarm seems to possess only
a collective stinger that, so far, has not stung anyone very
hard.

These young people appear to be extremely likable.
I suspect that there is nothing vicious about them;● but
they have convictions. I am willing to believe that if I
were coming of age now, that is, if I were their age and
were able to meet present events head on, I should be
marching by their side.●● Less burdened than we are
by memories, with one fell swoop they reach the spot
toward which we must toil, though laden with more
solid knowledge. They are at the age of quick conclusions; because we add a qualification to their sometimes
not ripely considered affirmations, they bristle with the
belief that we want to do combat. If I return once more
to the field, it is not as an adversary but as a gleaner of
truths. I beg their indulgence, nevertheless, if I call attention first to a certain lack of logic in their reply, for
this leads them toward unwarranted conclusions against
which I think it is of some use to lodge a protest.

Their reply is very brief. This is the gist of it:

"If we recognize with M. Ghéon—and how can we
avoid it?—that 'literary art realized its maximum of
perfection and equilibrium under Louis XIV,' we must
conclude that classicism is the high point of French letters. A second conclusion, which cannot be avoided, is
forced upon us: it is that, in the history of a language,

● They have shown since that they could be very nasty.
●● And sometimes that would have made me very unhappy.

there can be no two literary points of the same height. We are therefore condemned to the impossibility of ever surpassing the seventeenth century. We shall never write, from now on, anything except a few fine anthology pieces. It is for some other literature to become classical, to take up again, continue and develop the work of Athens. Let us manage, then, to die with dignity. Let the final works of our hands have at least the appearance of solidity and proportion."

So this is the only challenge these young beginners have to offer to their valor: a dignified death! My heart, too full of life, rebels at such conclusions; but I go beyond that, I even deny, Jean-Marc Bernard, that they necessarily follow from your premises. Let us look at them more closely:

Balance, proportion: Yes, these admirable qualities, so easy to imitate effectively, were brought by the seventeenth century to a point hard to surpass even in imagination; but are they the only qualities to which a literature may lay claim?

One expression keeps on turning up under their pen: *"haute littérature,"* M. Clouard said; *"haute littérature"* is what M. Bernard says. "Solidity of manners and morals is absolutely necessary for the development of an elevated literature," he writes in *L'Ame Latine* for the month of May. If we could only say that these words had no meaning! But in what direction will they lay their measuring rod? Do they think that literature develops only in one dimension?

No doubt they mean by *haute littérature* the counterpart of that "elevated" painting that Ingres called "historical," that Rubens and Vandyke, he thought, were forced to give up, and to which he was referring when he wrote: "No intense colors; that is antihistorical. Instead, go in for grays."

No doubt it was the hope of attaining to such elevation in literature that inspired Ronsard's *Franciade*!

No doubt it was from literature of such elevation that Boileau banished La Fontaine and La Bruyère, the *Fables* and the *Caractères* being less elevated genres!

No doubt Boccaccio aspired to such elevation in literature when he wrote his *Discourses* in Latin, to make up for insufficient altitude in the *Decameron*!

No doubt our eighteenth century owed the favor in which it was held all over Europe to the "elevated level" on which Voltaire and Crébillon succeeded in maintaining French tragedy!

No doubt we must give up considering the *Divine Comedy* and *Paradise Lost,* the products of deeply troubled periods, as literature of "high seriousness," since M. Jean-Marc Bernard has declared that "solidity of manners and morals is absolutely necessary for the development of an elevated literature"!

Let us give up this useless quarrel. The question remains of the first importance: it is the old quarrel of Ancients against Moderns that is being revived. Specifically, what we want to know is indeed whether "everything has been said" and whether "we have come too late after more than seven thousand years since there have been men, 'indulging in thought,' " as La Bruyère wrote at the head of his *Caractères;* whether, as M. Jean-Marc Bernard writes in our day, "we shall never write, from now on, anything except a few fine anthology pieces." Be that as it may, the short article in *Les Guêpes* is no more than a pretext to expound some ideas that are dear to me. I shall take a broader view of the question.

II

Our young traditionalists are doubtless acquainted with the theory of Ricardo; at least, if I explain it here, they will recognize it as their own:

In a domain under exploitation for some time the good places are already taken. The first cultivators having appropriated the best lands, those who follow attach themselves to less fertile soil, first come first served; soon only the worst lands remain uncultivated, which nevertheless offer a field of conquest for the ambitions of the late-comers, but these lands can only reward increasing labor with steadily decreasing returns. The wisest and the most fortunate, inheriting the lands of their ancestors, will be satisfied with the fields cultivated by them, whose soil, not too impoverished, though long since subject to the plow, yields even today a not inconsiderable harvest.

The illustrious English Jew thought only of tangible harvests. Is it permissible to carry over into the intellectual domain the theses he enunciated? The double meaning of the word "culture" invites such treatment, as does M. Barrès with his theory of uprooting and his eloquent phrase, only half metaphorical: "The soil and the dead." The dead teach us the method of cultivation for the soil that we inherit from them. The beauty of yesterday's harvests is a sure guarantee of the excellence of soil and method. Those terrains, freely and deliberately chosen —how could they be less than the best? O classical writers, Greek, Latin, French! You have taken the good places. The unprofitable tillage that became our heritage might spoil your tools; the hoped-for harvest will never repay our effort. Far better, taking the plow from your hands, to guide it over the deep furrow that you have traced. "Everything has been said"; one can only say it again but not so well. "We have come too late."

This doctrine, considered "pessimistic" in political economy, held the field for quite a while. The moral that any one derived from Ricardo's theses could vary with temperaments. Some thinkers wrestled with the conclusions of his reasoning; the premises at least seemed indisputable once and for all. Now, it is these very premises that Carey's theory attacks.

No, he pointed out, man's earliest efforts were not directed at the best lands. The first areas cultivated are those easiest to get at, those tilled with the greatest convenience—that is, not the rich areas but the poorest ones, those within immediate reach and long capable of satisfying man's needs. They are the high plateau lands (I am reminded of the term "elevated literature") with soil of no great depth, sparsely covered with natural vegetation, so that the plow (or the stylus) can easily work it.

Other land, rich areas, low-lying areas, man will consider only later. For a long time they will remain on the margin of cultivation as "wild" tracts, their riches unsuspected. Civilized man will not readily become aware of their promise; if he does venture to cross them, it will be at first with a sense of inconvenience and danger. "The richest land," says Carey, "is the terror of the first settler."

"What is a fertile soil? It is a soil that, in the state of nature, is invaded by a luxuriant vegetation that will have to be cleared away, or which, if made by alluvial deposits, will have to be reclaimed from the water." • Dark and luxuriant forests where the tangle of vegetation makes the pioneer's journey a weary one; a land peopled with cruel and cunning wild animals; marshy lands, with quicksands and noxious effluvia, fecund beyond any expectation are the last to be exploited. For a long time man will recoil before the dangers and the fevers of low-lying lands; for a long time the murky

• Charles Gide and Charles Rist, *Histoire des doctrines économiques.*

shores of a Stymphalian lake will in vain await their hero.

Yet, however deadly they may have been at first, the plains of the Metidja and of the Sahel, with their abounding fertility, have at last been domesticated. The soil, good or average, has finally been conquered; man has exploited just about the whole area from which he could hope to profit. Virgin forests to clear, marshes to drain become increasingly remote and rare. It is in agronomy that the applicability of Carey's theory first reaches its limit.

It remains longer applicable when it comes to natural forces. "The order of their domestication is in inverse ratio to their power." • Man began by utilizing the power of animals, then of wind and water; the subjugation of steam, then of the redoubtable power of electricity was attempted only later.

Need I say more? I am anxious to go on to the passions, to the forces of intelligence. I have an idea that in psychology Carey's theory maintains its full significance; perhaps it would shed new light on the history of literature—or at least on the particular point that engages us today.

Upon what would the first impulse to poetry tend to bear, the first effort toward stylization operate? On the most fertile areas of the spirit? Certainly not! On the most easily workable. Literature, in the beginning, and for a long time afterward, will be satisfied with exploiting the plateau lands: elevated thoughts, elevated feelings, noble passions; with the result that the earliest heroes of the novel or of tragedy, deprived of depth and complication of character, appear, in the book and on the stage, like sublime marionettes on whom the poet easily pulls the strings.

• Ibid.

And if the Latin elements of our race appeared very early to promise the best cultivation (I was going to say, the largest returns), and if, furthermore, they were the first to reach complete cultivation, it is because, having already been worked over, they yielded most easily to further effort. Latin culture, with its handsome and gracious arrangements, its fruit and branch disposed with such large and elegant economy—how much worry and indecision it spares us by its invitation to devote all our zeal and industry to the established pattern of a few ancient espaliers inherited from Greece!

Meanwhile the alluvial flood of barbarism was covering the plain and the low country—a kind of jungle where Jean-Jacques Rousseau came to botanize; as for the romantics, they bungled their way in.

Racine would not deserve such high honors had he not had a sense, equal to Baudelaire's, of the indescribable resources available to the artist in the wild, fever-ridden, swampy tangle of Orestes' nature, or of Hermione's, Phaedra's, and Bajazet's. He saw that high lands are poor lands. If as a man he finally attained to the high plateaus of virtue, isn't the secret reason for his silence at the height of his career the thinness he found in subjects that harmonized with his piety?

Two things seem to follow: that the richest natures are the hardest to cultivate (to what poverty of temperament is perfection of culture often due: an Anatole France offers a flagrant example); and that each one of us gives over to cultivation, at first, only the more superficial levels of his being, the thinnest, and often stops there, disdaining, scorning, even unaware of his lower depths with their thick vegetation and latent fecundities.

But, some neo-Latins will reply, we are not discussing questions of the greater or lesser fecundity of our lands, we only want to recognize those on which our talents, our methods of cultivation, can be used with the greatest convenience. It goes without saying that they would be Latin soil. Well, you are free, gentlemen, if you do not feel the strength to attack other areas and bring them to terms, you are free to restrict yourself to fields that have already known the plow! But grant at least that men challenged to a bolder adventure by their robustness, hardihood, curiosity, and perhaps a certain restless and passionate ambition shall devote themselves to conquest of newer lands, and not be considered less French for doing it.

I know only too well, alas! the confused romanticism in which such restlessness can eventuate when it is not mastered. The work of art demands order, but what can be given order if not forces still in tumult? Upon what shall our disciplines be worn to the breaking point, if not upon whatever rears up in resistence? What have I to do with the easy to express? I am the mortal enemy of any theory that does not teach me a maximum application of my strength and my virtue. I languish in lands without danger and recognize the Hesperides at a distance by the dragon's roar.

O alluvial soil, new acres difficult and dangerous, but infinite in fecundity!

From the fiercest of your hidden powers, heeding no constraint but that of a sovereign art, there will rise, I know, works that will make men marvel. I know that you are waiting for us. What do I care then for Trianons in all their finery and for the most solemn of Versailles! I will not permit my heart to give more room to regret than to hope, and of the past I will retain only what gives courage toward the future.

And that is why, my dear young traditionalists, if I admire our golden age as much as you do and share with you many of your thoughts, I will not be a party to either your pessimism or your impious act of renunciation.

TRANSLATED BY ANGELO P. BERTOCCI

License, Moral Depravity, and
Senator Bérenger's Declarations

In a campaign to purify the streets of Paris and outlaw pornographic publications, Senator René Bérenger, a self-appointed censor, had written in L'Echo de Paris *that he refused to recognize a special privilege for talent. André Gide answered him in the following witty and annihilating essay, which appeared in* L'Ermitage *of 15 April 1906.*

As an epigraph he used the Senator's words:

Let me make it clear that what I aim at is solely those drawings or writings where an undisputed licentiousness of subject matter cloaks itself in a certain form of beauty. It is alleged that talent and even mere reputation should be enough to allow the merchandise to pass. Thus the blunderer and the artist without skill could be prosecuted; but the man of talent, by a special privilege, would enjoy then an immunity denied the mediocre.

Here, we must confess, agreement is impossible. We cannot countenance the idea that, after having fought a revolution to win equality before the law, our country should put up with such inequalities.

SENATOR BÉRENGER

At the request of the *Echo de Paris,* Senator Bérenger has published in that newspaper "written declarations" where we note an effort to make clear and definite the expression, I won't say of his doctrine, but of his good will. In my desire to clarify my thinking on the most ungrateful of subjects, I went to the newspaper office to look up the articles "Against License and Moral Depravity." I am afraid it was a mistake to read them.

Yet the question was a simple one. It was just a matter of bad public sanitation. We are all agreed: the brazen display of these posters and newspapers is an ignoble thing; you, the moralist, attack their indecency; as an artist, I charge them with ugliness. But we are agreed in a common will to destroy them. They are not only immoral; they are also stupid. They not only shock your modesty; they also offend my taste, repel my eyes. They insult our intelligence.

There are certain places along the boulevards where, in shops open to all and always well stocked, a child boosted by a friend can, with a couple of sous in the slot, see wide-eyed a succession of images with the appetizing title: *The Bride Goes to Bed; Painter and Model; Hunting the Flea,* etc. Close up that place and I shall applaud. We shall see whether there is a single artist not in love with paradox who will protest. You will have them all on your side.

No talent is involved here, nor even a claim to it. These unsigned productions do not express anybody. We have nothing there but a profit motive.

While you are at it, take down a few posters, too. The street belongs to you as well as to me. It belongs to everybody; and not in the same way as a museum whose door I am free to pass without entering. No, I have to go this way; it is the street: unless I am blind or short-sighted, I have to see what's here. Get this stuff out of here!—Are you satisfied?—Your wives, your children, yourselves may circulate without danger. What more do you want?

What you're getting at is this: you want to pursue people into their own domain.

If you found some picture of Danaë shocking, you need not have stepped into the Louvre. If Beaumarchais seemed to you lascivious, you could have done without a ticket to the Théâtre Français. You were free not to buy *Les Fleurs du mal,* not to read *Madame Bovary.* But no. As you "confess": "Here agreement is impossible." With all due consideration you are warned when you approach a work of art: "Look out! There's talent here." But you are quick to take offense and to say: "What do I care?" and (I quote your very words): "It is alleged that talent and even mere reputation should be enough to allow the merchandise to pass. Thus the blunderer and the artist without skill could be prosecuted; but the man of talent, by a special privilege . . ." (I refer you to the epigraph for the rest.) There follows a well-meaning dissertation on ethics: "What makes art is not talent, but the pursuit of the ideal. . . ." "Nudity, which in its nobility of pose or gesture, its perfection . . . realizes a pure ideal of beauty, does not evoke a sensual impression. . . ." It would seem, M. Bérenger, that you have no great taste for the arts.

I am going to try to weigh my remarks carefully. I will grant that it is possible to be an artist without wanting to go to bed with Titian's courtesans like the Fortunio of Gautier; I will grant this unwillingly, but, to please M. Bérenger, I will grant it. But as for the further effort to strip art of all "sensual impression"; the claim that art is not addressed to the senses; the claim that what is addressed to the senses is not art—I say stop there! On this point I am indignant, but not against M. Bérenger alone. What is the difference if some particular Correggio or Watteau leaves him cold? After all, we cannot insist that everyone must be sensitive to painting. What rouses my indignation is the cowardice of certain artists who put on an innocent air and pretend not to understand; they get up on their high horses and cry out: "Our writings pornographic? Our painting sensual?"—I beg of you, don't confuse the question! The important thing is not whether you are licentious or not;

the important thing is that you should have the right
to be.

This is the right that art must defend at all costs.

There are productions of a shameless sort which have
nothing to do with art; but shall we insist because of
them that art has nothing to do with pornography? No
use quoting Aristophanes and the Greeks. I hold that
between one of these objectionable productions and the
"Chemise enlevée" of Fragonard, for instance, the difference lies not in the subject, nor in a quality of
"nobility" or the "ideal," but in talent. Where one man
creates a masterpiece, another would have painted an
obscenity. I hold that if you deprive talent of this "special privilege," you condemn at one stroke our literature and our arts. I hold that you condemn them even
if you accord such a privilege only to talent; for who is
going to recognize this talent, is it *you,* Senator? I am
perfectly confident that, when it first appeared, you saw
in Manet's *"Olympia"* nothing but a parcel of filth—
with which you contrasted, no doubt, the chaste nudity
of a Lefebvre and the ideal nudity of a Cabanel.

Out of the same horror for such mediocre special
pleading, out of the same disgust for such filthy and
inept publications, I thought I shared your feelings
fully. I read what you have to say. I can see the danger
you represent. Your motives are noble, but your disinterestedness carries you beyond the real task. Purify
the street by localizing pleasure and we shall back you
up. But do not pursue pleasure wherever it takes refuge.
Above all do not dislodge it from literature and the
arts; I should like to see talent make them an asylum
absolutely inviolable—yes! the asylum of pleasure.

You invoke the respect owed the child. I know; I
know—I remember the words of the Gospel: "But
whoso shall offend one of these little ones which believe
in me, it were better for him that a millstone were
hanged about his neck, and that he were drowned in

the depth of the sea." Alas, I am also aware of Socrates, condemned *quia corrumperet juventutem*. O pacific, O perfidious language! For whom, M. Bérenger, will you grind the hemlock? I know very well that your hands would never hold the cup of death; but, nevertheless, I shall be on my guard. Others will come who will not have your tact; after the newspaper and the picture, it will be the turn of the book, the painting; after "morals" will come philosophy. Out of respect for the child we shall render the man puerile; to protect the weak of mind, we shall make imbeciles of the strong. It is by very similar theories that, sometimes, certain of our nationalists . . . But this would lead me too far afield.

TRANSLATED BY ANGELO P. BERTOCCI

In Memoriam

Gide frequently spoke of the value of veneration and of the fact that recent generations were losing the faculty. Perhaps nowhere does his own capacity to venerate appear more clearly than in his memorial essays on Stéphane Mallarmé and Oscar Wilde, which appeared in October 1898 and June 1902 respectively in L'Ermitage.

Upon learning of the death of Mallarmé, the high priest of symbolism whose regular Tuesday gatherings he had attended since 1890, Gide wrote a friend that Mallarmé was "the only literary survivor of the preceding generation whom I admired." And by the time his essay had appeared, he had already arranged with Paul Valéry and Francis Vielé-Griffin for the three of them to pay the monthly rent of the famous apartment at 98, rue de Rome so that Mallarmé's widow and daughter could continue to live there. As late as 1948, he saw the bond linking together his generation (Valéry, Proust, Suarès, Claudel, and himself are the ones he mentions) as a scorn for things of the moment, in which "the more or less secret influence of Mallarmé" was the determining factor.

It is significant that, despite what he says of the folly of imitating Mallarmé's syntax and manner, Gide's essay on Mallarmé is written in Mallarmé's prose style. Many were those who, sixty years ago, unconsciously adopted the master's concise and stiffly articulated Latin style. Gide, Louÿs, Régnier, and Valéry inherited the manner

direct from Mallarmé's lips, but nowhere in Gide's writ-
ing is it more flagrantly apparent than in this pious
memorial to the dead leader of the group.

Gide first met Oscar Wilde in Paris in 1891, when the
latter was truly a "King of Life." Then a highly signifi-
cant encounter, which Gide described much later in his
memoirs, occurred in early 1895 at Blida, between Al-
giers and Oran. Apart from their common homosexual-
ity, the two men are about as different as men can be,
yet the writers share more than appears on the surface.
As the memorial essay (written in December 1901)
tells us, Gide was one of the first to visit the paroled and
chastened Sebastian Melmoth at Berneval, and he was
one of the last to sit on a café terrace with the pitiable,
soft Wilde who stares out at us from the Toulouse-
Lautrec portrait. On those occasions the thought may
never have crossed his mind to contrast himself with
his interlocutor, so different did he recognize his own
ethic and force of will to be. Yet Wilde's example even-
tually forced him to attempt a justification of his own
way of life in so many of his works.

STÉPHANE MALLARMÉ

Stéphane Mallarmé is dead. Our hearts are filled with
sorrow. How could I speak today of anything else? The
noble figure that has just disappeared is still almost
alive; we are even more aware now of its uniqueness.
Of that figure, before it gets farther from us, I should
like to speak especially, and of its admirable example.
There will be plenty of time to speak of his work; those
who come after us will speak of it even better; it covers

this beloved name with a quiet but pure celebrity, composed of beauty without sadness and almost without human emotion. Already marked by tranquillity and immortal serenity, it is the most beautiful kind of fame —the most beautiful and the bitterest kind of fame.

For even in the face of death, ridicule and spite have not laid down their arms. And there is reason to think that for a long time to come foolishness, superficiality, and self-satisfaction will not forgive what, by its brightness alone and simply by existing, humiliates them.•

Through a kind of cruel pride, or, rather, naturally and solely through the purity of his beautiful mind, Stéphane Mallarmé had preserved his work from life. Life flowed about him as a river slips past the sides of a ship at anchor; he was never swept along. The very lack of timeliness of his work is cause that it will not be short-lived. Already remote from the present by anticipation, it appeared, rather, like a distant work, already tested by time, upon which time has no hold. And I believe firmly that Mallarmé's work will endure almost intact. What rarer praise can be given this rare spirit, isolated in a society of men of letters who speculate, confuse fame and success, acquire the one only by scorning the other, and owe to the apparent timeliness of their work alone the clatter of quick applause, the vulgarity of their indiscriminate public, and then, the

• Let us mention, to set against the indecent article in *Le Temps*, M. Lalo's respectful and serious tribute in *Les Débats;* perhaps in atonement for the foolish and vile article that same paper once dared to print, entitled "Old Verlaine Pulls a Fast One," which was signed Georges Clément. These things must not be forgotten.

As for *L'Aurore*, we cannot ask that it understand so uncharacteristic a figure; it would have done better not to speak of him at all. Nothing seems more vain than an occupation of which the motives are not understood; had it not been for the practical invention of Greek fire, the scorn of the Syracusans for Archimedes would have known no bounds, especially when he let himself be killed. Here scorn tends even to become hatred; did not the philosopher indicate in this way that what occupied him and could not be seen by others was more important than Syracuse, more important than life itself?

immortal scorn or the immortal oblivion that follows?
The public thinks it chooses its authors; not at all; it is
the artist who chooses his public; one is always worthy
of the other. Some, little eager for trivial favors, find in
a huge and bustling crowd very few readers worthy of
them; they require a greater choice, in a crowd still
vaster and more widespread. To scorn the vulgar public
is to esteem certain individuals the more. Where is one
to find them? It is only in the long sequence of time
that they can of themselves make their choice, one here,
another there, each of them solitary. Slowly, through
successive generations, is formed a public that is itself
admirable.•

The flight of time carries along all that was attached
to it; it is outside of time that the anchor holds. Secured
against drifting, Mallarmé had long stood steady outside
the world; that is why, no longer receiving nourishment
from without, his totally abstract work, springing from
itself and using the world only as a representative instrument, can in its entirety appear vain to one who
seeks relationships with "its time"—but illuminated in
its entirety to one who is willing to penetrate it intimately, slowly, step by step, as one enters the closed
system of a Spinoza, a Laplace, or a geometry.••

• I know that many names, and among them the greatest, can be
cited, for whom popular favor did not bar more selective favor, whose
success did not kill fame, and whose fame, for being initially popular,
was neither less splendid nor less enduring; but this is because the
work of those admirable geniuses without containing walls stretched
far out over the public domain. Accordingly what the crowd admires in
them is not the very center of the work, the god in the secret of his
temple, but rather the outbuildings of easy access and the common
ground where it is easy to get one's bearings. Besides, there is no rule
for this, and in the face of a thousand bold examples in contradiction,
what I have said above can be reiterated.
•• Literature a priori in its orientation—and consequently distinctively
French and Cartesian—but more concise in form than the somewhat
discursive French mind can generally endure, and in appearance rather
Latin, by reason of its conciseness, its syntax, to such a degree that

It is essential that we should soon have a complete edition of the works of Stéphane Mallarmé. Aside from some poems admirable separately (almost all from an early period), Mallarmé's works require, for understanding, a very slow and progressive initiation. The last writings disconcert those who have not come to them from a study of their predecessors. Only under very close scrutiny do the words reveal the frightening density that inner meditation has given them, and as they count neither on picturesqueness nor on direct pathos, but on *that* alone, everything escapes the impatient reader who wants writing to speak quickly. He holds nothing more before him—nothing but a little black on white; "Words! Words! Words!"

But the attention we refuse to the living we grant more readily to the dead.

We do not flatter ourselves, certainly, that we have "understood" all of Mallarmé. Many passages remain under study. And the mind often balks, refuses to pursue further a thought so different from its own (for it seems often that the secret is revealed only as a reward for a most assiduous pursuit). But I know that never was the pursuit vain and that, the more patient it was, the more profound, joyous, fecund, full of delights, was the calm that followed, in the contemplation of this pure and beautiful imagination.

I must confess on the other hand to the irritation that certain pseudo admirers of the poet cause me, who, in truth, "understand" with a facility that suggests superficiality of mind rather than strength. Usually writers themselves and not satisfied with understanding, they imitate. A quick-blooming Mallarmé lives again in them. Against one of them Mallarmé turned a very gentle

---

certain passages in the *"Après-Midi d'un faune"* have brought us a poetic emotion very like what we seek in the Virgilian *Eclogues*.

irony, barely tinged with melancholy and so discreet that the one who reported it to me, the very author to whom the words were addressed, repeated them as though they were praise. "What I especially admire here," said the master, "is that what I spent thirty years seeking, you, who are now twenty, have discovered in one."

What madness, to imitate Mallarmé! At the very most one could employ his patient method for other ends, but to imitate the result of this method in the external oddity that is sometimes due to it is as foolish as walking through the streets in a diver's outfit, or writing backward on the pretext that you admire Leonardo's manuscripts. Mallarmé, in this respect, did much good and much bad, like every powerful spirit. Much good, because he singled out certain stupid plagiarists for deserved ridicule; much harm, because the authority of this magical mind, its involuntary despotism—all the more fearsome for being veiled with gentleness—could bend certain spirits not negligible, but overly flexible, or too young and insufficiently formed, bend them into insincere attitudes, cause them to adopt a syntax, a manner of writing, that assumed and necessitated a method and without it was but manner and pure affectation.

How could it have been otherwise? Those yet to come, and those who have come in the last three years, cannot adequately comprehend the disappointment in store for a youthful spirit eager for art and the emotions of the mind upon entering what was then "the literary world." Renan, Leconte de Lisle, and Banville, dead; Rimbaud, lost; Verlaine, wild, impossible to catch. Heredia's conversation, all verve, had little substance; Sully Prudhomme was off the mark; a certain disdainful infatuation with self made it difficult to recognize in Moréas the qualities of a true poet which were his; Régnier and Vielé-Griffin were just emerging. To whom could we turn? Great heavens, whom could we admire?

We would go to Mallarmé's; it was evening; at first one was struck by a great silence; at the door all the noises of the street died; Mallarmé began to speak in a soft, musical, unforgettable voice—forever stilled now, alas! Oddly, *he thought before speaking!*

And for the first time, in his presence we felt, we touched the reality of thought; what we were seeking, what we wanted, what we adored in life existed; to *that,* a man, here, had sacrified everything.

For Mallarmé literature was the aim, yes, the very end of life; here one felt it to be authentic and real. In order to sacrifice everything to it as he did, one had to believe in it to the exclusion of all else. I do not think that, in all our literary history, there is an example of a more intransigent conviction.

Closed to every other voice, we could not see in him the final and most perfect of the Parnassians, the summit, the fulfillment, the consummation of the school; we saw in him an initiator. That is why, perhaps, the reaction during these last years was so sharp, so wildly impassioned. It might have been taken for a rebellion in the name of freedom compromised, so completely had this calm and withdrawn spirit dominated minds and compelled the admiration of others. They kicked over the traces; they made a show of hating him; and never was his domination so plainly asserted as by those who broke loose from it. They could not do so without fanfare. They demanded the right to live as if Mallarmé had forbidden them existence in some other world than his own—solely by the tranquil manifestation of a moral beauty outside the world, blinding like that of the solitary of whom he speaks, who negates the external world through the power of his faith.

And I grant that the violence and passion of recent reactions came also from the violence and passion of certain admirers, among whom we count ourselves.

In an age when we needed to admire, Mallarmé

alone inspired a legitimate admiration; how could it have been other than violent and impassioned?

TRANSLATED BY JEFFREY J. CARRE

OSCAR WILDE

It was in Biskra, a year ago at this season, that I learned from the newspapers of the distressing death of Oscar Wilde. To my keen regret the distance made it impossible for me to be one of the meager escort that followed his remains to the ——— Cemetery.• I lamented in vain that my absence seemed to reduce still further the pitiably small number of friends that had remained faithful, but at least I intended to write these pages at once; then for a rather long period, Wilde's name seemed to become again the property of the newspapers. Now that all indiscreet gossip around this so sadly famous name has abated, now that the crowd, after having first praised, is at last wearied of sensation and condemnation, perhaps a friend can express an abiding sorrow and contribute, like a wreath to an abandoned grave, these pages of affection, admiration, and respectful pity.

When the notorious trial, which so aroused English public opinion, threatened to destroy Wilde's life, a few writers and artists attempted a kind of rescue operation in the name of literature and art. It was hoped that by praising the writer they would secure forgiveness for the man. Unfortunately, their action was based on a misconception, for it must be admitted that Wilde is not a great writer. The leaden life preserver that was thrown

• [Gide omitted naming the Père-Lachaise.]

out simply completed his ruin; his works, far from supporting him, seemed to sink with him. In vain a few
hands stretched out. The waters of the world closed
over him; it was the end.

At that time, a quite different mode of defense could
not occur to anyone. Instead of attempting to hide the
man behind his work, it was essential to show the man
at first admirable, as I shall now attempt to do—then
the work itself illuminated by the man. "I have put all
my genius into my life; I have put only my talent into
my works," said Wilde. He was not a great writer but
a great *liver,* if you will allow the word to assume its
full sense. Like the Greek philosophers, Wilde did not
write but talked and lived his wisdom, entrusting it
imprudently to the fluid memories of men, as though
writing in water. Let those who have known him longer
relate his biography; one of those who most avidly listened to him simply records here a few personal memories.

I

Those who met Wilde only during the last period of
his life can ill imagine, from the enfeebled and ravaged
creature that prison sent back to us, the prodigious being he was at first.

I met him for the first time in 1891. Wilde had then
what Thackeray calls "the principal gift of great men"
—success. His look and his gestures were triumphant.
His success was so assured that it seemed that success
preceded Wilde and that he had but to step forward.
His books surprised and charmed. His plays were to be
the rage of London. He was rich, tall, handsome—show-
ered with happiness and honors. Some compared him to
an Asiatic Bacchus; others to a Roman emperor; others
to Apollo himself—and it is a fact that he was radiant.

No sooner was he in Paris than his name ran from
mouth to mouth; absurd anecdotes were told about him;

Wilde was still known simply as the man who smoked gold-tipped cigarettes and who walked in the streets with a sunflower in his hand. For, skillful at gulling those who assure social success, Wilde had created, as a front for his real character, an amusing phantom that he paraded most wittily.

I heard him discussed at Mallarmé's: he was described as a brilliant conversationalist, and I expressed an interest in meeting him, but with little hope of success. A bit of luck, or rather a friend to whom I had spoken of my desire, came to my aid. Wilde was invited to dinner at a restaurant. There were four of us present, but Wilde alone did the talking.

Wilde did not really talk—he narrated. For almost the entire meal, he did not stop telling his stories. He told them softly, slowly; his voice was marvelous. He spoke French admirably well, but he pretended to grope a bit for the words that he wanted to postpone for emphasis. He had almost no accent, or at least only as much as it pleased him to keep, so as to give words an aspect sometimes new and strange. In pronouncing *"scepticisme"* he would retain the English "k" sound. The stories that he told us endlessly that evening were confused and not his best; Wilde, uncertain of us, was trying us out. Of his wisdom or his madness he would release only what he thought his listener could enjoy; he served to each, according to his appetite, his proper food; and those who expected nothing from him got nothing, or only a touch of froth; as his first concern was to entertain, many of those who thought they knew him knew only the entertainer in him.

When the meal was over we went out. As my two friends were walking together, Wilde took me aside:

"You listen with your eyes," he said to me quite abruptly. "That is why I shall tell you this story:

"When Narcissus died, the flowers of the fields grieved and asked the river for some drops of water that they might weep over him. 'Oh,' answered the river, 'if all my drops of water were tears, I should not myself have enough to weep over Narcissus. I loved him.' 'Oh,' said the flowers of the fields, 'how could you have failed to love Narcissus? He was beautiful.' 'Was he beautiful?' asked the river. 'Who should know that better than you? Each day lying on your bank, he would gaze at his beauty in your waters. . . .' "

Wilde paused. " 'If I loved him,' answered the river, it is because when he bent over my waters, I saw my waters mirrored in his eyes.' "

Then Wilde, puffing into a bizarre laugh, added:

"That is called 'The Disciple'!"

We had reached his door and we left him. He asked me to see him again. That year and the year following I saw him often and everywhere.

In front of others, as I have said, Wilde assumed a public mask, designed to surprise, amuse, or occasionally exasperate. He never listened and paid little attention to any thought that was not his own. As soon as he ceased to shine alone, he would take a back seat. You found him again only when you found yourself alone with him.

But once alone, he would begin: "What have you been doing since yesterday?"

And since my life then flowed on smoothly, the account I could give offered no interest. I obediently reported some minor details, and as I spoke, I saw Wilde's face darken.

"Is that really what you have done?"

"Yes," I answered.

"And what you say is true?"

"Quite true."

"Then why tell it? Don't you see? That has not the

slightest interest. You must understand that there are two worlds: the world that exists without having to talk about it is called *the real world,* because there is no need to talk about it to see it; the other is the world of art; one must talk about that world, for otherwise it would not exist.

"There was once a man who was loved in his village because he told stories. Every morning he would go forth, and when he returned in the evening all the workers in the village, who had labored all day long, would gather about him and say: 'Come! Tell us. What did you see today?' And he would say: 'In the forest I saw a faun playing a flute, and a circle of small wood-spirits danced to his music.' 'Tell us more. What else did you see?' the men would ask. 'When I reached the seashore I saw three sirens, at the waves' edge, combing their green hair with a golden comb.' And the men loved him because he told them stories.

"One morning he went out from his village as he did every morning, but when he reached the seashore, he saw three sirens, three sirens at the waves' edge, combing their green hair with a golden comb. Then he continued on his way and, coming near the forest, he saw a faun who was playing the flute and a circle of spirits dancing to his music. That evening when he returned to his village and they asked him as they did every evening: 'Come! Tell us. What did you see?' he answered: 'I saw nothing at all.' "

Wilde paused for a moment, let the effect of the story sink into me, and continued:

"I do not like your lips; they are straight like those of someone who has never lied. I want to teach you to lie, so that your lips might become beautiful and twisted like those of an ancient mask.

"Do you know what makes the work of art and what makes the work of nature? Do you know what makes their difference? After all, a narcissus is as beautiful as a work of art—it cannot be beauty that differentiates them. Do you know what the distinction is? The work of art is always *unique*. Nature, which makes nothing that endures, repeats itself always so that nothing it makes will be lost. There are many narcissi; therefore each lives but one day. And each time nature invents a new form, she repeats it immediately. A sea monster in one sea knows that in another sea there is another monster —his double. When God creates a Nero, a Borgia, or a Napoleon in history, He holds another in reserve; he is not known, but that is of no importance; the essential is that *one* succeed; for God invents man, and man invents the work of art.

"Yes, I know—one day there was on the earth a great disquiet, as though at last nature was about to create something unique, truly unique, and Christ was born on earth. Yes, I know that—but listen:

"When Joseph of Arimathea, in the evening, came down from the Mount of Calvary, where Jesus had just died, he saw seated on a white stone a young man weeping. And Joseph drew near to him and said: 'I do not wonder that your sorrow is great, for surely He was a just man.' 'Oh! I do not weep on that account. I weep because I too have wrought miracles! I too have given sight to the blind; I have cured the lame and I have raised the dead. I too have dried up the barren fig tree and changed water into wine. And yet they have not crucified me.' "

And more than once it was shown to me that Oscar Wilde was convinced of his representative mission.

The Gospel disturbed and tormented Wilde, the pagan. He could not forgive it for its miracles. The pagan miracle is the work of art: Christianity was trespassing. All robust artistic unreality demands an assured reality in life.

His most ingenious apologues, his most disturbing ironies, were devised to confront the two ethics, that is,

pagan naturalism and Christian idealism, with a view
to stripping the latter of all sense.

"When Jesus thought to return to Nazareth," he
would say, "Nazareth was so changed, that He no longer
knew His city. The Nazareth in which He had lived was
filled with tears and lamentation; this new city was
filled with laughter and song. And Christ, entering the
city, saw slaves bearing flowers, hastening toward the
marble staircase of a house of white marble. Christ
entered and saw, in the rear of a hall of jasper, lying on
a purple couch, a man whose disheveled hair was en-
twined with red roses and whose lips were red with wine.
Christ approached him and touched his shoulder and
said: 'Why do you lead this life?' The man turned
around, recognized Him, and answered: 'I was a leper
and you healed me. What other life should I lead?'

"And Christ passed out of this house. And in the
street He saw a woman whose face and garments were
painted and whose feet were shod with pearls; and a
man followed her whose cloak was of two colors and
whose eyes were bright with lust. And Christ approached
the man and touched his shoulder and said to him:
'Why then do you follow this woman and look thus at
her?' The man turning recognized Him and answered:
'I was blind and you gave me sight. What else should
I do with my eyes?'

"And Christ approached the woman: 'This path you
are following,' He said to her, 'is the way of sin; why do
you go on?' The woman recognized Him and smiling
said: 'The path I follow is pleasant and you forgave me
all my sins.'

"Then Christ felt His heart full of sadness and wished
to leave the city. But as He was going forth, He saw at
last, seated on the edge of the moat around the city, a
young man weeping. Christ approached him and touching his locks said to him: 'My friend, why are you
weeping?'

"And Lazarus looked up and recognized Him and answered: 'I was dead and you raised me from the dead; what else should I do with my life?' "

"Do you want me to tell you a secret?" began Wilde, another day—we were at Heredia's and he had taken me aside in the middle of a drawing room filled with people—"a secret, but promise me that you will never repeat it. Do you know why Christ did not love His mother?" He whispered this in my ear, as though ashamed. He paused briefly, seized my arm, stepped back, and then, breaking into a laugh, said abruptly: "Because she was a virgin!"

I should like to tell one more story, one of the strangest on which the mind can stumble—and let him who can understand the contradiction that Wilde hardly seems to invent:

"And there was a great silence in God's House of Judgment. And the soul of the sinner came naked before God.

"And God opened the Book of the Life of the sinner.

" 'Surely thy life hath been evil: thou hast . . .' (thereupon followed a prodigious, marvelous enumeration of sins).• 'Since thou hast done all that, surely will I send thee into Hell.'

" 'Thou canst not send me into Hell.'

" 'And for what reason can I not send thee into Hell?'

" 'Because in Hell have I lived all my life.'

"And there was a great silence in God's House of Judgment.

" 'Well, since I may not send thee into Hell, I will send thee into Heaven.'

" 'Thou canst not send me into Heaven.'

" 'And for what reason can I not send thee into Heaven?'

• The version that Wilde made later of this tale is, exceptionally, excellent—and excellent, too, the translation that our friend H. Davray has made of it for the *Revue Blanche.*

" 'Because I have never been able to imagine it.'

"And there was a great silence in God's House of Judgment." •

One morning Wilde had me read an article in which a rather obtuse critic congratulated him on "his ability to invent pretty stories to better clothe his thought."

"They think," began Wilde, "that all thoughts are born naked. They do not understand that I *cannot* think except through stories. The sculptor does not seek to translate his thought into marble; *he thinks in marble,* directly.

"There was a man who could think only in bronze. And this man, one day, had an idea, the idea of joy, the joy that abides for a moment. And he felt that he must express it. But in all the world there remained not a single piece of bronze; for men had used it all. And this man felt that he would become mad, if he did not express his idea.

"And he thought of a piece of bronze, on his wife's tomb, of a statue that he had made to adorn the tomb of his wife, the one woman whom he had loved; it was the statue of sorrow, of the sorrow that endures for a lifetime. And the man felt that he would become mad if he did not express his idea.

"And he took this statue of sorrow, the sorrow that endures for a lifetime; he broke it and melted it and made from it a statue of joy, the joy that abides but for a moment."

Wilde believed in a fatality for the artist; he believed that the idea is stronger than the man.

"There are," he would say, "two kinds of artists: some bring answers, the others bring questions. You must know if you are of those who answer or of those who question; for the one who questions is never the one who answers. There are works that wait and are not

• Since Villiers de L'Isle-Adam has let it out, everybody, alas, knows the Church's great secret: *There is no purgatory.*

understood for a long time: they brought answers to questions not yet asked; for the question often comes a terribly long time after the answer."

And he would say also: "The soul is born old in the body; it is to rejuvenate it that the body ages. Plato is Socrates' youth. . . ."

Then I did not see him again for three years.

II

Here begin the tragic memories.

A persistent report, growing with the news of his success (in London he was being played simultaneously in three theaters), attributed unnatural habits to Wilde, about which some deigned to be smilingly indignant and others unperturbed; it was said also that he made no secret of his habits and often flaunted them, some said courageously, others cynically, others affectedly. I listened, amazed, to this report. Nothing, in the time I had known Wilde, had ever led me to suspect anything. But already, prudently, a number of old friends were deserting him. They did not yet reject him outright, but they no longer made a point of having encountered him.

An extraordinary coincidence joined our paths once more. It was in January 1895. I was traveling; a black mood drove me to it, and the pursuit of solitude more than the novelty of places. The weather was abominable; I had fled from Algiers to Blida; I was about to leave Blida for Biskra. On the point of leaving the hotel, out of idle curiosity, I looked at the blackboard where the travelers' names were written. What did I see? Beside my name, touching it, was Wilde's. I have said that I was avid for solitude; I took the sponge and wiped out my name.

Before I reached the station, I was no longer wholly certain that a touch of cowardice was not hidden in this act; at once turning back, I had my valise taken up to my room and wrote my name back up on the board.

In the three years since I had last seen him (for I cannot count a brief encounter in Florence, the year before), Wilde had certainly changed. There was something less soft in his glance, something hoarse in his laughter and violent in his joy. He seemed at once more sure of pleasing and less intent on doing so; he was emboldened, strengthened, heightened. It is strange, but he no longer spoke in apologues; during the few days that I remained with him, I could not get the slightest story from him.

I expressed my surprise first at finding him in Algeria. "Oh," he told me, "it's because I am now fleeing from the work of art. Now I want to adore only the sun. Have you noticed that the sun detests thought? It drives it ever back, into the shadows. Thought once inhabited Egypt; the sun conquered Egypt. It lived long in Greece, and the sun conquered Greece; next came Italy and then France. Now all of thought is driven back to Norway and Russia, lands never reached by the sun. The sun is jealous of the work of art."

To adore the sun was to adore life. The lyrical adoration of Wilde was becoming fierce and terrible. A fatality was leading him; he could not and would not break with it. He seemed to put all his care, his virtue, into exaggerating his destiny and exasperating himself. He went toward pleasure as a man goes to his duty. "It is my duty to amuse myself terribly," he would say. Nietzsche came as less of a surprise to me later, because I had heard Wilde say: "Not happiness. Pleasure. One must always desire what is most tragic."

He would walk through the streets of Algiers, preceded, accompanied, followed by an extraordinary band of ruffians; he would talk with each one; he would look joyously at them all and scatter his money to them.

"I hope I have thoroughly demoralized this city," he would say to me.

I thought of Flaubert's remark when asked to what

kind of fame he aspired: "That of demoralizer," he
answered.

I stood astonished, admiring, and fearful before that.
I knew about his situation imperiled, the hostilities, the
attacks, and the somber uneasiness he hid beneath his
bold joy.• He spoke of returning to London; the Mar-
quis of Q.•• was insulting him, summoning him, accus-
ing him of running away.

"But if you go back, what will come of it?" I asked
him. "Don't you know the risk you are taking?"

"One must never know that. My friends are ex-

• On one of our last evenings in Algiers Wilde seemed to have resolved to say nothing serious. At last I became somewhat nettled by
his overly witty paradoxes.

"You have something better to offer than jokes," I began. "You are
talking to me tonight as though I were the public. Instead, you should
speak to the public as you speak to your friends. Why aren't your
plays better? The best in you comes out in your talk. Why don't you
write it down?"

"Oh, but my plays are not good at all!" he exclaimed at once. "They
mean nothing to me. But if you only knew how much people enjoy
them! Almost all of them are the result of a wager. *Dorian Gray*, too.
I wrote it in a few days because one of my friends claimed that I could
never write a novel. It bores me so to write." Then, leaning suddenly
toward me, he said: "Do you want to know the great drama of my
life? It is that I have put all my genius into my life; I have put only
my talent into my works."

It was only too true. The best of his writing is but a pale reflection
of his brilliant conversation. Those who have heard him talk find his
writings a disappointment. *Dorian Gray* was originally an admirable
story, much superior to *La Peau de Chagrin!* Far more *significant!*
Written, alas, it is a masterpiece that falls short. His most charming
tales are too literary; despite their grace you are too much aware of
affectation; preciosity and euphuism cover the beauty of the first inspiration; you feel in them, you cannot but feel, the three phases of
their development: the original idea is very beautiful, simple, profound,
and sure to impress: a kind of latent necessity holds its parts firm;
but here the gift comes to a halt; the development of the parts is done
in an artificial manner; they do not go together well; and when, later,
Wilde works over his sentences, strives for his effects, it is by a prodigious overlay of conceits, of petty inventions, amusing and bizarre, in
which emotion is brought up short, so that the surface shimmer con-
ceals from mind and eye the profound central emotion.

•• [Gide gives only Queensberry's initial.]

traordinary; they advise me to be prudent. Prudence! Is prudence possible for me? That would mean turning back on myself. I must go as far as possible. I cannot go further. . . . Something has to happen, something else. . . ."

Wilde took a boat back the following day.

The rest of the story is familiar. The "something else" was "hard labour." •

III

As soon as he was released from prison, Oscar Wilde returned to France. In Berneval, a quiet little village in the neighborhood of Dieppe, a certain Sebastian Melmoth took up residence; it was Wilde. As I had been the last of his French friends to see him, I wished to be the first to see him again. As soon as I found out his address, I hurried there.

I arrived toward the middle of the day. I had not announced my arrival. Melmoth, whom the hospitality of T. called rather often to Dieppe, was expected only that evening. It was the middle of the night before he arrived.

It was still almost winter. It was cold, nasty weather. All day I wandered over the deserted beach, dismayed and bored. How could Wilde have chosen to live in Berneval? It was lugubrious.

Night came. I returned to engage a room at the hotel where Melmoth was staying—the only one in town. The

---

• I have invented nothing, rearranged nothing, in the final words I quote. Wilde's words are present in my mind; I might almost say that they ring in my ears. I do not claim that Wilde saw prison rise up clearly before him; but I maintain that the great reversal that surprised and rocked London, abruptly transforming Wilde from accuser to accused, did not, strictly speaking, cause him any surprise. The newspapers, which insisted on seeing in him a mere buffoon, have distorted as best they could the attitude of his defense, to the point of divesting it of all sense. Perhaps in some distant future, it will be appropriate to raise this abominable trial out of the mud.

hotel, clean, pleasantly situated, sheltered only a few nondescript beings, inoffensive background figures with whom I had to dine. A poor society for Melmoth!

Fortunately I had a book with me. A lugubrious evening! Eleven o'clock—I was about to abandon my vigil when I heard the wheels of a carriage. It was M. Melmoth.

M. Melmoth was chilled. He had lost his overcoat along the way. A peacock feather which, the evening before, his servant had brought him (dreadful omen) had foretold his bad luck; he was happy that it was no more than that. But he was shivering and the entire hotel bustled about to prepare him a hot toddy. He scarcely acknowledged my presence. Before the others, at least, he would not show his emotion. And mine almost immediately subsided, at finding Sebastian Melmoth quite simply the Oscar Wilde he had once been; not the violent lyricist of Algeria, but the gentle Wilde I had known before the crisis; I found myself carried back not two years, but four or five; it was the same tired look, the same amused laugh, the same voice. . . .

He occupied two rooms, the best in the hotel, and he had had them furnished with taste. There were many books on his table, and he pointed out among them my *Nourritures terrestres (Fruits of the Earth)*, recently published. A pretty Gothic Virgin, on a large pedestal, in the shadows.

We were seated near the lamp with Wilde sipping his toddy. Now that the light was on his face, I noticed that the skin had become red and common; his hands even more so, although wearing the same rings; one that he was particularly fond of bore a lapis-lazuli scarab in a swiveled bezel. His teeth were shockingly decayed.

We talked. I recalled our last meeting in Algiers. I asked him if he remembered that I had then almost predicted the catastrophe.

"You really knew, didn't you," I said, "what was

waiting for you in England; you foresaw the danger and threw yourself into it?"

(Here I can do no better than transcribe the pages on which shortly thereafter I noted down all that I could remember of his words.)

"Oh, of course! Of course I knew that there would be a catastrophe—that one or another—I was expecting it. It had to end that way. Just think; it was not possible to go further; it could not last. That is why, you understand, it had to come to an end. Prison has changed me completely. I was counting on it for that. Bosy [Lord Alfred Douglas] is terrible; he cannot understand that; he cannot understand why I don't take up the same existence; he accuses the others of having changed me. . . . But one must never take up the same existence. . . . My life is like a work of art; an artist never begins the same thing twice over—or else it is because he had not been successful. My life before prison was as successful as possible. Now it is over and done with."

He lit a cigarette.

"The public is so terrible, that it never knows a man except by the last thing he has done. If I returned to Paris now, they would see in me only the—convict. I do not want to reappear before having written a play. Until then I must be left alone." And he added abruptly: "Didn't I do well to come here? My friends wanted me to go to the South to rest, because, at first, I was very tired. But I asked them to find for me, in the North of France, a very small beach, where I should see no one, where it is cold, where there is never any sun. . . . Didn't I do well to come to Berneval? [Outside the weather was horrible.]

"Here everyone is very kind to me. Especially the priest. I like the little church so much! Would you believe it—it's called Notre-Dame de Liesse! Oh, isn't that charming? And now I know that I shall never leave

Berneval, because the priest offered me this morning a permanent seat in the choir.

"And the customs officers! They were so bored here! Then I asked them if they had anything to read; and now I bring them all the novels of Dumas *père*. . . . I do have to stay here!

"And the children! Oh, they adore me! The day of the Queen's Diamond Jubilee, I gave a great party—a great dinner—to which I invited forty school children—all of them! All of them! And their teacher! To honor the Queen! Isn't that absolutely charming? You know that I like the Queen very much. I still have her portrait with me." And he showed me, pinned to the wall, Nicholson's caricature.

I stood up to look at it; a little bookcase was beside it; I looked at the books for a moment. I wanted to induce Wilde to speak more seriously. I sat down again, and with some trepidation asked him if he had read *The House of the Dead*. He did not answer me directly, but began:

"The Russian writers are extraordinary. What makes their books so great is the pity they have put into them. You know, I used to like *Madame Bovary;* but Flaubert wanted no pity in his work, and that is why it seems petty and closed; pity is the side by which a work is open, by which it seems infinite. . . . Do you know, André, that pity kept me from killing myself? Oh, during the first six months I was terribly unhappy—so unhappy that I wanted to kill myself; but what kept me from doing it, was to look at *the others*, to see that they were as unhappy as I, and to have pity. Oh, dear! Pity is an admirable thing; and I did not know what it was! [He was speaking almost in a whisper, with no trace of emotion.] Do you realize how admirable a thing pity is? As for myself I thank God each evening—yes, on my knees —I thank God for having revealed it to me. For I en-

tered prison with a heart of stone and thinking only of
my pleasure, but now my heart is completely broken;
pity has entered my heart; I have now understood that
pity is the greatest, the most beautiful thing on earth.
That is why I bear no resentment against those who condemned me, or against anyone else, because without
them I should not have comprehended all that. Bosy
writes me terrible letters; he tells me that he doesn't
understand me; that he doesn't understand why I do
not resent everyone; that everyone has been hateful to
me. No, he does not understand me; he can no longer
understand me. But I repeat to him in every letter: we
cannot follow the same path; he has his; it is very lovely;
I have mine. His is the way of Alcibiades; mine is now
that of Saint Francis of Assisi. Do you know Saint Francis? Oh, admirable! Admirable! Do you want to make
me very happy? Send me the best life of Saint Francis
you know."

I promised to do so, and he went on:

"Yes, then we had a charming warden, oh, quite
charming! But during the first six months, I was terribly unhappy. There was a very bad warden, a Jew, who
was very cruel, because he was totally lacking in imagination." This last sentence, said very rapidly, was irresistibly comic; and as I burst out laughing, he laughed
too, repeated it, and continued:

"He did not know what to devise to make us suffer:
You will see to what a degree he lacked imagination.
You must know that in prison they let you out only one
hour a day; they walk you in a court, in a circle, in single
file, and it is absolutely forbidden to speak to one another. Guards are watching you and there are terrible
punishments for anyone who is caught. Those who are
in prison for the first time can be recognized because
they don't know how to speak without moving their lips.
I had been in prison for six weeks, without saying a
word to anyone—to anyone at all. One evening we were

walking in single file during our hour of exercise, and suddenly, behind me, I heard my name: it was the prisoner behind me saying: 'Oscar Wilde, I pity you, because you must suffer more than we do.' Then I made an enormous effort not to be noticed (I thought I was about to faint), and I said without turning around: 'No, my friend, we all suffer equally.' And from that day on I no longer had any desire to kill myself.

"We talked like that for several days. I learned his name and what he did. His name was P.; he was an excellent fellow; oh, excellent! But I still did not know how to talk without moving my lips, and then one evening: 'C.33! (I was C.33) C.33 and C.48, step out of line!' So we stepped out and the guard said: 'You will appear before the war-rden!' And as pity had already entered my heart, I had absolutely no fear on my account; on the contrary, I was happy to suffer for him. But the warden was really terrible. He sent for P. first; he wanted to question us separately—because I must tell you that the penalty is not the same for the one who talks first as for the one who answers; the penalty for the one who talks first is double that of the other; ordinarily the first has two weeks of solitary confinement, the second only a week; so the warden wanted to know which of us had spoken first. And, naturally, P., who was an excellent fellow, said that it was he. And when, afterward, the warden sent for me, naturally, I said that it was I. Then the warden turned purple, because he was baffled. 'But P. says too that he was the one that started it! I don't understand. . . .'

"Just think, André! He didn't understand! He was very embarrassed. He said: 'But I have already given him two weeks confinement.' And then he added: 'Well, if that's the way it is, I'm going to give you each two weeks.' Isn't that extraordinary! That man had no imagination at all!" Wilde enjoyed hugely what he was saying; he laughed; he was happy to be telling the story.

"And naturally, after the two weeks were over, we were far more anxious than before to talk to each other. You don't know how comforting that could seem, to feel that we were suffering for each other. As we did not every day occupy the same position, gradually I was able to talk to each of the others; to all of them. All of them! I learned the name of each one, his story, and the date he was to leave prison. And to each I would say: 'When you leave prison, go straightway to the post office; there will be a letter for you with some money! That way I remain in touch with them, because I like them very much. And there are some who are absolutely delightful. Would you believe that three of them have already come to see me here! Isn't that really wonderful?

"The one who replaced the bad warden was a charming man. Oh, remarkable! very friendly with me—and you can't imagine how much good it did me in prison to have *Salomé* played in Paris, just at that time. There, they had completely forgotten that I was a writer! When they saw that my play had some success in Paris, they said to themselves: 'Well, that's strange! So he has talent!' And from that moment on they let me read all the books I wanted.

"I thought first that Greek literature would please me most. I asked for Sophocles, but I could take no interest in him. Then I tried the Church Fathers, but they did not interest me either. And suddenly I thought of Dante. Oh, Dante! I read Dante every day—in Italian, and I read him entire, but neither *Purgatorio* nor *Paradiso* seemed written for me. It was his *Inferno* that held me; and why not? Don't you understand? Hell is where we were. Hell was prison."

That same evening he told me of his plan for a play about Pharaoh and an ingenious fable concerning Judas.

Next day he led me to a charming little house, two hundred yards from the hotel, which he had rented and had begun to furnish. There he planned to write his plays: his *Pharaoh* first, then an *Ahab and Jezebel* (he pronounced it "Isabelle"), which he told marvelously well.

The carriage that was taking me away was hitched up. Wilde got in with me, to accompany me for a space. He talked again of my book, praised it, but with a reticence I could sense. Finally the carriage came to a halt. He said good-by, was about to get out, then said suddenly: "Listen, André, now you must promise me something. *Fruits of the Earth* is fine . . . fine . . . but, André, promise me: never write 'I' again."

And as I did not seem to comprehend, he continued: "In art, you see, there is no *first* person."

IV

Upon my return to Paris, I went to give news of Wilde to Lord Alfred Douglas. He said to me:

"But that is completely ridiculous. Wilde is totally unable to stand boredom. I know that very well: he writes to me every day, and I, too, am of the opinion that he must first finish his play; but, then, he will come back to me; he has never done anything good in solitude; he needs to be amused constantly. He has written his best things when he was with me. Besides, here is his last letter." Lord Alfred showed it to me and read it aloud. It begged Bosy to let him complete his *Pharaoh* undisturbed, but said, in fact, that once the play was written he would return, would be with him again, and ended with this glorious phrase: ". . . and then I shall again be the King of Life."

V

Shortly thereafter Wilde returned to Paris.● His play was not written; it was never to be written. Society

● The representatives of the family assured Wilde of a very good situation if he would agree to certain conditions, among others that of never seeing Lord Alfred again. He could not or would not agree to them.

knows very well how to go about suppressing a man and has methods more subtle than death. Wilde had suffered too much for two years and in too passive a manner. His will had been broken. During the first months, he could still delude himself, but he soon surrendered. It was a kind of abdication. Nothing remained in his shattered life but a painful echo of what he had once been; a momentary need to prove that he had not ceased to think; there was wit, but it was farfetched, uneasy, tarnished. I saw him only twice more.

One evening on the boulevards, where I was walking with G. I heard someone call my name. I turned around; it was Wilde. How he had changed; "If I reappear before having written my play, the world will see in me only the convict," he had said to me. He had reappeared without his play and, as some doors were closed to him, he no longer sought to enter anywhere; he roamed the streets. Friends on several occasions attempted to save him; they tried all sorts of things; they took him to Italy; Wilde would soon break away, would fall back. Among those who had remained longest faithful, some had repeated so often to me that one could no longer be seen with Wilde that I was somewhat embarrassed, I confess, to see him again, and in a place where so many might pass. Wilde was seated on the terrace of a café. He ordered cocktails for G. and for me. I was about to sit down facing him, so that my back was turned to the passers-by, but Wilde, hurt by this gesture, which he thought inspired by an absurd sense of shame (he was not, alas, completely mistaken) said, pointing to a chair beside him: "Oh, sit down there, beside me. I am so alone now."

Wilde was still well-dressed; but his hat no longer shone; his collar still had the same form, but was no longer so clean; the sleeves of his frock-coat were somewhat frayed.

"When, formerly, I would come across Verlaine, I did

not blush to be seen with him," he went on, with an effort at pride. "I was rich, gay, famous, but I felt that to be seen with Verlaine honored me, even when he was drunk." Then, afraid of embarrassing G., I think, he suddenly changed tone, tried to be witty, tried to joke, then became gloomy. My memory of this is excruciatingly painful. Finally G. and I got up. Wilde insisted on paying for the drinks. I was about to take leave of him when he took me aside and, embarrassed, said in a low voice: "Listen, I must tell you—I am absolutely without resources."

A few days later, for the last time, I saw him again. I shall report only a word of our conversation. He had told me of his straits, of the impossibility of continuing, of even beginning any work. Sadly I reminded him of his pledge to return to Paris only when he had completed a play.

"Ah," I began, "why did you leave Berneval so soon, where you had resolved to stay so long? I cannot say that I reproach you for it, but . . ."

He broke in, placed his hand on mine, and with a look of profound suffering, said to me: "You must not reproach a man who has been struck down."

Oscar Wilde died in a wretched little hotel on the rue des Beaux-Arts. Seven people followed the body, and they did not all continue to the end. On his bier, some flowers, a few wreaths: one alone, I have been told, bore an inscription. It was from the owner of the hotel and read: "TO MY TENANT."

TRANSLATED BY JEFFREY J. CARRE

Baudelaire and M. Faguet

Gide reached literary maturity at a time when critical judgments were commonly handed down ex cathedra *by university critics, such as Ferdinand Brunetière, Emile Faguet, Jules Lemaître, and that "university professor who had missed his calling," as Remy de Gourmont has been called. This may account, in part at least, for the breezy playfulness of much of Gide's criticism. Frequently in his* Journals *and at least twice in his essays (notably this one on Faguet's view of Baudelaire and another on Lemaître's* Fénelon*) Gide openly took issue with the academic critics.*

The comparison between Baudelaire and Chopin suggested in this essay, which appeared in the Nouvelle Revue Française *for November 1910, prefigures the more extended comparison in his* Notes sur Chopin *of 1931.*

In the *Revue* for September first M. Faguet has written an important article on Baudelaire, an article so important that it should really be better. A quotation taken out of context, verses quoted out of order, an incomprehensible sentence,• due either to careless writ-

---

• "And then, finally, I am perhaps sensitive to the sublime, and that is why I am insensitive to this, a well-known passage, but which I won't deny myself the pleasure of transcribing. [The quotation follows; then M. Faguet continues.] There is no getting away from it; that is incomparable.

ing or to careless proofreading—yet the article seems important to those of us who consider Baudelaire important, which is not true of M. Faguet, who rates Baudelaire a poet of the "second rank" for whom the vacation article, the article hastily thrown together, would do well enough.

For professors and critics of the Ecole Normale and the Sorbonne, for M. Faguet particularly, I am far from sharing the indifference and disdain affected by certain poets.[•] If his portraits of the nineteenth century have rarely seemed sufficiently clear-sighted, his eighteenth-century portraits, on the contrary, still are and will remain, I think, among the best. May I add that M. Faguet early showed toward me, and maintained, a kindness to which I had hardly been accustomed by official critics? My gratitude today calls for a careful and patient examination of his article. And since M. Faguet has in the past been so kind as to notice my critical writings and hold my critical judgment in some esteem, perhaps he will not find me wholly unqualified to speak.

Let us follow him step by step:

I am a contemporary of Baudelaire [he declares at the beginning of his article]; I was beginning to read the newer poets when *Les Fleurs du mal* was only five years old; I was twenty years old when he died. Yet throughout all my youth I kept thinking: "He is certainly worthy of attracting attention and awakening interest; but he won't survive; one generation and he is done for."

Brunetière, who in 1887, just after the publication of Baudelaire's posthumous works, wrote some of his most unjust pages, thought the same:

[•] I cannot share the rather waspish joy of some lyrical poets upon hearing M. Faguet declare that he was not acquainted with Paul Claudel. Before venting their indignation let them wait until M. Faguet does become acquainted with him; until then, of course, they have no right to conclude that M. Faguet will see nothing in him.

Now that all sources of information are exhausted, all his works published, and all his letters too, all the anecdotes and all the documents, we can feel sure we shall hear no more talk of that artist in mystification whose sole excuse is that he was himself the dupe of his mystification.

He had already said:

What surprises me, and what is hardly a credit to our perspicacity [!], is that we allowed ourselves to be deceived by such rhetoric and that we failed to see that it served even in *Les Fleurs du mal,* especially in *Les Fleurs du mal,* as a disguise for pure banality.

An heir to the astonishment, M. Faguet says today:

A generation has passed, alas, another is in full career, and Baudelaire has not sunk out of sight; indeed, he has managed to keep afloat; he is not popular; he never was; but he certainly has about as many admirers as he did during his lifetime. I made a mistake in my diagnosis. If I were to say I'm not a bit surprised at that, you would not believe me.

What should surprise M. Faguet even more than their number is the quality of his admirers, musicians and poets whom Baudelaire recruits from all civilized countries with every new generation. One cannot deny the fact, it is the elite. Decidedly he was correct in writing: "I made a mistake in my diagnosis." But what does he mean by that? That he had misjudged Baudelaire? Not at all!

I am rereading Baudelaire, and I am still surprised that "he had the stuff" for more than a generation; I find him, as I did before, a good poet of the second rank, far from negligible, but essentially of the second rank.

How does he explain, then, such an embarrassing persistence in public favor? It's a fad, they said at first. But fashions pass; critics too; Baudelaire remains. Might it not be just possibly that here is something more in *Les Fleurs du mal* than M. Brunetière and M. Faguet saw there?

M. Bourget and M. Barrès—who nevertheless are also members of the Académie Française—having managed to see something more in Baudelaire, once spoke of Baudelaire with much better judgment; one of them at the beginning of his *Essais de psychologie,* the other in the first two numbers of *Tâches d'encre.* But, however justified their appreciations may have appeared in their day, their point of view does not seem quite ours today. Against fresh attacks (if M. Faguet's may indeed be considered fresh) our times require a fresh defense.

If M. Bourget and his fellows sought perhaps above all in *Les Fleurs du mal* a reflection of their own "spleen," and a consent to their own melancholy (against which we could only praise M. Faguet for reacting), this is not, I think, what Baudelaire holds for a generation that is no longer given to reverie but is active, steeled by the Dreyfus case, galvanized by Barrès's example, with a definite horror for the deliquescent and the morbid. If this new generation still manages to enjoy Baudelaire, it must be because Baudelaire offers it something else. For it is with Baudelaire as it was with Rousseau and as it will be with Barrès: what makes for an initial success does not serve to maintain a lasting reputation. Indeed, I might say, what favors a first success the most will injure true fame the most. Enduring fame is promised only to those writers who can offer to successive generations a substance constantly renewed; for every generation arrives upon the scene with its own particular hunger.

What is more repulsive, more tiresome in Rousseau than the theories about the return to nature, the breast feeding of children, Italian music, etc., points where the favor of the multitude seized hold of him in the beginning—or if you prefer: where he seized hold of the favor of the multitude. He is great in spite of, and not because of this. Likewise, it seems evident to the clear-sighted that the celebrated doctrines of Barrès, of such an excellent practical effect today, both for himself and for France, will lay their dead weight heavy on his work, and that very soon. Likewise what will live in the poetry of Francis James, as it is possible to tell already, will surely not be what seems most obvious in his verse today. A work survives only through its deeper qualities; these hidden qualities give the work at first an air of uncertainty and vague elusiveness, mysterious, disturbing for those who think they can discover at one fell swoop everything the writer was "trying to say," something enigmatic, and let us risk at last the frightful word, "unwholesome!" •

What made the work of Baudelaire seem so disturbing and unwholesome in its day is exactly what keeps it so young today, so gripping.

In art, where expression alone matters, *ideas* seem to retain their youth but a day. "Observe that this innovator [it is M. Faguet's ironical term for Baudelaire] has not a single novel idea. *We must, after Vigny, wait for Sully Prudhomme before we can find new ideas in French poets.*" (The italics are M. Faguet's.) This is badly put yet very true; and that's what makes so medi-

---

• I marvel that this is the word most often used to qualify—that is, disqualify—the music of Chopin, whose perfection—and it is the case in point—offers such subtle and constant relationships with the poetry of Baudelaire.

ocre a poet, alas, of so lovable a man as Sully Prudhomme. For Vigny's big mistake had been precisely the
idea that *novelty* in poetry consisted in "putting into
verse" novel ideas; and Chénier wrote, in this spirit:
"Sur des pensers nouveaux faisons des vers antiques"
("On modern thinking fashion ancient verse"), but was
in fact a great poet only when he forgot his precept.

As a result, looking only to the novelty of the *idea*, it
is easy for M. Faguet to say: "Baudelaire never deals
with anything but the commonplace worn threadbare.
He is the sterile poet of banality"; then he will enunci-
ate the "subject" of some of these poems: " *'La Beauté':*
beauty makes things beautiful. *'Confession':* in this
world there is nothing to trust. *'Les Phares':* artists are
the beacons of humanity," • etc., and will conclude:
"such are the novelties that Baudelaire has broadcast
throughout the world."

As a result I, in turn, find it less surprising that the
profound novelty of Baudelaire escapes him,•• so that
he does not quite know how to handle its expression,
which seems to him almost everywhere faulty:

> But let that pass [banality]; for there are very great poets
> who never have done anything but unfurl their common-
> places like banners; nevertheless, there is a way to do it,
> and you must have form. Baudelaire is often a very bad
> writer. . . . Inappropriate terms abound, as well as the
> awkward or cumbersome turn of phrase and the platitude.
> Rare are the spots where for four consecutive lines the lan-
> guage doesn't fumble.

Form! How dare we, after such declarations, propose
to M. Faguet the only plausible explanation for the

• ". . . short, detached poems, with *no appreciable subject* (like the
others, who wrote a sonnet to narrate something in poetic form, plead
a case, etc.)," Laforgue notes in the margins of *Les Fleurs du mal.*
•• "Emotions cannot be analyzed like intellectual phenomena," Barrès
wisely notes, with specific reference to Baudelaire.

mystery that astonishes him so much today: Baudelaire owes his survival to his very perfection of form. Does an artist ever owe it to anything else?

A very different perfection, obviously, from that of the sonnets of Heredia, for instance, so Latin, logical, and explicable. With that kind of perfection our tongue has often been too easily satisfied; not that traces are lacking, here and there, in Racine's verse especially, and sometimes at the expense of the external perfection, of a more hidden perfection, already of a musical nature, but as though unintentional—and it is hardly an exaggeration, I think, to say that we have just discovered it. Baudelaire was the first to make this secret perfection, consciously and deliberately, the aim and the justification of his poetry; and that is why poetry—and not merely French poetry, but English and German as well—European poetry in general, after *Les Fleurs du mal,* has never been quite the same.•

In this little volume there was indeed something else, and much more than the contribution of a "new idea" or even many "ideas": poetry from now on was to knock at other portals of the intelligence and set before itself a different aim.

Insensitive to a hidden perfection, it is the other perfection alone, rhetorical and logical in form and purpose, oratorical, in a word, that M. Faguet seeks; and which, with little good will, he will concede that *"L'Homme et la mer"* and the fourth *"Spleen"* have almost attained—these poems that are among the least successful in the collection. He writes: "I recognize that *'Don Juan aux enfers,'* as a picture, is very noteworthy;" the very *"Don Juan"* that Barrès would like to excise.

• "Prophet of a new kind of art," Barrès writes.

Quoting another poem, "I admit," he says, "that the first five stanzas, with their abundance of 'filler' for the verse and their insignificant or simply silly observations (which I shall underline), are of a great intrinsic beauty, where the poet's idea is firmly grasped [*sic*] and sometimes forcefully expressed." He admits that " '*La Charogne*' . . . has firmness of outline, distinctive color, a splendid central image in an admirable place, and *movement* [the italics are M. Faguet's], a very fine movement." "It is perhaps the only poem of Baudelaire's with a marked progression," he finally declares, content to find once more the eloquence he seeks. How much more would he find in the odes of Jean-Baptiste Rousseau! •

Therefore I am ready to believe that when he quotes his author, choosing the least successful poems in the book, and which have about the same place in the work of Baudelaire that the verse in *terza rima* of the "*Romancero*" have in *Les Trophées* of Heredia—I should like to believe it was the result not of malice aforethought, out of simple insensitivity to the beauty of the companion poems. And yet the mediocre bits he quotes, why does he quote them so incorrectly?

Why, in the poem without title where he can see nothing but "platitude . . . , filler material . . . , images of a shocking inappropriateness" (he likes to add up this kind of thing; and unfortunately for Baudelaire, the "beauties" of his poems are of the kind that can never be catalogued), why invert the order of the verses so that

---

• As if the greatest novelty of his art had not been precisely to *immobilize* his poems, to develop them in depth!

"I hate movement," he will have "*La Beauté*" say.

The periodic return of the same verse, of several verses, of an entire stanza, ought to have warned M. Faguet, it would seem, that the extraordinary absence of movement that he calls to our attention might well be deliberate and premeditated. See "*Mœsta et Errabunda*," "*Le Balcon*," "*Réversabilité*," "*Le Beau Navire*," "*L'Invitation au voyage*," "*Le Jet d'eau*," etc.

their connection is completely lost? I will grant that he did not do it on purpose; it is too bad nonetheless.

Why, as he quotes with patronizing air the disappointing poem entitled *"Confession,"* and criticizes two lines:

> *Une note plaintive, une note bizarre*
> *S'échappa tout en chancelant.*•

why does he put a period after *"chancelant,"* which throws the rhythm completely off, denatures the meaning, and invites the remark, *"A note that escapes stumbling!* how farfetched the metaphor, hard to grasp, *forming no visual image* [the italics are M. Faguet's]." Why a period when Baudelaire did not use even a comma, and when the reconstructed sentence reads as follows, presenting a metaphor one may not like at all, but which, nevertheless, forms more of a *visual image* than M. Faguet will allow:

> *. . . en chancelant*
> *Comme une enfant chétive, . . .*•

I will grant that M. Faguet failed to see that the sentence went on, just as, in general, I prefer to think that he read only a little of Baudelaire and that little badly. But, just the same, to criticize so harshly—counting the mistakes on one's fingers—a misquoted passage, which serves as a basis for conclusions, once more I say that is too bad.

"If Baudelaire were worth the trouble" (the words are Brunetière's), doubtless he would have paid attention.

As for *"Le Balcon," "La Chevelure," "Le Jet d'eau,"*

• A plaintive note, a note bizarre
Escapes, though stumbling
Like a sickly child, . . .

"L'Invitation au voyage," the "magnificent" *"Crépuscule du matin"* (the epithet is M. Bourget's), etc., M. Faguet doesn't even mention them; and I would rather have him ignorant of these poems, for I should hate to think that if he had read them, even without really liking them,* he would not at least have sensed, had some slight intimation, that there was something more here than in Hégésippe Moreau, for instance (I mention a name he brought up), something disturbing, something suspicious—something musical.

Musical! The word should be allowed to express not merely the flowing caress or the harmonious impact of the verbal sonorities through which poetry may please even a foreigner with a musical ear but no knowledge of the language; but also that sure choice of expression which is dictated not by logic alone, and which escapes logic, by which the "musical" poet succeeds in formulating, as exactly as a definition would do it, the essentially indefinable emotion:

> *Mais le vert paradis des amours enfantines,*
> *Les courses, les chansons, les baisers, les bouquets.*
> *Les violons vibrant derrière les collines,*
> *Avec les brocs de vin, le soir, dans les bosquets.*
> *—Mais le vert paradis des amours enfantines,*
> *L'innocent paradis, plein de plaisirs frutifs,*
> *Est-il déjà plus loin que l'Inde et que la Chine?*
> *Peut-on le rappeler avec des cris plaintifs,*
> *Et l'animer encor d'une voix argentine,*
> *L'innocent paradis plein de plaisirs furtifs?* **

---

* "Criticism begins with this: to understand what you don't like," he says at the end of the article, as if he had really understood Baudelaire!
** But the green paradise of childhood loves,
   The races, the songs, the kisses, bouquets.
   Violins vibrant behind the hills,

I quote this sequence of lines because they are perhaps a little less famous than the even more beautiful sequences, from *"La Chevelure"* or *"Le Balcon,"* for instance—and because they seem to me significant. M. Faguet might doubtless like, except for the word *"parfumé,"* the stanza that preceded, and in it especially the third line:

> *Comme vous êtes loin, paradis parfumé,*
> *Où sous un clair azur tout n'est qu'amour et joie,*
> *Où tout ce que l'on aime est digne d'être aimé,*
> *Où dans la volupté pure le cœur se noie;*
> *Comme vous êtes loin, paradis parfumé!* •

because almost everything can be explained; but what of the two following stanzas, the ones I quoted first? Why these *"brocs de vin"*? Why *"furtifs"*? he will ask, and we shall not know what to answer. Then he will say: you should have animated *"avec"* a voice; you do not "call back" paradise, you "recall" it "for yourself" with a *"se."* *"Avec les brocs de vin"* is mere filler; you should have written *"Les brocs de vin,"* in order to continue the enumeration; *"Chine"* is there only for the rhyme; one, two, three, four, five mistakes! Brunetière had already written: "The fellow had a veritable genius for feeble and inappropriate expression!" and in another place: "What am I expected to admire here?" and in a third

---

Sundown in the woods with our jugs of wine.
—But the green paradise of childhood loves,
Innocent paradise, filled with furtive pleasures
Is it farther off now than India and China?
Can we bring it back with our plaintive cries,
And still give it life with our silvery voice,
Innocent paradise, filled with furtive pleasures?
• How far you have gone, o perfumed paradise,
Where under clear blue sky there's only love and joy,
Where all we love is worth our love,
Where the heart drowns in thrilling sense;
How far you have gone, o perfumed paradise!

place: "Do we have to understand?" Of course not: we don't have to understand! Any more, fortunately, than we have to agree with Brunetière! It is certainly true of the poetry of Baudelaire, and that is precisely the source of its power, that it knows how to win from the reader a kind of connivance, that it invites a collaboration. The seeming inappropriateness of terms, which will irritate some critics so much, that skillful impreciseness of which Racine already made such masterly use and which Verlaine was to make one of the conditions of poetry:

> . . . *surtout ne va pas*
> *Choisir tes mots sans quelque méprise . . .●*

that air-space, that interval between image and idea, between the word and the thing, is just where there is room for the poetic emotion to come and dwell. And if nothing is more compromising than to be permitted not to speak clearly, it is precisely because the true poet alone can manage it successfully.

Failure to find the exact word? How is it, then, that in Baudelaire's better poems (which are more numerous than one might think), if you try to replace a single word, the harmony of verse and stanza in its entirety, the entire poem sometimes in its sound becomes no more than some fine, flawed bell?

"You do not yet seem to have realized," my professor, M. Lyon, used to write as he corrected a philosophical exercise of mine, "that there are in our language *certain words that are made to go together!*" Baudelaire cannot tolerate stereotyped expressions, hackneyed metaphors; he will often take pleasure even in putting the reader off the track through a relationship whose exactitude is not perceived at first, and having an aristocratic preference

---

● You choose your words on the oblique.

for the strange over the commonplace, he will judge
that an association of images and words is perfect, not
when it can be used over and over, but on the contrary
when it can serve but once.

I have saved for the end the first point of accusation
in the article; certainly not because it is very hard to
handle, for I do not aim to contradict it. On the contrary
I mean to accept it and acknowledge its justice, since I
believe that this very objection, for which I myself
would praise him, must serve to bring out the secret
virtue of Baudelaire: "He has almost no imagination."

Barrès had already written: "Baudelaire really toiled
over his writing. . . . Yet, after many a night of labor,
the poetic production of this indefatigable worker is
rather meager." To be sure he was quick to add, quite
judiciously: "In him the simplest word betrays the effort
by which he attained so high a level." • A phrase of
Brunetière's is even more to our purpose: "The fact is
that the poor devil had nothing or almost nothing of the
poet about him. . . . He lacks animation and imagination." I should be the last to raise a protest. Agreed that
he lacks animation and imagination; whether he gets
along without them out of *necessity* or *choice* matters
little if the poetic result is the same. The question arises,
since, after all, we do have *Les Fleurs du mal,* whether it
is indeed essentially the imagination which makes the
poet; or, since MM. Faguet and Brunetière certainly
are in favor of giving the name of poetry to a kind of
versified argument, whether we should not do well to
hail Baudelaire as something other and more than a
poet: the first artist in poetry.

"The imagination imitates; it is the critical spirit

• The name of Mallarmé would fit this situation as well as Baudelaire's.

which creates." • This aphorism of Oscar Wilde's, which certain superficial or prejudiced minds will insist on considering mere paradox, throws light upon a profound truth; it explains, particularly in the case of Baudelaire, how a certain infertility of imagination did him an actual service, forcing him never to relax his control over his intelligence—so precise in all its vigor, constantly exercised in close conjunction with so responsive an organic sensibility—and over his critical sense, so scrupulous and tenacious and never in abeyance.

Baudelaire was with Stendhal the most admirable critical intelligence of his time. What is romanticism compared to these two inventive spirits?

To be sure, Stendhal, too, was completely misunderstood by Brunetière (and neither of these two great names figures in M. Faguet's nineteenth century).

For Brunetière I feel now and then what comes pretty close to admiration; he interests me, and often he intrigues me, with his obstinate rigor, his exclusions, his sheer misunderstandings, his hatreds that are so much more amusing than his loves; yes, even with his loves, bestowed on such worthy objects. His rhetoric in its enveloping movement knots itself around his subject and all that pertains to it, like the endless bronze serpent

---

• I am putting into a single sentence the idea more or less scattered through the first dialogue of "The Critic as Artist," in *Intentions*—of which I quote some significant passages:

It is so now, and it has always been so. We are sometimes apt to think that the voices that sounded at the dawn of poetry were simpler, fresher, and more natural than ours, and that the world which the early poets looked at, and through which they walked, had a kind of poetical quality of its own, and almost without changing could pass into song. . . . But in this we are merely lending to other ages what we desire, or think we desire, for our own. Our historical sense is at fault. Every century that produces poetry is, so far, an artificial century, and the work that seems to us to be the most natural and simple product of its time is always the result of the most self-conscious effort. Believe me, Ernest, there is no fine art without self-consciousness, and self-consciousness and the critical spirit are one.

around the family of Laocoön. He is not without his moments of awkward grace oddly illuminated by a crabbed smile; but when he writes: "When Baudelaire was not ill, or more exactly, when his malady let up a little, like everybody else he would write his *salons,* which of their kind were no better and no worse than so many others"—he comes pretty close to irresponsibility.

With hardly less impertinence M. Faguet can write: "As a translator, all seem to concur in granting him the highest rank; as a writer of articles (literary, artistic, *salons*) he is simply a man who writes very well." This last hardly seems in agreement with criticisms I have just quoted: "Baudelaire is often a very bad writer." Yet we still remain unsatisfied, for Baudelaire has done nothing less than to create modern art criticism.

Nevertheless, when I talk about *criticism,* I mean of course the kind that is applied not so much to another person's work as to one's own work. "Without the critical faculty," Wilde writes, "there is not artistic creation at all, worthy of the name. You spoke a little while ago of that fine spirit of choice and delicate instinct of selection by which the artist realizes life for us, and gives to it a momentary perfection. Well, that spirit of choice, that subtle tact of omission, is really the critical faculty in one of its most characteristic moods, and no one who does not possess this critical faculty can create anything at all in art."

It is by his ever-present critical sense that Baudelaire detaches himself so definitely from the romantic school, little though he knew it,• and that, like Stendhal, thinking to represent romanticism, he stands opposed to it— or at least, after rejecting its rhetoric and conventional utopianism, he retains no more than a vital sense of its *modernity.*

• "The imagination, that queen of the faculties," he says (*Curiosités esthétiques,* p. 227).

How far misunderstanding of Baudelaire must have gone, to find fault with him precisely on grounds of rhetoric and declamation! If occasionally, in *Les Fleurs du mal,* one or the other is found, his times are responsible. Nothing is more alien to Baudelaire, to the art of Baudelaire, than useless exaggeration of gesture and raising of the voice. Some, who have failed to understand, may be easily shocked by a sudden, and rare, grandiloquence; we shall praise it instead, and for this reason: it is not sincere—and it makes it possible for the rest to be profoundly so.

"He was the first," as Laforgue so well says, "to talk of himself with moderation in the confessional style and without putting on an air of inspiration." And that is doubtless the reason why, practically alone among his contemporaries, Baudelaire deserves to remain untouched by that unfavorable wind blowing in our day against the romantics. Here, too, he is rather closely affiliated with Racine; the choice of words in Baudelaire is not untroubled in its precision and may aim at effects of somewhat greater subtlety: but I maintain that the tone of voice is the same; instead of working up expression, like Corneille or Hugo, toward the greatest sonority possible, they both speak quietly, and we are glad to listen longer.

"It is through *Les Fleurs du mal,* perhaps, that we shall come back to the great classical tradition, modified no doubt to suit the modern spirit, but contemptuous of the loud clash of colors and of plastic barbarisms, convinced that what does honor to the intellectual is the quiet effect, and with the ideal of expressing in terms themselves clear and sensitive to every shading things that are obscure and subtleties of the most intimate sort." This is what Barrès wrote in 1884. I prefer to leave such things for Barrès to say to M. Faguet; but, though with no great liking for "things that are obscure" and "subtleties of the most intimate sort," I think for my part that Barrès has never written more perceptively.

TRANSLATED BY ANGELO P. BERTOCCI

Political Essays

Soon after the First World War, André Gide wrote two
significant essays on subjects of political interest. In both
he returned to his favorite concern with nationalism.
"Reflections on Germany," inspired by the meditations
of his friend Jacques Rivière in a German prison camp,
appeared in the Nouvelle Revue Française in June 1919.
"The Future of Europe" was published in January 1923
by the Revue de Genève as part of a symposium to
which Keyserling, Middleton Murry, Pareto, Merezh-
kovski, and Unamuno also contributed.

REFLECTIONS ON GERMANY

After reading Jacques Rivière's book *L'Allemand,* I was
curious enough to go through my notebooks of the war
period and to look up the few isolated pages having to
do with our enemies. I reproduce them without making
any changes in them, although some of the thoughts
that I express have lost that air of originality which they
had when I wrote them; although certain others are not
yet widely enough accepted to have ceased to appear
shocking. Considerations of timeliness which kept me

from publishing them earlier now urge me to publish them today.

We hope for some things; we fear others. We should like to have some things happen; we think others will happen. But since the beginning of the war, a confusion has grown between the one and the other. It is certain that the value of an army depends upon its confidence in victory; it is certain that the nature of this war has enlisted everything in the army. At this point, we no longer admit any other truth than that which is expedient; for there is no worse error than the truth that may weaken the arm that is fighting.

How much we have had to accept in the name of this aphorism! As if *our* cause had to be sugar-coated to appear good! As if truth were not more encouraging, more convincing, more beneficial than any lie! But let truth appear the slightest bit embarrassing, it will be avoided and thus alienated, whereas it approached us like a friend, whom we should have merely tried to understand.

And you who want to reject everything that comes from Germany, why do you not understand that by doing so you are working toward German unity?

We were holding Goethe as a hostage and you give him back to them!

Nietzsche enlists in our foreign legion and you fire at him!

You skip over the texts where Wagner indicates his admiration for France and find it more advantageous to prove that he was insulting us!

You say we do not need applause from beyond the Rhine.

Why do you not understand that it is not a question of what these men bring to us, but of what they take away from the Germans. And this is not to be minimized if they are the elite of the country.

This is not to be minimized—whereas the best of French thought, all French thought, works and struggles with France—the best of German thought is raised against Prussia, which is leading Germany into combat.

We have the most extraordinary trumps in our hand and we do not know how to use them.

Nothing can be more demoralizing to thoughtful German youth (and all the same they do exist) than to feel that Goethe is not with them (or Leibniz, or Nietzsche).

In France, where our great writers are so numerous and where we honor them so little, we cannot realize completely what Goethe means to Germany. Nothing can please Germany more than a thesis like that of Louis Bertrand, who finds an invitation to the present war already stated in *Faust*. The absurdity of this thesis reassures us. On the contrary, what can grieve the thoughtful young of Germany is to feel that neither Goethe nor any of the writers of the past whom they admire would have approved of this monstrous war into which their country has been dragged. It is probably flattering, even heady to tell oneself and to hear others constantly telling one that the nation to which one belongs is chosen to govern the earth; but if this sophistry has already been pointed out ahead of time by the wisest men of the nation, is it skillful on our part to treat these wise men as brigands, impostors, or madmen?

To crush Germany! I am astonished that any serious-minded person can want this, even without thinking it possible. But to divide Germany, to break up its enormous mass into small pieces is, in my opinion, the plan that wins over the most reasonable men, that is, the part

of us which is most French. The essential is not to prevent Germany from existing (on the contrary, it is important, even for us, that she exist), but to keep her from
harming, that is from devouring us. Divide Germany—
and in order to divide her, the first thing to do is not to
put all Germans into the same bag (and if you affirm
that they are all alike at bottom, be careful; you are admitting that in your opinion it is impossible to dis-
criminate among them, and that if they are so similar,
they will not accept that division you would like to impose upon them). How much more clever are those who,
from now on, by exposing the Prussian idea as a poisonous virus in modern Germany, excite Germany itself
against this Prussian element, and instead of seeking
weapons against ourselves in Goethe, read this, for example, in his memoirs (has it already been quoted? I do
not think so):

"Among these objects, so proper to the development
of the feeling of art [he is visiting Dresden], I was frequently saddened by traces of the recent bombardment.
One of the main streets was only a pile of rubbish, and
in every other street could be seen bombed-out houses.
The massive tower of the Kreuzkirche was cracked, and
while I was contemplating these ruins from the top of
the cupola of the Frauenkirche, the sacristan said to me
with concentrated anger: 'The Prussians did that.' "

Goethe, Nietzsche (and several others to a lesser degree) are our hostages. I maintain that of all the blunders
in which our country excels, undervaluing our hostages
is one of the greatest.

Yes, as you have said: the Germans are miserable psychologists, and their most noticeable errors in this revealing war are errors of psychology. But it is not sufficient merely to note this: we must explain why.

Their power, on the contrary, and what might be called their virtue, comes from the extraordinary difficulty the individual of their race has in breaking away from the common run, the mass; let us be specific: in becoming an individual. He stands in contrast to nothing, has no form of his own, so to speak, or if you prefer, takes form from the group; hence his submission to method, to rules, to all traditions; he finds no interest in disobedience and feels no need to do so. He thinks it is because *his* law and order is perfect, but it is also because, without law and order, he is imperfect.

In literature their inability to create characters is noticeable. They have neither dramatists nor novelists. The surrounding people do not have faces for them, and if they did, they would not know how to sketch them; they do not know how to sketch themselves, and to put it more absolutely, they do not know how to sketch.

That is where their culture is bankrupt. The great instrument of culture is draftsmanship, not music. Music requires each one to unlearn himself, to radiate vaguely. Draftsmanship, on the other hand, exalts the detail, is precise; through it criticism triumphs. Criticism is at the basis of all art.

You go around exclaiming that the Germans detest us and you do your best to deserve their hatred, without understanding that their secret weakness, quite to the contrary, is their inability to hate us.

Why do you not understand that you give France all the weapons you take away from Germany, and that you will never be overarmed against Germany.

It is not just a question of fighting, but of being victorious. Make an effort, anyhow, not to prefer the combat to the victory.

"We would have suffered less severely had we been more numerous." This is what I read at the beginning of an article on the decrease in the birth rate.

The decrease in the French birth rate is the proof and not the cause of the decadence of our country. It is obvious that the progressive depopulation is deplorable and that we must try the possible and the impossible in order to check it. But we err in thinking that number would have been sufficient where quality is lacking; or that quality is sufficient without order and a reasonable distribution. Such an error made us shout victory when the Rumanians first entered upon the scene. With one more ally, triumph was assured. We had to be convinced, just the same, that number does not make strength; at least not without an orderly arrangement. The more numerous the disorderly elements, the more confused and vulnerable the mass.

We have been fooled by the amorphous aspect of Germany. Because every living thing in France immediately acquires contours, we saw a lack of cohesion in the absence of profile among the masses beyond the Rhine. The absence of definite form allowed the elastic German substance to flow into all the holes. In peacetime we had already seen how it penetrated the spongelike neighboring countries. To be precise, Germany owes her prodigious force of expansion to her lack of contours. She belongs to the family of the ficus, and like the banyan tree, is without a principal trunk, without definition, without axis, but her slightest twig (even detached from the trunk) grows very quickly, wherever it is, at the tip of a branch or at the end of a root; it lives, grows, prospers, thickens, and becomes in turn a forest. Germany gets along without the theories of Barrès; she laughs at them. I have always said that it was a great shame that Barrès had botany against him.

When I go to see Jacques Rivière in Switzerland, where he is finishing out his military captivity, he talks to me, concerning a book he plans to write, about the extraordinary German will. In my opinion, this is depreciating somewhat the word "will"; I think "tenacity" would be sufficient. I am well aware that the examples he gives me tend to prove especially that the German "wills" the feelings that he thinks it expedient to have. But as for the rest, I mean this bull-like stubbornness that allows him to accomplish formidable tasks and to write such thick books—I remember a statement of S., whom I went to see in Zurich two years before the war (we talked only about the war, which he foresaw as inevitable; how well he knew the Germans!). "They are," he said to me, "incomparably more stupid, formless, nonexistent than the French can imagine. But for this very reason, they are never inattentive. Think of all that goes on in a Frenchman's head while he is working, whatever may be that work. The German never thinks of anything; he has no personal existence; he is completely absorbed in his task. He is capable of going on a wild spree certain evenings, of getting dead drunk, but the next morning he will be back behind his counter or in his office as if nothing had happened."

They are never inattentive. How often I have remembered this sentence. In my opinion nothing more true has ever been said about the German. And what an explanation for us French, who constantly allow ourselves to be distracted by delicacy, sensitivity, emotional, mental or physical curiosity, by that innate, irrepressible generosity which comes before our own interests.

Near me, in an armchair, my old cat is nursing two little mongrel kittens that they let her keep.

If everything were challenged once again (and it must be), my mind would still find repose in the contemplation of plants and animals. I have ceased being interested in anything that does not come from nature. A truck gardener's cart bears more truth than the most beautiful phrases of Cicero. France is ruined through rhetoric; an oratorical nation accustomed to take words at face value, adept in taking words for things, and prompt in setting formulas above reality. Forewarned though I am, I do not escape this myself, and although I denounce it, I am oratorical myself. . . .

Before the war, the question was asked: Can a civilization, a culture, aim to maintain itself indefinitely along a direct, uninterrupted trajectory? And as the answer is negative, of necessity, the second question comes immediately as a corollary to the first: Can *our* civilization, our culture still be prolonged?

Does this new world we are entering upon follow directly after the preceding one? Are we continuing the past? But if we are entering a new era, who then can maintain that the first chapter of this new book is not a French chapter and a new French book?

Everything that represents tradition is doomed to be upset, and only long afterward shall we be able to recognize in the upheaval, the continuity of our temperament and our history, in spite of all that has happened. What has had no voice until that time must speak. It is a cowardly error to believe that we can struggle against Germany merely by withdrawing into our past: Rimbaud, Debussy, even Cézanne may in no way resemble our past tradition, but nevertheless, they do not cease being French; they can differ from all that has represented France up to the present and still express France. If France is no longer capable of originality, why should she struggle?

The artist who is preoccupied with being French

when he creates, and with creating "a very French"
work, is condemned to being worthless. It is no longer
a question of what we were, but of what we are.

To tell the truth, this new culture promised to be not
so much specifically French as European; it seemed that
it could no longer get along without the collaboration of
Germany. And from certain angles, this war tends to
prove this. Perhaps we needed Germany to bring our
finest gifts into play, just as she needed our leaven to
make her thick dough rise.

It is absurd to exclude anything whatsoever from the
European concert. It is absurd to imagine that anything
in this concert can be done away with. I speak without
any trace of idealism: Germany has shown sufficiently
that she could be useful, and we have shown sufficiently
what we lacked. The important thing is to prevent her
from dominating; this brass instrument must not be
allowed to dominate. But it is mystical to claim that its
voice would not be missed from the orchestra if it were
suppressed; mystical to believe that we should do better
to get along without it—and by "mystical," I mean not
practical at all (you, Barrès, I think, gave this meaning
to the word when you were speaking of Michelet). But
all that tries to enslave will be enslaved.

You poked fun at what we called our European culture and failed to understand what we meant by it. You
let us think, made others think, yourself thought or pretended to think, that we meant the denationalization of
literatures, when on the contrary, we found value only
in those works that revealed most deeply the soil and the
race that had borne them.

And the strange thing is that this accusation came
from you who reproached us, on the other hand, for
our individualistic tendencies, you who claimed that the

individual should be deflated for the greater advantage of the state. We, on the contrary, maintained that the most accomplished work of art will also be the most personal and that there is no advantage for the artist in trying to sink into the stream. We have always maintained that the individual serves the state not by leveling himself off, but by individualizing himself, so to speak; and in the same way, literature, by becoming more national, takes its place among humanity and assumes meaning in the concert. But convinced of the profound truth contained in Christ's teaching: "Whosoever shall seek to save his life shall lose it; and whosoever shall lose his life shall make it truly living," we have believed that the height of individualism is in the sacrifice (but voluntary) of the individual; that the most personal work is the one that involves the greatest abnegation and in the same way, that the most deeply national work, the most particular, ethnically speaking, is also the most human, the one that can touch most strongly the most foreign peoples. What is more Spanish than Cervantes, more English than Shakespeare, more Italian than Dante, more French than Voltaire or Montaigne, than Descartes or Pascal, what more Russian than Dostoevsky; and what is more universally human than these men? It is true that I dare not say: more German than Goethe? For in what concerns Germany, Prussia is responsible for a terrible misunderstanding. Prussia has enslaved Germany so thoroughly that she has forced us to think: Goethe was the least German of the Germans.

If among all French literature, I had to choose the book of which the German genius would be the most incapable, I think I should choose the *Caractères* of La

Bruyère.• In my opinion, there is nothing more French
or less German than what I call the spirit of discrimination. The German, who is never an individual himself,
does not sense the individuality of anyone or anything;
he has never learned draftsmanship. France is the great
drafting school of Europe and of the entire world.

TRANSLATED BY BLANCHE A. PRICE

THE FUTURE OF EUROPE

If I had to teach a child geography, I should start with
the plan of his garden, it seems to me—as Rousseau did
—with the space that his pupil Emile can embrace, with
the horizon that his own eyes see; then I should project
his curiosity beyond the limit of his vision.

But on the other hand, I should be careful to keep the
child from overvaluating the importance of the little
garden from which we have set out; I should take great
care to teach him early what a small place this tiny field
of vegetables and flowers occupies in the region, what a
small place this region occupies in France, and France

• In the same way, it seems to me that *Jean Christophe,* out of all
our literature, is the book that we might think could be the most
easily written in Germany, and this probably accounts for its success
beyond the Rhine.
It is a grave error to think that we work toward European culture
by denationalized works; quite to the contrary, the more *particular* the
work, the more useful it becomes in the concert. It is important to
repeat this unceasingly, for there tends to be a growing confusion between European culture and denationalization. Just as the most in-
dividualized writer is also the one who presents the most general human interest, the work most worthy of being included in European
culture is the one that first of all represents most specifically the country of its origin.

on the terrestrial globe, the image of which I should often show him.

I should not let him know too soon what an imperceptible point in space is this globe itself, for fear of discouraging him, and probably I should not invite his mind to these latter considerations until after I had persuaded him that these questions of dimension are, after all, of no importance in respect to the mind. I should not restrain him from thinking that such vastness was perhaps necessary to allow us to exist and to permit the slightest creation of the spirit to come into being through us; that all these worlds were needed to maintain our world in equilibrium, to balance its rhythm, to temper its humor, to regulate its tides; that on this globe, in sum, a fortunate proportion of earth and water, a certain distance from the sun were to favor our Europe among all the continents. Should I allow him to think that France occupies a privileged rank in Europe itself? Perhaps; but only to use this as a start to teach him to require a great deal of himself. As I talked to him of Greece and Italy, I should not allow him to be ignorant of that darkness which covered our land during the remarkable splendor of the ancient world. I should bring him around to admitting that we are not the sole heirs of that splendor, to understanding that the centers of civilization have slowly shifted and can shift again, that those centers have spread out, and that when we speak of Western civilization, it is not a question of considering any one country, but Europe as a whole.

The generation to which I belong was home loving; it was very ignorant of foreign lands, and far from suffering from this ignorance, it was ready to glory in it. Too easily convinced that what it did not know was not worth the bother of knowing, it saw a guarantee of superiority in its very ignorance. In my opinion, the generation which follows ours is more curious; it recognizes the pleasure and profit of adventure; it no longer feels as our generation did, as if it had lost its illusions and returned to itself without having gone anywhere. It understands correctly the story of Lot's wife: by looking backward, by contemplating continually "the Land of the Dead," one becomes a statue of salt. What it seeks in tradition and in the study of the past is an impetus to go ahead.

After all, I am not very certain that the new generation is really like this, but this is the way I should like it to be—holding that it is a serious error to think one knows his own country the better because he knows others less well. As for me, I can say that I best understood and loved France most when I was in foreign lands. In order to judge properly, one needs some distance; and that is the reason why, too, one must renounce self in order to know oneself.

Not having been able as yet to go to China in order to judge Europe well, but thinking at least that a judgment from that country might be instructive, I accepted with eagerness the opportunity offered me two years ago by Arthur Fontaine to dine with a Chinese. This Celestial, of whom we are speaking, an ex-minister of the Interior or of Finance, had been in Europe for several months; he was traveling from country to country, desirous of gathering information, of improving his mind, and probably, also, of getting away from his country a little so as to judge it.

He was very late in arriving at this dinner given in his honor. His lateness was explained in the course of the dinner, when it was noticed that he just barely touched the food offered to him and only out of politeness did he pretend to eat. Evidently he distrusted European cooking and had taken care to eat beforehand. Whatever his acquaintance with Occidental civilization, he spoke no French and never went out unless accompanied by another Chinese gentleman, his interpreter—who seemed to be under twenty, but was perhaps more than forty.

People age slowly in that country. The ex-minister wanted to interview me on French literature, said Fontaine to me; that is why I had the honor of being seated at the table between him and his interpreter.

With the soup began the interrogatory. I felt extremely ill at ease, for there were numerous guests, and as they were silent, out of politeness, to listen to the questions of the Chinese, they heard my answers as well. At each new question, I turned first toward the minister, who asked it, smiling, and then toward the interpreter, who transmitted it to me, smiling. I answered something or other, smiling first to the interpreter, then to the minister when the transmission reached him. It was long and drawn out, very awkward. Preoccupied with saying nothing that could not be easily translated into Chinese, I gave only the most rudimentary answers. Nevertheless, after each answer and before each new question, the minister did not fail to inform me that my subtlety delighted him, and finally the excess of his politeness disconcerted me completely. It was important to China to know what I thought the repercussion of the war might be on the novel, poetry, the arts. I understood that I was lost if I did not take the offensive, and suddenly sliding out from under the questioning, I begged the interpreter to express in Chinese my great desire to go to China. There was nothing untrue in this remark. China has always greatly attracted me. (The remarkable book of Hovelacque on that country, which I have since read, has only quickened my desire.) The interpreter transmitted it. The minister smiled even more, emitted a short sound—which the interpreter interpreted as:

"Hurry!"

The other guests, however, discouraged by the first part of our conversation, began to talk among themselves; and I think that the minister, as well as I, was more at ease, no longer feeling that we were being listened to. The conversation really began.

"Thrown into confusion by the revolution, China is rapidly changing in appearance," answered the minister, "in a little while the traveler will no longer be able to recognize anything that made up its value."

I was curious to know if this revolutionary movement had preceded, accompanied, or followed some religious reform? The minister excused himself for not having understood my question clearly.

"The Chinese," he said to me, "lives according to ethics, but has never had, properly speaking, any religion. No need of mysticism torments him."

"Has this revolution been born spontaneously in the country," I asked him, "or do you think it must be attributed to an outside cause?"

"Certainly," he answered. "The youth of China, who are restless, who are rising up and unwrapping the swaddling of their past, were in the beginning awakened by Western ideas."

"I suspected as much," I said, but as I saw him continuing to smile, I thought momentarily that he was congratulating himself on this awakening.

"No, no," he then said, "I am not one of those in favor of change; and nothing, to my eyes, can be worth the China that is about to disappear. But what can be done about it? And what is the use of grieving? Your Western world has spread ferment among us. Three of your authors in particular have acted profoundly upon our minds: Dostoevsky, Ibsen, and Shaw."

I was astonished: I could understand Dostoevsky, for he seems to us Far Westerners almost Asiatic at times. But Ibsen? As for Bernard Shaw, the institutions against which he revolts are so specifically Western. In what way could he interest the Chinese?

"To them, what he demolishes makes little difference," I was told. "The important thing is that he demolishes. What young China venerates in him is disrespect."

I asked him what had struck him especially in his travels. He told me that in Europe, he was especially sensitive to the expression of fatigue, sadness, and care on all the faces, and that it seemed to him that we knew all the arts excepting the simple one of being happy. While he spoke to me, I admired his tranquil smile; his eyes were filled with serene kindness and reminded me of the eyes of certain monks whom I had formerly associated with at Monte Cassino; like theirs, his face and body were not marked by any sign of age.

"Humanity," he continued, "had the choice of setting as its aim progress accompanied by attrition, or the prevention of attrition by the refusal of progress. Up to recent times, at least, the whole effort of China, like that of Egypt formerly, has been to prevent time from taking a hold." He then pictured for me the voluptuous numbness that had gone on for centuries behind that Sacred Wall which inventions, modern discoveries, torments, desires, and inordinate ambitions had found no way of scaling. Seeking happiness in the norm, each individual took care not to stand out from the mass; each day was not to stand out from the past.

"But what astonishes me in your country," he continued, "is not that you have preferred life to slumber and progress to stagnation: your civilization has certainly raised man to a higher point than we ever thought he could reach—mechanically speaking at least, and you have a right to think that this was indeed worth a few wrinkles. What astonishes me is that your religion, at least the one you profess, Catholicism, Christianity, has taught you something quite different. Did not Christ repeatedly say to you that happiness lies in the renunciation of precisely that in which you glory the most and for which you fret so much? That state of childhood he wanted to bring you back to, that immediate and constant enjoyment, is the very state in which we Chinese live, but it is a state of which the inhabitants of your world, even those who call themselves Christians, have little knowledge."

"Precisely because the Church understood that," I said to him, "it opposes respect and love of tradition and the past, to innovations and reforms."

"Do you not think," he continued, "that all of Europe's suffering of these times comes from the fact that having decided in favor of civilization, it allies itself with a religion that denies civilization? By what juggling do you succeed in reconciling the one with the other? But in truth, you reconcile nothing. You live in a state of compromise; even the Church is constrained to compromise in order not to lose its contact, its hold; it has had to consent to take all progress of thought into account and because of this, it is more and more separated from the pure spirit of the Gospels. But as soon as Christianity was not contented to have brought a system of ethics to the world, as our great Oriental sages have done, as soon as it imposed its dogmas, required faith in those dogmas, and demanded that reason yield to faith, at that moment it accepted conflict. If reason is opposed to dogma—as seems to me to be the case (for if it were not opposed, why then require faith where simple good sense and reason would suffice)—the Church is compelled to evolve along with reason. Leo-tse, Confucius, and Sakyamuni forearmed themselves against this necessity by not placing their teaching on a level that reason could attain only as an enemy; by not making it rest upon anything supernatural, finally, by not separating morals from wisdom, so that the most virtuous among us is also the most reasonable. Thanks to this, we achieve on earth the happiness that you postpone until heaven.

"I have traveled a great deal. I have seen Moslems, Buddhists; everywhere I have seen customs, institutions, the very nature of society fashioned according to beliefs —yes, everywhere, excepting among Christians. Here is a religion that says to man: 'What are you troubled about?' It teaches him to possess nothing on this earth, to help one another, to love one another, not to want to add an inch to his stature, to offer his right cheek to the one who has struck his left. Yet this religion is precisely the one that has formed the most troubled nations, the most rich, learned, and civilized (all forms of wealth), the most ingenious, industrious, inventive, clever, the most restless and turbulent, ever desirous of puffing themselves up, of raising themselves, in short, those whose honor (as you call it) is the most easily wounded, who are most often opposed to pardon and remission. Will you not agree with me that there is something strange, a misunderstanding and a deception in this—in fact, an indefinable discordant note that is leading you to failure?"

I dared reply: "I think that I glimpse the secret reason for this discordant note that strikes you so strongly, but to which we are so accustomed that none of us is astonished any longer; it is because Christianity, without seeming to be so (and Catholicism not much less than Protestantism), is a school of individualism, perhaps the best that man has ever created up to the present."

I quite felt that I should have developed my thought a little, but fortunately he did not leave me time to do so.

"Yes," he continued by way of conciliation, "that is truly what characterizes you Europeans. With us, on the contrary, the individual tends to melt into the mass; with you all things work toward forming individuals."

We had risen from the table. And while the Chinese was refusing coffee, I said to myself, "individuals," and I tried to remember the words that Montesquieu ascribes to Eucrates in his dialogue with Sylla: "It costs too much to produce them. . . ." Yes, that was approximately it: it costs too much—and the whole sad comedy that was being played in our Occidental world bore the

title: The Search for the Individual, or the Sacrifice of
Happiness.

The Chinese had understood well, I thought: our
whole Western world was comparable to "him whose
heart is divided," who, as the Scripture tells us, "is in-
constant in all his ways." Our restlessness indeed comes
from the fact that religion and civilization pull us about
in opposite directions, and that in no direction do we
achieve anything pure. Since we consent to giving up
neither the one nor the other, we have made of Europe a
place of lie and compromise. On the one hand, however
much culture has been opposed by the Gospel, it has
not been able to deny religion any more than it has been
able to cast it out from its bosom; on the contrary, does
it not give religion the advantage of its infidelities? On
the other hand, while religion protests against those infidelities of culture, it willingly accepts its benefits;
though it protests against culture, it does not dare oppose it completely and allows itself to be carried along
by it far from its point of origin, the Gospel. Finally, far
from rendering unto Caesar what is Caesar's and keeping for God what is God's, as Christ taught, we have
seen it enter into partnership with Caesar and enroll
itself. We have seen the monstrous fruit of this adul-
terous alliance: we have seen the nations of Europe
strike out against one another and kill in the very name
of God, in the name of Christ, who had said to the one
who also had drawn a sword to defend Him: "Put up
thy sword into the sheath."

These were all reflections that I preferred not to reveal to a Chinese. So when he asked me to tell him in
turn what I thought of Europe, I answered that I
thought a great deal of good of it.

And now that you urge me, my dear De Traz, what
should I say? That I believe we are witnessing the end

of a world, of a culture, of a civilization, and that everything must be re-examined, and that the conservative
parties are deluded if they think they can accommodate
the future in the institutions of the past, for old forms
cannot suit young forces.

But you ask what the Europe of tomorrow will be, and
you receive answers from different countries. I believe
that your correspondents will agree on certain points;
these in particular: that no country in Europe can henceforth claim a real progress of its own culture by isolating
itself or without having an indirect collaboration with
other countries; that from the political, economic, and
industrial point of view as well—indeed, from any point
of view whatsoever—Europe as a whole is speeding toward ruin if each country in Europe is willing to think
only of its own particular salvation.

But you have only the particular opinions of several
very carefully chosen correspondents; and perhaps your
choice was somewhat dictated by the anticipation of
their answers. To tell the truth, the question of Europe
preoccupies people's minds very little—or to be more
exact, preoccupies only a very small number of minds.
The feeling of a common interest awakens only in the
face of a common danger, and until now, the feeling of
danger has merely set the peoples of Europe one against
the other. The habit is formed, and that is why it is so
difficult today to agree to think of bankruptcy as a common danger.

The true European spirit is opposed to the isolating
infatuation with nationalism; it is equally opposed to
that depersonalization that internationalism would like.
Over a long period I have often said: *one best serves the
general interest by being the most particular;* and this
holds true for countries as well as for individuals. But
this truth must be reinforced by the following: *one finds
oneself by giving up oneself.*

And so long as politics dominates and subjugates

ethics, we are not permitted to glimpse the truth of this last statement as applied to countries. To tell the truth, political questions interest me less and seem less important to me than social questions; social questions less important than ethical questions. I think that the greater part of the former can be reduced to the latter, and that in all we deplore today, institutions should be blamed less than man himself—it is primarily, above all, man who must be reformed.

TRANSLATED BY BLANCHE A. PRICE

Notes to Angèle

In early January 1921 Gide noted in his Journals *that he had made up his mind to "extract from" himself a "Letter to Angèle," which "will make certain of my friends pursue me with invective, yet I owe them frankness." He did revive at that time the naïve and silent correspondent whom he had not addressed since 1900, and thus a series of lively "Notes to Angèle" came out in the* Nouvelle Revue Française *between March and June 1921.*

Inasmuch as the first two notes concern classicism and derive directly from Gide's "Reply to an Inquiry of La Renaissance *on Classicism"—in which he had so succinctly set down his thoughts on the subject—that "Reply" is given here before the "Notes to Angèle."*

The third note marks Gide's first public homage to Proust, although he had written Proust two contrite and admiring letters in January 1914 (at a time when very few critics had yet come to appreciate Proust) to atone for his error of rejecting the manuscript of Swann's Way *in 1912. And by 1919 he had succeeded in acquiring the rights from Proust's original publisher and bringing the whole of the novelist's work under the N.R.F. imprint.*

Notes Four and Five concern the Nouvelle Revue Française *itself, that vastly influential literary monthly which Gide and a group of friends had founded in 1909. And Note Six with its detailed comments on Maurice Barrès continues the ideological quarrel that had begun in 1897.*

REPLY TO AN INQUIRY OF
"LA RENAISSANCE" ON CLASSICISM

I do not think that the questions you ask me about classicism can be understood anywhere but in France, the home and last refuge of classicism. However, even in France, have there ever been any greater representatives of classicism than Raphael, Goethe, or Mozart?

True classicism does not result from outer constraint; this type remains artificial and produces only academic works. It seems to me that the qualities that we are pleased to call classical are above all moral qualities, and I am likely to think of classicism as a harmonious group of virtues, the first of which is modesty. Romanticism is always accompanied by pride, infatuation. Classical perfection, to be sure, does not imply the suppression of the individual (I almost said: quite the contrary) but the submission of the individual, his subordination, as well as that of the word to the sentence, of the sentence to the page, of the page to the work. It is a demonstration of a hierarchy.

It is essential to consider that the struggle between classicism and romanticism exists inside each mind as well. And the work of art must be born from this struggle; the classical work of art tells of the triumph of order and measure over inner romanticism. The greater the initial revolt of the object brought under subjection, the more beautiful is the work of art. If the material is subdued ahead of time, the work is cold and without interest. True classicism is composed of nothing that restricts or suppresses; it is not so much conservative as creative;

it turns away from archaism and refuses to believe that everything has already been said.

 I add that not everyone can become classical; and that the truly classical are those who are classical in spite of themselves, unconsciously.

TRANSLATED BY BLANCHE A. PRICE

My dear Angèle:
 Too much time has gone by. I have lost the knack of writing to you. You were listed among the missing. But since you have once more opened your salon to friends and would like to see our correspondence resumed, do accept sometimes a very brief note from me, and irregularly at that.
 Before leaving Paris I put my library in order; what a lot of rubbish! My rule now is to write as little as possible; and as I took that resolution, I immediately thought of you.

CLASSICISM

I have been interviewed. The *Renaissance* wanted my opinion on the question of classicism.
 Since I believe that those who talk most are often those who produce least, I began by declaring that I had nothing to say. But Emile Henriot, who came to get my answer, brings so much intelligence, courtesy, and persuasiveness to his interviews that it is not enough to say that it is easy to talk with him; with him one cannot

keep from talking. You may already have seen my answer in print.

Having identified modesty as the essence of classicism, I can now tell you that I see myself as the best representative of classicism today. I was about to say the only one; but I was forgetting MM. Gonzague Truc and Benda.

And now if you will allow me a few supplementary remarks, I will note down my ideas as they come.

The triumph of individualism and the triumph of classicism merge. But the triumph of individualism resides in the renunciation of individuality. There is no single quality of the classical style that has not been bought at the sacrifice of some self-indulgence. The painters and writers we most praise today have a manner; the great classical artist makes an effort not to have a manner —he strives for the commonplace. If he achieves this banality without effort, he is manifestly not a great artist. The classical work will be strong and beautiful only by virtue of a romanticism brought under control. Twenty years ago I wrote:

A great artist• has but one concern: to become as human as possible—or, to put it better, to become *commonplace.* . . . The wonderful thing is that he thus becomes more personal. But he who flees humanity for himself alone, succeeds only in becoming special, bizarre, incomplete. It is perhaps appropriate to recall the words of the Gospel here—I do not think I am distorting the sense: "Whosoever shall seek to save his life [his personal life] shall lose it; and whosoever shall lose his life shall preserve it." (Or, to translate more faithfully the Greek text: ". . . shall make it truly alive.")

I judge that the successful work of art will be that which will first pass unnoticed, which will not even be

• [Gide misquotes himself: the original reads "great man." See p. 31.]

singled out; in which the most unlike qualities, apparently the most contradictory, strength and softness, erectness and grace, logic and impulse, exactness and poetry, will breathe so easily, that they will seem natural and not at all surprising. Accordingly, the first sacrifice to require of oneself is that of startling one's contemporaries: Baudelaire, Blake, Keats, Browning, Stendhal wrote only for future generations. On this matter Proust has said some very sound things.

And yet I do not believe that the classical work is necessarily first misunderstood. Boileau, Racine, La Fontaine, Molière himself, were at once appreciated; and if we see in their writings many qualities that were not those to which their contemporaries were most responsive, those whom we recognize today as supreme were from the first celebrated. Despite the rather unintelligent attempt of Gautier to turn up neglected geniuses among the *"grotesques"* of the seventeenth century, their position is in no way comparable to that of Baudelaire with respect to a Ponsard or a Baour-Lormian. The public itself was classical and demanded of the work of art those very qualities that make us today judge it classical.

The word "classical" is today in such honor and carries such weight that we incline to call classical every great and beautiful work. This is absurd. There are giant works that are not in the least classical. This does not mean that they are romantic. The classification is meaningless except in France, and even in France what could be less classical often than Pascal, Rabelais, Villon? Neither Shakespeare nor Michelangelo, neither Beethoven nor Dostoevsky, not Rembrandt—not even Dante (I cite only the greatest) is a classicist. *Don Quixote* and Calderón's plays are not classical—they are not romantic—they are purely Spanish.

Indeed, since antiquity I know of no other classicists but the French (with the exception of Goethe—and he is classical only by imitation of the ancients). Classicism seems to me so completely a French invention, that I would almost make the two synonymous—classical and French—if the first could lay claim to exhausting the French genius and had romanticism not succeeded in making itself French; at least it is in its classical art that the French genius has been most fully manifested. But among other peoples every attempt at classicism will remain artificial, as, say, in the case of Pope. Moreover in France and in France alone intelligence tends always to win out over feeling and instinct. This does not mean (as some foreigners are likely to believe) that feeling or instinct is absent. One has only to go through the recently reopened Louvre galleries, both sculpture and painting. To what a degree all those works are dominated by reason! What balance, what moderation! It is necessary to examine them at length before they yield up their profound meaning, so secret is their vibration. Sensuality overflows in Rubens; is it the less powerful in Poussin for being completely inward?

Classicism—and by that I mean French classicism—tends wholly toward litotes. It is the art of expressing the more by saying the less. It is an art of restraint and of modesty. Each of our classicists is more moved than he lets first appear. The romanticist, because of the splendor of his expression, appears always to be more moved than he really is, so that among our romantic authors the word continually precedes and overstates the emotion and the thought; it corresponded to a certain blunting of taste as a result of an inferior culture, which allowed them to doubt the reality of what was so modestly expressed by our classicists. For lack of knowing how to penetrate them and catch their allusions, they found our classicists cold, and judged as a shortcoming their most exquisite quality—reserve.

The romantic author remains always this side of his words; but one must seek the classical author over and

beyond his words. A certain faculty for passing too rapidly, too easily, from emotion to word is characteristic of
all French romanticists; hence their lack of effort to seize
emotion other than by words, their lack of effort to master it. The essential for them is no longer to be moved, but
to *seem* to be moved. In all Greek literature, in the best
English poetry, in Racine, in Pascal, in Baudelaire, you
sense that the word, while revealing emotion, does not
contain it entire, and that, once the word is uttered, the
emotion that preceded it continues. In Ronsard, Corneille, Hugo, to cite only great names, it seems that the
emotion ends with the word and is held within it; it is
verbal and the word exhausts it; the only overtones to be
found in it are supplied by the voice.

TRANSLATED BY JEFFREY J. CARRE

CLASSICISM

Did you read in the January issue of the *N.R.F.* the
translation of a remarkable English article, called to my
attention by your friend Arnold Bennett? As is cus-
tomary, the article appeared unsigned in the *Times
Literary Supplement.* I thought that it might interest
our readers, and that they would profit from hearing
something of what is said abroad about us, the French.
It seemed to me that few answers to M. Henriot's inquiry threw more light on the question of classicism
than did this article. It points out the danger of applying to the concept of order and classicism the restrictions and suppressions that Maurras attempts to impose.
"No art," it states, "can lay claim to the epithet 'classical' that does not meet the problem of totality." And

further: "The splendor of the art and thought of the Greeks resided precisely in the equilibrium they maintained between two forces, one of which Maurras sacrifices. Greek art and thought were at one and the same time individual and universal; they were classical because *they took everything into account.*" This is precisely what I attempted to express in my answer. And finally: "M. Maurras is a man who likes restrictions; his love of the classical is *the love of what is completed* and not of the power that completes. In our opinion there can be only one kind of true realism, as there can be only one art which is true—which is classical; the criterion in both cases is intellectual and emotional integrity. We are, no less than M. Maurras, concerned with moderation and harmony; but we recognize that moderation and harmony are merely modes of existence; the task of our time lies in instituting not any chance order but our own order. Such order alone can satisfy us—an order in which our nature is expressed in all its fullness, in which all the elements in ferment in the modern world after having . . ."

I cannot here reproduce the whole article; but you will read it, will you not? I am less convinced by the anonymous *Times* correspondent when he undertakes to persuade us that the true classical period in French—in the perfect sense that he assigns to the word classical—was that of the cathedrals, the Middle Ages. "This period was classical," he says, "in the sense that at that time all the energy of the people was directed toward a single goal." At any rate, the paradox is an interesting one. And he adds that if "the French had no literature of a classical nature in the Middle Ages," it is because "their language was not ready to serve this final expression of thought and faith." Our seventeenth century compared to this age of complete integration seems to him "a period of formalism." I cannot here espouse the critic's thought. On the contrary, all that he had said

previously helps me understand the signal grandeur of
the century of Molière, La Fontaine, and Racine. It
seems to me that the importance of the writers of this
period—the classical character of their works—stemmed
precisely from an integration within themselves of the
totality of the ethical, intellectual, and emotional preoccupations of their times; the barrenness of today's
neoclassicists (I am speaking of the majority of them)
results from their persistence in aspiring to the grand
style through negation, restriction, and ignorance.

The sole legitimate classicism today, the only one to
which we can and must aspire, concludes the *Times*
critic, is that in which "all of the elements in ferment
in the modern world, after having found free expansion,
will organize themselves according to their true reciprocal relationships." And I adopt willingly his concluding
formula: "The goal to which we aspire is a broad
integration."

Let us integrate then, my dear Angèle. Let us integrate. All that classicism refuses to integrate threatens
to turn against it.

TRANSLATED BY JEFFREY J. CARRE

MARCEL PROUST

It has often been said: the judgments we pass on our
contemporaries are distorted. Not only are we under
obligations to friendship, but we lack the necessary
perspective, and according to our humor, disparage or
magnify to excess those whose work is too close to us.
Some who appear important, whose reputation thanks to
the complicity of the critics seems even in foreign eyes

to bring new luster to France, will soon surprise us by their insignificance. I deserve to be forgotten if before two generations have passed Curel, Bernstein, and Bataille are any more esteemed than is Mendès now.

I had resolved to speak henceforth only of the dead, but it would grieve me to leave in my writing no trace of one of the most intense admirations I have ever felt for a contemporary writer; doubtless I would say *the most intense,* if Paul Valéry did not exist. Despite what I have said above, I do not think I overstate the importance of Marcel Proust; I do not think it can be overstated. It seems to me that it has been a long time since any writer has brought us such riches.

Mme B. was telling me yesterday that she had always been nearsighted; her parents were not at first aware of it and she was about twelve before they had her fitted to glasses. "I remember so well my delight," she told me, "when for the first time, I could make out all the pebbles in the courtyard." When we read Proust, we begin suddenly to perceive detail where until then we had seen only a mass. He is, you will tell me, what is termed an analyst. Not so. The analyst separates with effort; he explains; he takes pains. Proust's response is utterly natural. Proust is someone whose eyes are infinitely more subtle and attentive than our own, and who lends us his eyes so long as we are reading him. And as the things he looks at (so spontaneously that he never seems to be observing) are the most natural things in the world, it seems always that he permits us to see within ourselves. Through him all the confusion of our being emerges from chaos and becomes conscious; and, just as the most diverse feelings exist in each man at the larval stage most often unknown to him and await sometimes only an example or a designation—I was on the point of saying, an attestation—before declaring themselves, we imagine, thanks to Proust, that we have ourselves experienced the detail; we recognize it, adopt it, and it is our own past that is enriched by this multiplication. Proust's books act like powerful developer solutions for the cloudy photographic negatives that are our memories, in which suddenly reappear a particular face and a forgotten smile, together with the emotions that the fading of face and smile had carried into oblivion with them.

I do not know which is more to be admired—the hyperacuity of the inner glance, or the dazzling artistry that seizes this detail and offers it to us enchantingly fresh and alive. Proust's style is the most *artistic* I know (to employ a word against which the Goncourts had prejudiced me but which, when I think of Proust, ceases to displease me). He never feels hampered by it. If, in order to give form to the ineffable, there is no word, he turns to the image; he has at his disposition a whole treasury of analogies, equivalents, and comparisons so precise and so exquisite that sometimes you wonder which lends the other more life, light, and pleasure; you wonder whether the emotion is abetted by the image, or if this airy image were only waiting for the emotion before alighting. I look for the shortcoming of this style and I cannot find it. I look for its dominant qualities, and I cannot find them either; it does not have this or that quality; it has them all (but this is not perhaps altogether praise), not in turn but at one and the same time; his suppleness is so stunning that every other style by comparison seems stiff, dull, imprecise, summary, inanimate. Must I admit it? Whenever I plunge into this lake of delight, for days I stay without daring to take up my pen again, not admitting—as happens during the whole time that a masterpiece dominates us—that there are other ways of writing well, and seeing in what you call the "purity" of my style only poverty.

You have said to me that often the length of Proust's sentences fatigues you. But just wait until my return, when I can read those interminable sentences aloud to you; you will see how everything falls into place, how the different planes stand out, what depth the landscape of the idea assumes. I picture a page of *The Guermantes Way* printed in the manner of Mallarmé's *Coup de dés;* my voice gives relief to the structural words, I orchestrate in my own way the parenthetical remarks, I shade them, moderating or quickening my reading; I shall prove to you that there is nothing superfluous in this sentence, that every word was needed to maintain the different planes in position, to permit a total flowering of such complexity. However detailed Proust may be, I never find him prolix; although luxuriant, he is never diffuse. "Minute" but not "meticulous," Louis Martin-Chauffier has said very perceptively.

Proust clarifies for me in exemplary fashion what Jacques Rivière meant by "lump," a word he used to point out the sloth of those who are content to embrace the feelings that custom has bound together, the group of which presents a deceptive unity. On the contrary, Proust opens up the sheaf carefully, and sets straight the tangle. Indeed, he is not satisfied unless he shows us together with the flower the stem and the delicate net of roots. What curious books! You move into them as into an enchanted forest; from the first pages you are lost and happy to be lost; soon you no longer know your point of entrance or your distance from the starting point; at times it seems that you walk without advancing, at times that you advance without walking; you know not where you are or where you are going.

Suddenly my father would stop us and ask my mother: "Where are we?" Exhausted by the walk, but proud of him, she would confess affectionately that she had not the slightest idea. He would shrug his shoulders and laugh. Then, as if he had taken it from the pocket of his coat together with the key, he would point out directly in front of us the little back-door of our garden which had joined with the corner of the rue du Saint-Esprit to wait for us at the end of those strange paths. My mother would say to him admiringly: "You are remarkable, my dear. . . ."

You are remarkable, my dear Proust! It seems that you were speaking to us only about yourself, and your books are as crowded as the entire *Comédie humaine;* your narrative is not a novel: you do not contrive a plot or a denouement, and yet I know none we follow with keener interest; you introduce your characters to us only incidentally and it might be said by a fluke, but we soon know them as intimately as we know Cousin Pons, Eugénie Grandet, or Vautrin. It seems that your books are not "composed" and that you scatter your wealth haphazardly, but though I wait on your following books to judge with certainty, I suspect already that all the elements unfold according to a hidden order like the branches of a fan, which are fastened at one end and the spread of which is joined by a light fabric whereon the varied colors of your Maya are displayed. And you find the means, along the way, to talk about everything, mingling with the apparent fragmentation of memory observations so penetrating and original that I find myself wanting an appendix to your work, a kind of lexicon to permit us to turn readily to certain comments on sleeping and insomnia, sickness, music, the drama and the art of acting, a lexicon that would even now bulk large but in which I think it would be necessary to enter substantially all the words in the language when the books you promise us will have appeared.

If I now seek what I most admire in this work, I believe it to be its gratuitousness. I know no work that is less utilitarian, no work less bent on proving something. I am well aware that every work of art has this pretension and that each one finds its justification in beauty. But—and this is characteristic—the component

parts are under tension, and although the whole is useless, nothing appears or should appear that is not useful
to the whole, and we know that all that is not useful to
the whole is harmful to it. In *Remembrance of Things
Past* this subordination is so deep-hidden that in turn
each page seems to find its perfect end in itself. Hence
this extreme deliberateness, this reluctance to quicken
the pace, this continuous satisfaction. I find a similar
nonchalance only in Montaigne, and it is doubtless on
that account that I can compare the pleasure I find in
reading Proust only to that given me by the *Essays*. They
are works of long leisure. And I do not mean merely
that the author in order to produce them must have felt
his mind perfectly free from the rush of hours, but also
that they require on the part of the reader a like freedom. They both require and obtain it; that is their gift.
You will say that the character of art and of philosophy
is precisely that of escaping the demands of time; but
Proust's book is characterized by an attention to each
moment; it could be said that the flight of time itself is
his theme. Having broken free of life, he does not turn
away from life; bending over it, he contemplates, or
rather he contemplates within himself life's reflection.
And the more disturbed the image, the steadier is the
mirror and the more contemplative the gaze.

It is strange that such books have come at a time when
the event triumphs everywhere over the idea, when time
is lacking, when action scorns thought, when contemplation seems no longer possible, no longer permissible,
when, not yet recovered from the war, we esteem only
what can be useful, only what can be of service. And
suddenly the work of Proust, so disinterested, so gratuitous, appears to us more profitable and of greater relief
than so many works whose goal is usefulness alone.

TRANSLATED BY JEFFREY J. CARRE

"LA NOUVELLE REVUE FRANÇAISE"

It has come to my attention that the *Nouvelle Revue Française* disappoints a number of its readers, its best friends among them. They expected something else from it. Michel Arnauld writes to me: "I cannot reconcile myself to seeing the *N.R.F.* abandon what its initial effort had so well prepared: a revision of French values —and European values—without prejudice of school or party. . . ." And I assure you that I should not be reconciled to that either, for I judge that this function has never been more useful. But first, if there be such an abandonment, I doubt that it is conscious; above all I do not believe that it is solely imputable to the new editor• of the review. It stems principally from this fact, that a number of the first and most active participants, having "evolved" during the war, no longer brought the same spirit to the criticism of these "values" and, indeed, judged them differently. For my part, not approving them always, and not approving Rivière any more often, I kept my own counsel for fear of poisoning the discussions inspired by the resumption of our review; and particularly anxious to strengthen rather than diminish the authority of our editor, I accorded him at least the support of my silence. There were additional reasons that can perhaps now be told.

When I allow my thoughts their natural course, they go toward the extreme Left, and I swing them back toward the Right only through an effort of my reason. I made this effort during the war, because of circum-

• [Jacques Rivière.]

stances, because of necessity, and I still make it out of
consideration for some friends whom I dislike displeas-
ing—and who certainly do not suspect what I assume on
their behalf. I do not say that my reasoning is distorted
in the process of *rectification* of my ideas; I say simply
that this direction is not natural to them. And I cannot
persuade myself that the natural bent of thought is not
the best. I am easily swayed by patriotic or personal interest, by sympathy; but I see value in my thought only
if I feel that it is not directed. That is why I said nothing during the war.

We have passed through doleful times when all the
thoughts of heart and mind were enlisted; the one concern was to aid France, each to the limit of his powers,
to help France to victory, to bring her out of it alive.
France emerges victorious but exhausted. And now we
are told that submission of the mind is more necessary
than ever. Some who during the war heroically con-
signed their brains to their knapsacks are trying now to
persuade us that the arrangement is a satisfactory one,
that there is no point to shifting position, that, at the
very least, it is *useful* to leave their brains packed away
so as to permit the revival of France. And worst of all,
they believe it. The dilemma is, then, to run the risk of
disturbing momentarily an artificial and manifestly
provisional order, by airing certain ideas that do not adjust to it, or to consent to compromises of the mind, to
allow our judgment to be adulterated, to blunt our critical sense, and in a word, to tarnish the fair mirror that
France held up, wherein truth best saw her own clear
face.●

● "French intelligence, in this state of permanent mobilization, would
soon be in danger not only of being no longer intelligence but also
of being no longer French," your friend Thibaudet wrote in his excellent article on "The Demobilization of Intelligence" (*N.R.F.*, 1 January 1920) , an article to which I can really add nothing.

The concept of "nation" is a most complex one. There are not only fields, interests, and cathedrals to be protected; there are also incalculable intellectual and ethical values, whose progressive diminution may go unnoticed, because there is lost with them the sense of their worth; they are in great danger.

I realize that such considerations are deadly; if you prefer silence from me, do tell me. But first let me read you these few lines from a letter of Michel Arnauld:

What frightens me is to see how separate are now the noblest activities of the mind. Everything I see, everything I read, demonstrates that taste is in no danger. Art flourishes; it takes its place among the newly rich; it leaves thought among the permanently poor. If there was a time when knowledge and abstract logic hampered intuitive judgment, we are no longer in that fix, and today's problem is worse. When the assembling of information and the construction of a logical order are called for, we make decisions as though selecting a line or a value for a painting. It is maintained that we think as we feel, and feeling rightly, we think falsely. In regard to our country and to social peace, the votes of a Congress of Tours are less threatening than this absence of reflection among the cultivated classes.

I hesitate to send you these pages; this letter is ill adapted, I feel certain, to what you had hoped for from me. May I better meet your expectations another day. But because I have been so long silent, I must at the beginning remove this first barrier to my speech.

TRANSLATED BY JEFFREY J. CARRE

"LA NOUVELLE REVUE FRANÇAISE"

The more I withdraw from the *N.R.F.* the more it is thought that I direct it. It is true that Rivière often does me the honor of asking my advice; and I, who am particularly concerned with instilling confidence, encourage him in his projects; but it is always in those projects most unlike my own view of things that the public is inclined to recognize my mind. It would be futile to protest and so I keep silent; but in doing so a false image is allowed to form. Of all the monsters it is the one most difficult to combat. You have already pointed out to me that in the matter of the false image, I have often only myself to blame and that with *La Symphonie Pastorale* I threw many readers off the track. True enough. This, abetted by my moroseness, kept me from thanking any critic, however laudatory he might be, however appreciative I might be, however excellent his article might seem to me. I was particularly moved, I think, by a letter from a young writer who took me to task, divining that I could have no pleasure in this book, puzzled that I had written it after *Les Caves du Vatican* (*Lafcadio's Adventures*), asking me to justify myself. . . . I could only reply, in the most awkward way possible, with a Goncourt observation: "One does not write the books he wants to"; that I did not so much want to write the book as the book wanted writing by me; that in writing it I but paid an old debt I had formerly contracted to myself; that until the present I had not written a single work that had not been conceived before my thirtieth year, so that each one drew me back in time and in no way corresponded to the most recent state of my mind; but that now, at last, I was free and clear; that this book was my last debt to the past; that I had written it to exonerate myself; that to write it and write it well I had to assume a form not my own, or at least to fit myself again into an old garment; that during all the time of writing I fumed at the needlepoint that the conditions of the problem demanded, at those half-tones, those nuances, while what I now wanted was to—but I will tell you about that another time.

TRANSLATED BY JEFFREY J. CARRE

MAURICE BARRÈS

My dear Angèle:
On the appearance of Thibaudet's book on Maurice Barrès, I bring out for you, from the bottom of a drawer, these few notes made before the war. Most of them are very old (I trust you will not find them dated). I wrote each following a reading—shortly after the publication of the book in question.

DISCOURS À L'ACADÉMIE

"If these books have any value, it is due to their logic, to the consistency of thought that for five years I have maintained in them. As for the art that readers or indulgent critics find therein, that is but a passing fad" (Barrès, letter to *La Plume*, 1 April 1891).

On the contrary, the "passing fad" is your opinions, your ideas. Moreover, what you call here your "logic" seems to me most often only a clinging to theories contradicted by the logic of God or, if you prefer, the logic of "natural history." And what we like best in you are those inconsistencies in which the man of instinct steps ahead of the dogmatist and inspires in you, a nationalist, the most exquisite praise for Heredia, Chénier, and Moréas, your three best-loved poets: a Cuban and two Greeks. . . . And it is because of this art, which fortunately you repudiate only verbally, that your best writing will outlive your theories.

LES DÉRACINÉS

Could Barrès really have believed, could he have supposed for a moment, that his theories apparently so opportune (and I take the word in its most urgent sense), so therapeutic for our ruined country, so calculated to galvanize the middling intelligences of numerous elderly adolescents, would still find, these theories of his, an audience for as much as thirty years? And does he not understand that his theories atrophy in the very act of restoring vigor to France? For it is not appropriate to a healthy people, or to a robust mind, to remain with eyes rooted to the ground, intent only on seeing tombs there; it may well be, and I want to so believe, that the medicine will save the country; but, once saved, the country will be revolted by it.

LES AMITIÉS FRANCAISES

Fortunately for him, in his books Barrès does not supply answers as much as others do for him. The unresolved question persists in his writings, and it is the best thing in them. Woe unto works that draw conclusions; they first satisfy the public most, but after twenty years the conclusion crushes the book.

There are "circumstantial thoughts" that are the equivalent of "circumstantial laws." Rousseau's writings owed their initial success neither to their style, nor to their essential pathos, nor to their psychological novelty, but precisely to what was most specious and false in their theories: excellence of the instinct, return to nature, superiority of Italian music, etc., and even to certain practical recommendations (nursing of children by the mothers, etc.), which the dullest minds could grasp readily. I sense in Barrès's books, alongside a most noble will and a keen common sense, a great clutter of sophistries. For twenty readers capable of appreciating the real qualities of the writer, there are a hundred or a thousand capable of taking his sophistries for truths; Barrès owes the major part of his fame today to these very sophistries and not to the great talent that will permit his survival.

He maintains that the animal or the plant flourishes nowhere so well as in its place of origin; that may appear "logical," but it is false; as it is false to say, conversely, that on each soil must flourish especially the species native to that soil.

Bérénice "who died through having placed her confidence in the adversary . . ." Unquestionably that should have been the *subject* of the book; but it is just *this* that the book does not demonstrate.

Would it not also have been interesting—indispensable, indeed, to destroy the doctrine of a Bouteiller—that the doctrine ("to act in such a way, always, that I can wish my action to serve as a universal rule") be the direct cause of his ruin? Nothing of the sort. On the contrary, it is following an infraction of this rule of conduct that Bouteiller is disgraced and perishes.

SCÈNES ET DOCTRINES DU NATIONALISME

What Barrès condemns, what he calls the "Protestant spirit," is that "dangerous" spirit of equity which made the Jansenists write:

"To whatever order, and to whatever country you belong, you must believe only what is true, and only what
you would be disposed to believe if you were of another
country, another order, another profession."

And further: "We judge things, not by what they are
in themselves, but by what they are in regard to us; and
truth and usefulness are but one and the same thing"
(*Logique de Port-Royal,* Part III, Chapter XIX, 1).

Barrès makes the basis of his ethics what the great
Arnauld notes and deplores; Barrès thinks that we must
not seek to judge things by what they are in themselves,
indeed, that we cannot judge them except in their relation to us. From that point to confusing the concept of
truth and the concept of usefulness is but a step—a step
that expediency readily takes—and the whole reasoning
is falsified.

In the interest of greater usefulness Barrès depicts as
Kantian and German, or Protestant and un-French, and
consequently to be shunned, a form of thought that is
properly Jansenist and on the contrary more profoundly
French than the Jesuitical and Barrèsian form, to which
it has always been opposed.

AU SERVICE DE L'ALLEMAGNE

The gesture that supports his writings is a defensive one
and has no reason for existence except before the enemy.
Once the danger is gone I doubt that our successors will
understand the eloquence of the gesture. His emphases
and repetitions will weary as soon as they are no longer
timely. Even *Au Service de l'Allemagne,* an excellent
little book, but of a very restricted interest, will be less
interesting than, say, the narrative of Astiné Aravian,
*La Mort de Venise, Les Deux Femmes du bourgeois de
Bruges,* or *L'Amateur d'âmes*—these will doubtless inspire the thought that of all the "dissolvent" minds
against which Barrès protests he would have been the
best and most subtle, had he been more natural.

PASCAL

Barrès will perhaps some day become a Catholic; I came close to writing: Barrès will surely become a Catholic; but there is no fear that he will ever turn to Jansenism. I grant that the figure of Pascal impresses him; but, by temperament, he remains nonetheless closer to Sanchez and Loyola. At the very beginning of his lecture (on Pascal) a word, an exclamation, alerts us: "Gentlemen, our object is to place you on Pascal's path, to permit you, not to accompany him (Good Heavens, that is not our concern) . . ."

Is this "Good Heavens" mocking? Is it involuntary? I do not know and it is no matter; but we sense at once that it is not a question of accompanying Pascal; and when immediately afterward we read: "Accordingly I am going to focus all my remarks on a single point (a very brief text, but the most significant one) in order to lead you as close as possible to this great soul"—we feel ourselves too far from God to be really very close to Pascal, and we fear that the pathos is essentially literary in: "I shall try to guide you there *where the sublime moments pulse* . . ."

Anguish, true anguish; Pascal, the true Pascal—the anguish of Pascal: that is no subject for a fashionable lecture. Barrès is aware of that: "Here is a state of mind," he says speaking of *the state of mind* of Pascal, "of which you and I, gentlemen, can have no exact sense." And we share Barrès's awareness.

L'APPEL AU SOLDAT

Barrès furnishes a criterion, a new yardstick with which to measure minds and things of the mind. Hence the gratitude of young minds whose indolence he thus encourages. One judges by . . . or according to . . . such and such is recognized as good or bad, because . . . Barrès does not so much appeal to reason as to principles; the principles are there so that reason may be idle. It is forgotten that the originator sought the principles to aid in the development of his personality; the particular situation that brought them forth is forgotten; at a distance, they are attributed an absolute quality.

One mind out of a hundred, and a select hundred at that, succeeds in judging by itself. Hence the triumph of the schools, of systems of thought, in politics as in religion and art.

LE VOYAGE DE SPARTE

Barrès's mind recalls a machine for making hats of which I remember seeing an extraordinary advertisement some ten years ago: a drawing represented in summary fashion the machine and the hats it produced. Everything fed into the machine came out in the form of a hat—any material whatsoever would serve. At last, among the admiring spectators, a very young child, who was leaning too close, got caught in the mechanism; the machine swallowed him up. The parents were depicted and their gestures of despair; but their child, the delicate creature, emerged a moment later, at the other end of the machine, to the delight of all eyes, to the joy of his parents, in the form of a perfect little hat: "A hat, ladies and gentlemen, which it is my pleasure to doff to you," concluded the inventor. The child was at last *useful* for something.

We might initially have doubted that Greece could be useful; and at first, it is true, Barrès himself hesitates, turns, doubts, looks for his opening, his way of using Greece. But, lo and behold, in Sparta he comes upon the castles of his *uprooted* Normans.

TRANSLATED BY JEFFREY J. CARRE

Open Letters

After the Nouvelle Revue Française *resumed publishing at the end of the First World War, its pages contained several "Open Letters" by Gide, another form in which he enjoyed couching his literary criticism.*

The thirty-nine-year-old Gide met the twenty-three-year-old Jacques Rivière in 1909, and struck by his intellectual qualities, encouraged him to write for the newly founded N.R.F. *Rivière soon became managing editor under the general editorship of Jacques Copeau. Early in the war, Rivière was taken prisoner and during four years of prison camp he wrote several moving essays, a spiritual autobiography, and a penetrating analysis of the German character. On his return to Paris in 1919, he became editor-in-chief of the* N.R.F., *to which he devoted himself unstintingly until his untimely death in 1925.*

Gide's association with Jean Cocteau began in 1912 with the latter's third volume of verse at the age of twenty-three. Gide followed his young friend's work with interest as Cocteau's ballets, poems, and plays established him more and more as a leader of the avant-garde. *But this open letter hurt the younger writer who retorted with an "open reply" that Rivière refused to publish, despite Gide's urging, because it simply attacked Gide on personal grounds. Instead, Cocteau's "Reply to André Gide" appeared in* Les Ecrits Nouveaux *for June-July 1919.*

Gide's correspondence with the poet Francis Jammes

*began in 1893, although the two writers did not meet
until 1896, and continued until Jammes's death in 1938,
after the relationship had progressively cooled as a result
of incidents such as those discussed in this open letter.*

TO JACQUES RIVIÈRE

My dear Rivière:

I am delighted that so many readers have found complete satisfaction in your book. Moreover, I understand
the relief it brings them after the highly charged and
incoherent imprecations to which the state of war has
accustomed us. It is with emotion that I come upon the
exquisite qualities of your criticism in your book: your
scruples, your pertinence, your subtlety; but as you state
in your preface, just as you wrote your book for the utmost relief of your mind, so do I, in turn, write you this
letter to relieve my mind, for I must confess that your
book left me ill at ease.

In it you offer many a fact that our press would rather
neglect, pass over, or deny, because the facts seemed to
be of such a nature as to temper our feelings of hatred
toward our enemies, a feeling considered indispensable
to victory.

However, you sensed in us that extreme uneasiness
aroused by our noticing certain manifestations of apparent virtues in those whom we were supposed to hate and
whom we wanted to hate. Desirous once more of recov-
ering an easy flow of breath and thought, as you say, you
sought and found an explanation for those facts, an interpretation that made them all the more detestable to
us because at first glance they might seem to us to be

worthy of esteem. Certain people will be extremely grateful to you for this. But at times it happens that your
explanation of the facts is so subtle, that the mind forgets it shortly after reading it and remembers only the
facts themselves. Since this may fool us, you do well to
forewarn us. You will not deny that sometimes your
interpretation has cost you some effort and is a little
forced. To tell the truth, I am not even certain that you
are always right; in reading you, our interest comes
doubtless from the fact that when you portray the German, contrasting yourself to him, you are often portray-
ing yourself at the same time. It is not a question only
of the German in your book, but also of the French
reaction. In the main, you justify our reasons for not admitting the German virtues when we are confronted by
them.

May I say, further, that your knowledge of the German people is still perhaps a bit youthful? Not that I
think the passing of years will give you occasion to mod-
ify it very much subsequently; but probably you will
be led to find in other peoples, as yet imperfectly known
to you, certain of those characteristics that you note in
your book as peculiar to the German race, and of which
it would probably suffice to say that they are peculiarly
foreign to the Latin races and to the French. Here is
what an Englishman of superior culture who has just
read your book writes me on this subject:

That incapacity for objectification, which Jacques Rivière points out, does not seem to me to be especially peculiar
to the German race. We find this defect, this uneasiness, in
all the northern nations under one form or another. I dare
affirm that it can be found in another form in America as
well, and if it is not immediately apparent to you in England, it is perhaps only thanks to that small minority of
people who control the English civilization but who are in
violent reaction against the feelings and the attitude of the
mass of their contemporaries.

In the second year of this war, I happened to read a page of my journal to a Danish lady, a friend of mine and of France. It may, I think, interest you.

Here it is:

Yesterday morning (26 January 1914), Rainer Maria Rilke came to show me several pages of his translation of my *Enfant prodigue* with which he was not completely satisfied.

It gave me pleasure to see his delicate face once again. Now I have learned to perceive the purity and sensitivity of his soul under the ineloquence of his features. Happy to find the big Grimm dictionary in my library, he opened it to the word *"Hand"* and plunged into a patient search where I left him alone for awhile. He had been entertaining himself by the translation of several of Michelangelo's sonnets and he told me of his perplexity when he came to the word *"palma,"* and of his surprise in perceiving that the German language had a word to designate the back of the hand but not any to designate the inside.

"The best they can say is *'Handflächen'*: the plain of the hand; the inside of the hand, a plain!" he cried out. "But then *'Handrücken'* is constantly used. So what they consider is the back of the hand, that surface without interest, without personality, sensuality, gentleness, that surface preferred to the warm, caressing, gentle palm, which reveals the mystery of the individual."

By thumbing through Grimm, he finally discovered the word: *"Handteller"* with several sixteenth-century examples:

"But," he said, "This is the palm of the hand held out to collect, to beg, to ask for alms. What a confession in this deficiency of our language."

Once more I was able to ascertain the revealing irritation of a German writer at his own language, an irritation that I have already noted down elsewhere, which to my knowledge no writer of any other country has ever experienced. (It is proper to note here that Rainer

Maria Rilke, one of the greatest poets of present-day
Germany, is a Czech.)

After I had read this page to her, my Danish friend
exclaimed: "But, alas, we have no word either . . . in
none of the Scandinavian languages is there a special
word to indicate the palm of the hand. The philological
observations of Rilke that you report are indeed revealing, but be careful, for your conclusions drawn from this
fact may extend beyond the German race, and if you
decide to use them as a weapon, may wound with the
same blow a number of your friends."

TRANSLATED BY BLANCHE A. PRICE

TO JEAN COCTEAU

My dear Cocteau:

I have already told you of my pleasure in reading the
Cap de Bonne-Espérance and my even greater pleasure
in hearing you read it, for you read with amazing talent.

I was awaiting the *Coq et l'arlequin* with great impa-
tience, mixed, I must indeed confess, with a perceptible
apprehension. I had a feeling that I was going to find
the key, not to your talent, for talent is "the man himself," but to your aesthetics, and the explanation of what
disconcerts me in you, precisely because I feel that it is
preconcerted. I have long recognized the accuracy of
your maxims, but certain of them seem to me to be less
in keeping with the person you are than with the one
you would like to have people think you are. I tell myself that in writing you this, I shall stir up a very lively
protest in you; however, I do not feel that I am making
a mistake. And I do not claim that your aphorisms lack

sincerity, but that you are deceived about yourself and deceive us.

For example, I think you have nothing to gain by limiting the colors on your palette. On the contrary, your most pleasing lines are those in which you abandon yourself to your charming genius for analogies, and this seems to me to be your special poetic gift.•

Likewise, when you say that an artst must not "skip steps," what do you uphold, and what have you ever done but just that? I have often said to you that each time I talk with you, I think of a dialogue between the bear and the squirrel. There where I drag myself along, you leap. Of course I do not blame you for leaping, but for wanting to persuade us and yourself that you are a logician. I blame you for sacrificing your most charming and brilliant qualities for the benefit of heavier ones which you perhaps do not possess.

Finally I must confess my feeling of embarrassment when I read your "defense" of *Parade*. In general it seems to me that it is neither becoming nor adroit for an artist to explain his work: first, because by so doing, he limits it, and because a deeply sincere work goes beyond the meaning that the author himself can give it;

• For example, that exquisite description of a modern dance which I can not refrain from quoting, although you thought you had to relegate it to a footnote, perhaps because of overrefined affectation, or rather, I fear, because you were afraid to allow your true gifts to be too evident (and this is exactly what I blame you for).

This is what the dance was like:

The American band accompanied it with banjos and thick pipes made of nickel. To the right of the little troupe dressed in black, under a golden pergola, there was a barman, laden down with bells, rods, boards, motocycle horns, who was serving up sounds. With these he made cocktails, adding from time to time a little peel of cymbal, getting up, jazzing around with a beatific smile.

M. Pilcer, in a dress coat, thin and rouged, and Mademoiselle Gaby Delys, looking like a big ventriloquist's doll with a porcelain face, straw-colored hair, and a dress of ostrich plumes, danced a sort of tamed catastrophe to this hurricane of rhythms and drums, which left them quite tipsy and blinded, under a shower of six spotlights.

and then I maintain that the best explanation of one work must be that which comes after it. In the particular case of *Parade,* my embarrassment is increased by the fact that the reader of your explanation cannot refer to the play, so that the most courteous thing he can do is to acquit it by default.

But if the public and the critics received *Parade* in the way against which you protest, I should like to be more certain that it is because of their stupidity; the comments that you made about it seem to me to justify not so much your play as their incomprehension. Could you reasonably hope for these spectators to understand that *the real play* was not the one you were showing them? And it even seems to me that your error lies not only in the presentation of your fundamental idea, but in the idea itself: the true play is within.

For though, according to the mystics, that is true of the apparent world and of the whole human comedy, it just happens that a work of art, on the contrary, has no other reason for being and no other aim than to reveal, to display this secret reality, and whosoever neglects to do so, fails.

But probably this very embarrassment that I picture to you sharpens the great pleasure that I take in your little book, and since "the worst fate of a work is not to be blamed for anything," as you say, I am certain that you will take these few remarks in as friendly a spirit as I write them.

TRANSLATED BY BLANCHE A. PRICE

TO M. FRANCIS JAMMES

Paris, 24 April 1923

My dear Jammes:

When I went through Paris, I looked into the *Nouvelles littéraires* of 14 April and read the account of the visit to Claudel that we made together in 1900. In spite of my most friendly effort, I am not able to inhabit the sentences that you ascribe to me. What alters their character profoundly is that your account does not make it clear that Claudel and I could have known each other at that time, other than through you. Of the 125 letters of Claudel which I have kept (our correspondence stops in 1920), the first (from Ki Liang, 28 August 1899) antedates this visit, and the unusual praise that it contains, together with the admiration I had devoted to Claudel since the publication of *Tête d'or*, explain that I could have wanted to become acquainted with him. My fear of importuning people is so great that it was quite a long time before I saw him again. This is what he wrote me in September 1905:

Thank you, my dear Gide, for the information that you so graciously give me and which I shall turn to my advantage.

We could have spent a long time looking at each other like china dogs. You are certainly one of the men I hold in high esteem and whom I should most like to see upon my return to France. But I did not dare be importunate, and as you have never answered my letters, I wondered if it would please you to renew our acquaintance. Now my doubts are dissipated. . . .

You will decide from these lines of Claudel whether it is fitting to keep the passage in question in your memoirs. If you do, I count on you to be willing to quote my letter in an appendix. It displeases me to appear to be a tactless, begging individual here.

Let me take this opportunity to go back: in the preceding volume of your memoirs, you speak of your trip to Biskra and of a conversation you had upon your return from Touggourt with a certain M. Colombo. According to you, this man told you that I came and wept on his shoulder because the level of water for irrigation was going down on my property at Biskra. It is true that when I first stayed at Biskra, I bought a little piece of land with the intention of building, but this land, which was along a road and not cultivated, receives no water at all. Colombo is mistaken. Or you.

I remain very affectionately yours,

André Gide.

P.S. At this moment I am reading your poetic description of La Roque in the *Revue Universelle:* drawbridge, worm-eaten beams, an owl in your bedroom slipper, etc.; all that is delightful. I cannot refrain from thinking that a little truth would have been of greater interest; but probably, in your opinion, it would have stood out like a sore thumb.

TRANSLATED BY BLANCHE A. PRICE

Thoughts on Greek Mythology

During many of his best years, André Gide planned to write a "Treatise on the Dioscuri" or "Castor and Pollux," of which, unfortunately, only a few highly suggestive pages ever appeared—under the more descriptive title "Thoughts on Greek Mythology." They were published in the September 1919 issue of the Nouvelle Revue Française. *In emphasizing the inner fatality of the heroes and the psychological truth of the myths, Gide was following the lead established in the mid-nineteenth century by the brilliant Louis Ménard, as Gilbert Highet points out in his stimulating study of* The Classical Tradition, *adding: "It was through him and his pupil Leconte de Lisle that Greek legends, instead of being merely pretty rococo decorations, became, for the French Parnassians, grand and beautiful expressions of profound truths." It so happens that Gide encountered Greek mythology in Leconte de Lisle's translations.*

FRAGMENTS OF "THE TREATISE ON THE
DIOSCURI"

I

The Greek fable is like Philemon's pitcher, which no thirst can empty, if one drinks with Jupiter. (Oh! It is the god whom I invite to my table!) And the milk my thirst draws from it is assuredly not that which Montaigne drank, I know—nor was the thirst of Keats and Goethe that of Racine or Chénier. Others will come like

Nietzsche, whose lips burn with a different fever. But he who, lacking respect for the god, breaks the pitcher, on pretext of seeing the bottom and exposing the miracle, is left with shards in his hands. Most often the mythologists offer us but the shards of myth, bizarre bits in which we still admire here and there, as on the fragments of a Etruscan vase, a chance form, a gesture, a dancing foot, a hand stretched toward the unknown, an ardent pursuit of some fleeing game, a link detached from the perfect chorus of the Muses, whose unbroken garland encircled the vase we recreate in our imaginations.

The first condition for understanding the Greek myth is to believe in it. I do not mean that one needs a faith like that called for by the Church. The consent given the Greek religion is of a quite different nature. It is strange that a great poet like Hugo has understood that so little; he took pleasure like so many others in stripping the divine figures of all sense so as to admire only the victory over them of certain elemental forces and of Pan over the Olympians. It was not smart of him, if I may say so, and his Alexandrines suffer from it less than does our reason. "How could anyone have believed in that?" Voltaire exclaims. And yet, it is to reason first and to reason alone that each myth appeals: you have understood nothing of the myth if you have not first accepted its reasonableness. The Greek fable is essentially reasonable, and one can say, without Christian impiety, that it is easier to believe in the Greek fable than in the doctrine of Saint Paul, the characteristic of which is precisely to humble, supplant, stultify, and shackle reason. It is for want of intelligence that Pentheus refuses to admit Bacchus; on the other hand, it is Polyeucte's intelligence that at first interposes itself and clouds his triumphant vision. I am not saying that intelligence does not eventually find in Christian dogma a supreme satisfaction, or that skepticism is of greater profit for reason than faith; but the Christian faith is based on renunciation of the intelligence; and if reason perhaps emerges enhanced from this renunciation, it is in accord with Christ's promise: All that you sacrifice for love of me, you will recover a hundredfold—while he who here wishes to save his reason shall lose it.

Strictly speaking, there are no mysteries in pagan mysticism: even those of Eleusis were but the whispered teaching of a few great natural laws. But the error is deigning to recognize in the myth only the figurative representation of physical laws, and to see in all the rest only the workings of *fatality*. With that frightful word we have given too great an advantage to chance; it casts its blight wherever we abandon explanation. But I maintain that the more we reduce the role of fate in the fable, the more we learn from it. In the absence of the physical law the psychological truth comes clear, which speaks more compellingly to me. What does fate teach us, whenever we let it appear? To submit to what we can not resolve. But the great souls of the legendary heroes were in point of fact unsubmissive souls, and to allow chance to lead them is to misunderstand them. Doubtless they know this *amor fati,* which Nietzsche admired, but the fatality here at issue is an inner fatality. The fatality is in them; they bore it within them; it was a psychological fatality.

Nothing has been understood about the character of Theseus, for example, if it is accepted that the bold hero *"Qui va du dieu des morts déshonorer la couche"* ("Who to dishonor the couch of the god of the dead goes forth") left quite inadvertently the black sail on the vessel bringing him back to Greece, the "fatal" black sail which, deluding his grief-stricken father, caused him to hurl himself into the sea—thanks to which Theseus entered into possession of his kingdom. An oversight? Come now! He forgot to change the sail as he forgot Ariadne in Naxos. I understand full well that fathers do not teach that to their children; but if we wish to lift

the story of Theseus above the insignificance of an old
wives' tale, we have only to see the hero as fully conscious
and strong-willed.

It gives me great pleasure to find this inner fatality
that leads him, that drives him to his exploits, in the
words: *"Compagne du péril qu'il vous fallait chercher"*
("Companion of the peril you had to seek"). It is true
that I bend somewhat the sense of the words to my own
purposes. I admit it. And why not? The complete work
of art has the miraculous quality of offering to us always
more than was imagined by the author; it permits us
continually a richer interpretation. Do you believe for
a moment that Hugo writing his funeral song to the tune
of *"Malbrough"* imagined all that Péguy, in his *Clio*,
would find in it? And yet who will dare say that Péguy
was not right in seeing what he saw?

I picture Theseus at the court of Crete, *"Charmant,
jeune, traînant tous les cœurs après soi"* ("Young,
charming, drawing all hearts after him"), with whom
the eldest daughter of Minos will fall in love, but who
will fall in love with the younger. He comes to triumph
over the monster, son of the Queen and the bull (I have
already given my opinion on the Minotaur: if Pasiphaë
had heard any talk about Leda's amorous adventure,
she might very well have imagined that the bull hid
Jupiter himself. A certain school of critics deigns to see
in the bull merely a certain Taurus, the King's gardener,
or his general, but if you allow me, we will send this
explanation packing to join that of the solar myths and
the Totems).

Son of a king (I am speaking again of Theseus), he
comes to fight a royal bastard; he comes, eager for adventure, muscles still taut from the efforts of lifting
away the rocks—for it was under one of them, his father
had let it be understood, that he would find his weapons.
Admirable test of training. Each of these heroes has his
own weapons, fitted to no one else. It is only when he

had recovered from Philoctetes the bow of his father Achilles that Neoptolemus was able to kill Paris; and we know that the bow of Ulysses could be strung by Ulysses alone.

He embarks (I am speaking again of Theseus) with the band of twenty youths and twenty maidens which Greece paid in annual tribute to Crete to be devoured by the Minotaur, so says the old wives' tale; personally I think that the monster in the depths of the labyrinth counted on them for his seraglio. Why so? Simply because I do not see such carnivorous tastes as inherited from Pasiphaë or the bull progenitor—I see it as lust. Pasiphaë, Ariadne, the Minotaur—what a family! And at the head Minos, the future judge of Hades! I know not how Minos judged the conduct of his wife and his children; nor why, before being called to judge the dead, he was compelled to see in his own home examples of every crime. I know not why, but I do know that there is a reason for it. In the Greek fable there is always a reason.

I wonder, too, why—of all the Greek heroes that fought at the siege of Troy—Ulysses alone, tireless wanderer, whose return was so exasperatingly deferred, was the only hero who came home to conjugal peace? Calypso, Circe, Nausicaä, the Sirens detain him for ten years (is he not the son of Sisyphus?) while in Ithaca the faithful Penelope waits for her husband. But the others, so impatient to return, is it not to find on their abandoned hearths only disorder, terror, and ruin?

I do not know the answer, but there must be one. Agamemnon, Ajax son of Oïleus, Idomeneus, Diomedes, all, I say, thrown toward a peril *"qu'il leur fallait chercher"* ("they had to seek") are greeted upon their return by adultery, murder, betrayal, exile, and the most fearsome crimes; toward them they hasten. While Ulysses who alone, of them all, is to find at his hearth fidelity, virtue, and patience, remains for ten years separated by many an obstacle, and, I believe, by his vagabond curiosity, the restlessness of his genius. There is something of Sindbad in Ulysses; I am well aware that he longs for Ithaca, but it is under the spur of ill-fortune and in the manner of Sindbad, which did not prevent the latter, once home, from setting out again. It seems that Ulysses had a presentiment that on his hearth there waited no food for his restlessness, that his energy would find there no employment. Is it his anticipation of the security and tranquillity of Ithaca that makes him thus delay his return?

I admire in Theseus an almost insolent rashness. No sooner is he at the court of Minos than he seduces Ariadne. There is no evidence that he loves her. But he allows himself to be loved by her as long as this love can be useful. Is the thread that she ties to his arm there solely to guide him? No. It is the "apron string" and straightway Theseus finds it a bit short: he feels it tugging at him at the moment when, with horror and delight, he advances into the unknown depths of his destiny. And doubtless, we have there the subject of an operetta. I should very much like to know if he was thinking already of Phaedra? On leaving the court of Minos, did he carry off the two sisters at the same time?

II

It is doubtless plausible and agreeable to recognize in the Augean stables a cloud-filled sky, swept clear by a solar Hercules. It is enough that it should not be irrational for it to be Greek. But how much more meaningful it is to me to consider, for example, the following:

That Hercules, of all the demigods, is the only *moral* hero of antiquity, the one who, before setting forth, finds himself momentarily hesitating between "vice and virtue"; he is the only uncertain hero, the one whom the sculptor will for that reason represent to us as a melancholy hero; and we remember that, true enough, he is the one child of Jupiter whose birth is not the result of a victory of instinct over modesty and propriety; in order to possess the virtuous Alcmene the god was compelled to take on the appearance of her husband. If, doubtless, the theory of the laws governing heredity is of more recent formulation than the myth, I admire all the more that the myth can offer us this exemplary interpretation.

TRANSLATED BY JEFFREY J. CARRE

Conversation with a German Several Years Before the War

Between the lines of Gide's second essay on "Nationalism and Literature" can be read the implication that he was as much interested as Dostoevsky or Baudelaire in the chartless underground of human psychology. And this explains his curiosity for the criminal, the vagabond, the outcast, for whom he had a fellow-feeling as if studying in them what in other circumstances he might have become himself. His Journals show that everywhere he went he seemed to attract such individuals, some of whom even found their way into his books in the guise of Protos and Strouvilhou.

One such encounter, which Gide fully recorded in 1904 and published in the N.R.F. in 1919, was with Félix-Paul Grève, then twenty-five years old, who later translated into German Paludes, Saül, and La Porte étroite. His "Conversation with a German," though it discreetly concealed Grève's name, proved to be perhaps the most self-damaging of his writings because of the sentence: "I would rather cause action than act myself." Years later, after that remark had been frequently used against him, Gide explained that back in 1904 he had wanted to hold at a distance an adventurer who, by adopting Gide's own ethic, had forced him to the right of his real position. " 'If it may be that my teaching leads to crime, I prefer that it should be you who commit the crime.' This is what my sentence meant. Grève was

playing the role of drunken helot in my presence.
Through self-esteem I tried to save face; but I felt his
advantage and that he got the better of me. I was beaten
by my 'disciple' and was disavowing my ethic if that was
where it was to lead." In actual fact, the only people
Gide ever caused to act in his stead were his fictional
characters, and it is not negligible that each of them
suffers the consequences of his action.

Yet, it is difficult not to believe that when he pub-
lished the conversation with Grève in 1919 and again five
years later in Incidences *he was not motivated by a char-*
acteristic spirit of bravado compounded of scorn for
his detractors and the pleasure of misleading opinion.
Depicting himself in the company of a time-server who
talked casually of murder doubtless flattered in him a
puerile tendency to shock the conventional virtues.

I should like no one to be mistaken as to the feeling
that makes me give these notes here. I think they have
a certain psychological interest; but although some of
the features of B. R.'s portrait show a disquieting re-
semblance to those handed out to us today by certain
people as being the most typical of the Germanic race,
I doubt if it is prudent to cling too closely to their
representative value. The reader is free to generalize;
in them I merely sketched from the model a portrait of
an individual at a time when none of the considerations,
which today might falsify our painting somewhat, could
then intervene. Without any changes, I transcribe these
notes as I took them in June 1904, the day following
this single encounter.

B. R. had already been waiting for me for a half hour
in the lounge of the hotel where I arrive very exactly at
the specified hour; seated opposite the door, he held in

his hand, presumably to help me recognize him, the envelope of the message in which I had made the appointment with him. Uncertain, I went forward into the lounge. Right away I saw that smooth face, looking as if it had been bleached with chlorine, that body too tall, for which all seats are too low. I wished ardently that it might be he. It was. Von M. had not exaggerated his elegance. B. R. was perfectly dressed, looked English rather than German, and I was not astonished when he told me a little later that his mother was English.

I take him to the restaurant of the Hôtel Terminus. The conversation, which at first drags a little at the beginning of the meal, soon becomes animated. However, B. R. speaks extremely slowly, searching for words or even his ideas, but very correctly, without any accent. Toward the end of our conversation he said to me: "Monsieur Gide, you must understand that I should not speak any more quickly in German. At present I can no longer speak quickly."

He has just come out of prison; I know it, but he thinks I know nothing about it; admirably he hides a slight anxiety when he learns that Von M. has spoken of him to me. He is returning to Bonn this very evening. So he has come to Paris solely to see me.

"What made you want to know me?"

"Suddenly, when in your *Immoralist*," he says, came to the passage where Moktir steals a pair of scissors, and where Michel, who saw him do it, smiles."

A long silence, and then very slowly: "Monsieur Gide, do you know that—I have just been released from prison?"

In a very low voice, taking his hand: "Yes, I know."

When my hand touches his, he becomes slightly excited, and in a slightly warmer tone, says: "But do you know that I have been out just four days—and I was in for fourteen months—"

"I thought it was only three months."

"I haven't slept for four days."

"You seem extraordinarily tired."

"During those last days in prison, I could hardly eat any more—nervous tension, and look, my chin. . . . When I came out of prison my wife was waiting for me; it was a half-hour before I was able to talk to her, before I was able to utter a word. . . ."

At one and the same time, fatigue, the hypertension of all his features, the trembling of his muscles. . . .

"But now I absolutely have to talk. In Germany I can no longer talk to anyone; it's you I have to talk with; talking to my wife isn't the same thing. When I told her I intended to go and see you, she approved; told me right away I was to leave. I would even have come sooner, but before leaving, I wanted to try to speak, to explain myself to the friend who—with whom—well—

"Who had you sentenced."

"Yes, had me sentenced. I knew very well that if I had *asked* him for that amount, he would have given it to me right off; but—he didn't understand why I had acted the way I did—I wanted to explain to him—oh! not why I—but that he ought not to have insisted on that sentence—because in five years I knew I should be able to pay my whole debt; but on the condition that they left me something to live on till then."

"And what did he answer?"

"He rang for his servant to have me put out."

A silence; he continues with a little more animation: "Yes, in five years, I know that I could have paid everything with my translations and my books; but they put an interdiction on everything that could bring me money. I am now forced to appear under my wife's name or under assumed names. I am a terrific worker. Do you know that during those fourteen months in prison I translated forty volumes? All the correspond-

ence of Flaubert, *Bouvard et Pécuchet,* all of Wells, four
volumes of Meredith, three of De Quincey, your two,
in fact—

"What! you have already translated them?"

"Completely. My wife is reading them at present. I
have always had an enormous capacity for work. At six-
teen I lost my father; he was a very rich industrialist
from Mecklenburg, who, the year he died, was completely ruined. My mother and my three sisters had only
the money I earned with my lessons to live on. I must
tell you that physically I looked exactly the same at six-
teen as I do now. (That is not saying so much, for today
at twenty-six he looks scarcely twenty-two.) The parents
of my pupils did not know, did not suspect my age.
Lessons in Greek, Latin, French, English; I have given
up to eighty lessons a week. And add to that the fact
that I knew neither Latin nor Greek; I had to learn
Latin and Greek while I was giving my lessons. In Latin
and in Greek I am a—you would say an *autodidacte,*
wouldn't you?"

"You had three sisters?"

"I had nine and lost them. All died of—" He seeks
the word and says in German: "*Eklampseien.* I am the
tenth child. Doctor X., who is very well-known in Germany, claims that I escaped only because I was the only
one not breast-fed. It doesn't bore you to have me talk
of my family this way? Yes, my mother saw her nine
daughters die, or that is, I kept from her the death of
the last one, who was married in America; my mother
herself was very sick at that time, and several weeks
later I lost her."

"You were now how old?"

"Eighteen."

"So that now you are alone."

He repeats mechanically: "Yes, alone," then continues: "My mother was a wonderful woman. She summed

up in herself all earthly goodness, yes, all that was noble
and good. I cannot think of her without tears."

I look at him mechanically; his eyes are absolutely
dry.

"On her deathbed she said to me: *'Kind, dass du stolz
bleibe,'* • then she turned toward a friend who was at-
tending her and murmured: *'Ich furchte es gehe schlecht
mit ihm.'* " ••

"Was there something in you that could make her
foresee that—"

"Nothing as yet."

A long silence. Then:

"I must let you know, Monsieur Gide, that I lie constantly."

"Von M. informed me of that, too," I said to him.

"Yes, but he never understood the import of my lies.
I should like to make you understand; it's not what you
think. I feel the same need for lying and the same satisfaction in lying that others feel in telling the truth. No,
it's not what you think. Take this, for example: when
someone hears a sudden noise beside him he turns his
head." (He seizes my arm.) "But I don't, or when I turn,
I turn deliberately! I lie."

"When did you begin to lie?"

"Right after my mother's death."

A silence: "Lying is what binds me to my wife; my
extraordinary ability to lie. When she sensed it, she left
her husband, her child, for me; she left everything to
follow me. At first I wanted to abandon her; then I
understood that I could not do without her; it's to her
that I lie most readily. Sometimes that leads to horrible
scenes between us. But lying always ends up by being
the stronger. This evening I am going back to join her;
we are to be married in two months. Until then we are

• May you always remain proud.
•• I'm afraid he may go to the bad.

going to live in Switzerland; when I go back I am sell-
ing all that I have and we shall both live on one hundred
francs a month."

The lunch is ended; he offers me a cigarette from the
most elegant case I have ever seen. I admire the match-
box, too, in silver like the case; his slightest accessories
are in perfect taste with a sober and unpretentious
elegance.

"Yes," he says, "I love elegance passionately. But all
this is going to be sold. Oh, the clothes I am wearing
have been in my suitcase for fourteen months; it shows
a little."

We get up from the table. "At what time is your
train?"

"Eleven forty-five tonight; it is the only one with
third class."

"Have you someone to see, something to do in Paris?"

"No, nothing. I came solely to talk with you."

Fearful that the day may be long, I ask him if he
would not be interested in seeing a little painting.

"Oh," he said, "no, not yet. Look, if you want to do
something to please me, take me to the Champs-Elysées."

A carriage takes us to the Bois, going through Parc
Monceau.

While we were having lunch I saw him full face.
Beside him now, I notice how different he is in profile.
Full face, his almost childish smile is charming; in pro-
file, the expression of his chin is disturbing.

We talk again of his imprisonment.

"It did me good in this respect," he said, "it completely suppressed in me all remorse, all scruples."

"And now that society has struck you, you feel that
you have rights against it?"

"Yes, every right."

"It is thrilling to struggle against society, but it will conquer you."

"No, I am terribly strong."

He said that without boasting, with a simple, firm belief.

At least, I thought, in case he asks me for money (for I retain a vague fear that he has come to Paris to touch me for money), my sentence is ready: "If I helped you, you would interest me less." But to be more on my guard, I take advantage of the moment when he is affirming his love of opulence. "I do not," I retorted, "although it does not displease me in others. I should not like to have been Byron, but I should like to have known him."

I feel that he is a little less attentive and to recapture him: "That is the way in which your first booklet [on Oscar Wilde] interested me so much. I think that the antagonism between art and life that you pointed out is very true—"

He interrupts me. "But I don't find it true at all. Or rather—if you will—yes, it is dangerous for the artist to try to live; but precisely just because I intend to live, I say that I am not an artist. The need for money makes me write. The work of art is only an excuse. I prefer life."

"But in your book you affirmed exactly the contrary."

"Yes, I was lying. But then you, too, were lying when you wrote *Les Nourritures*. . . . Look . . . (and he extends his arm with an admirable gesture) just stretching out my arm gives me more joy than writing the most beautiful book in the world. Action is what I want; yes, the most intense action—intense—even murder—"

A long silence.

"No," I finally said, desirous of making my position clear, "action does not interest me so much for the sensation it gives as for its results, its reverberations. That is why, though it interests me passionately, I think it interests me even more when it is done by someone else. You understand, I am afraid of compromising myself by an act. I mean, of limiting what I could do, by what I do do. The thought that because I do *this,* I can no longer do *that* is what becomes intolerable. I would rather cause action than act myself."

"No other will ever act as you would have acted yourself. It is not the same thing. Monsieur Gide, I should like to tell you something else." (He hesitates.) "I do not find the words."

"Say it in German."

"I would not say it any better in German. I have been looking for the words for a long time. No, I am still too upset. I cannot. I feel as if I had a horrible weight on my head and as if my body no longer belonged to me. I wrote you as soon as I was out of prison, a long letter. No, you didn't receive it. Before I sent it to you, I wanted—to see you."

"Am I, at present, the reason why you can't speak to me?"

"No, today it's useless; I shall not be able to tell you."

The carriage enters the city gates.

"Where shall I drop you?"

"May I ask you a favor of a purely practical nature?" He seems extremely hesitant, and I begin to think again: "The time has come for the handout." But no, very simply he continues, "Do you know where I can find some henna?"

We are driving along rue Saint-Honore. I take him to Philippe the hairdresser. And there suddenly I say good-by to him, feeling that it is particularly difficult to take leave of someone at four o'clock who came from Cologne just to see you, and whose train does not leave before midnight.

TRANSLATED BY BLANCHE A. PRICE

The Ten French Novels . . .

Before its inclusion in Incidences, *this essay appeared in the* Nouvelle Revue Française *for April 1913. Years later Gide had to protest against those who assumed that he had listed here his ten favorite books in the whole world of literature and point out that he had been obliged to limit himself to* French novels. *"If, in exile, I could take along only ten books," he wrote, "not one of these would be among them."*

Representatives of a large daily paper came and asked me to indicate the ten French novels that I prefer.

It was Jules Lemaître, I think, who brought into style the little game that Pierre Louÿs and I used to play when we were in the upper classical form at school: "Supposing you had to spend the remainder of your days on a desert island, what twenty books would you want to take with you?" Twenty books! For us that was too few to people a wilderness and adorn a whole life; so we used to write down the names of authors rather than the titles of works; for example, we used to name simply Goethe and thus were not forced to choose among *Faust, Wilhelm Meister,* and the poetry; then we had recourse to trickery: we would choose Amyot, and by this choice we won, along with Plutarch, the delightful *Daphnis and Chloé* as a premium; we chose Leconte de Lisle, whose translations seemed to us then to be of unsurpassable beauty. In this way, we brought our library of twenty authors up to three or four hundred volumes.

I have kept several of these lists, which we used to draw up anew every semester. In vain do I look for the name of a novelist.

The novel, last born, is most favored today. In literature as a whole, and particularly in French literature, it has a small place; we were not so shortsighted as to fail to recognize this fact even then. It is true that at twenty we had not yet discovered Stendhal. But even now, if I had to make a choice among his works, would I indeed take his novels, or would I not prefer his letters, his *Henri Brûlard*, his *Journal*, and his *Souvenirs*?

Today, however, I am asked to name novels, and what is worse, French novels!

For a long time I hesitated between *Le Rouge et le noir* and *La Chartreuse de Parme*. In doubt, I nearly wrote down *Lucien Leuwen*, for which I had some fondness, as long as I had not reread the other two. But no, the *Chartreuse* is without equal, even though *Le Rouge et le noir* is more surprising on first contact. The *Chartreuse* possesses this truly magical quality: each time one comes back to it, it is always a different book that one is reading.

When I reopen Montesquieu, La Fontaine, Montaigne, I can still enjoy some sentence in them from which I had not at first extracted all the marrow, or which I had even failed to notice; my mind can listen to their counsel more docilely, more intelligently, or if it refuses to listen, it will have more judicious reasons for doing so. Constantly I refuse to yield to Stendhal; all that gives him pleasure would only bore me; too much of his company would be deadly to me; but like the *Britannicus* of Racine, Mosca, Fabrice, the Duchess, always smile at me with new and different faces, as does, indeed, the whole book. What grace in its detail! What elegance in the clarity of its line! How lightly it moves!

I leave it; I pick it up again; never will I finish speaking of it.

The great secret of this diversified youthfulness is that Stendhal, particularly in the *Chartreuse,* is not specifically trying to affirm anything; the entire book is written *for pleasure.* Stendhal hardly takes sides in it, except here and there (much less than in his other books); this is where he could have aged. On the contrary, how I like him when he writes: "I fear that the credulity of Fabrice will deprive him of the sympathy of the reader, but after all, that is what he was like; why flatter him in preference to any other?" And even how much more I should like him if he wrote these words with less pretense, with more sincerity.

In man there remain many regions that he will not learn how to discover, and we can even say that he likes to discover only what he will be able to explain: the ultraviolet tones, the very ones we are most concerned with today, escape him; a certain theory of pleasure precipitates his thought a little too much; he fastens upon himself a little too deliberately. No matter! If I had to choose ten novels without any care as to their origin, I would take two French ones: the *Chartreuse* would be the first.

Les Liaisons dangereuses of Laclos would be the other.

I liked this book so much when I first read it—I wonder if, now, I overestimate it a little. I must reread it. Very fortunately, I discovered it only quite late; I mean nearer the age of thirty than twenty. Readers who are too young tire of the resistance of Mme de Tourvel; they think the book would gain if she yielded more quickly to Valmont and did not complain at such length afterward. They deserve to prefer *Faublas.*

Everything in *Les Liaisons* is disconcerting to me, and nothing that I have found out about Laclos throws any light upon his motives in writing this novel. I come almost to the point of being in doubt as to whether the author is mocking in his impertinent preface, or whether he truly does not delude himself into thinking that he is "rendering a service to morals," as he says. I wish the latter were the case and that this book, basing itself upon the truth that to serve morals is to render a disservice to art, would be a proof *ab absurdo*. It must indeed be acknowledged that he becomes rather mediocre toward the end when he takes pride in making amends and sides, not with Mme de Tourvel, the President's wife, in whom sincere love and virtue are incarnate, but rather with Mme de Volanges, Mme de Rosemont, and other of their friends, who represent the side of so-called good morals—against which true love and true virtue will always have to struggle, even more so than the Valmonts and the Merteuils.

And sometimes, on the contrary, I half suspect that under the cover of a virtuous intention, Laclos perhaps wanted to compose the true manual of debauchery. Nevertheless, it is not on the part of Merteuil and De Valmont, but rather of Danceny and the young Volanges; debauchery begins when pleasure begins to disassociate itself from love. I do scarcely any violence to my thought if I now see only a libertine, not a debauchee, in Valmont; in Don Juan, a dissolute man, at the worst, without faith. Danceny is no longer a debauchee if, on the other hand, he stops loving Cécile. The seam that joins the sensations of pleasure and the feelings of love is neither predetermined nor perfectly natural. "Love, vaunted to us as the cause of our pleasures, is at most only a pretext for them." This little sentence, which Laclos puts into the mouth of Merteuil, illuminates with simplicity some of the so-called "mysteries" of the human heart.

In this book also, and still in this same letter of the

Marquise de Merteuil, I find the most subtle and pertinent criticism, though very circuitous, of the theories of Barrès. "Believe me, Vicomte," she says, "we rarely acquire the qualities we can do without." And what Barrès advocates about taking roots, puts man precisely in such a position that only the slightest effort and the least little virtue is required of him. We have stressed this elsewhere.

After these two novels, if my choice were not restricted to France, I should no longer name any but foreign novels.

"What, you don't esteem France any more than that?"

"Simply this. In my opinion, where France excels is not in the novel."

France is a country of moralists, incomparable artists, composers, architects, orators. What do foreigners offer to compare with Montaigne, Pascal, Molière, Bossuet, Racine? But on the other hand, what is Lesage in comparison to a Fielding or a Cervantes? What is an Abbé Prevost beside a Defoe. And even: What is a Balzac compared to a Dostoevsky? Or, if you prefer, what is a *Princesse de Clèves* in comparison to a *Britannicus*?

However, I shall have to name the *Princesse de Clèves*, since my choice is restricted to the French. But I confess that I feel only a moderate admiration for this book. There is nothing new to say about it, nor anything that has not been very well said. Probably there are different ways of reacting to the *Princesse de Clèves*, and it is possible not to like this novel at all; but if one does like it, this cannot be for different reasons. There is nothing secret, reticent, circuitous, no hidden spring; everything is brought out, emphasized, made the most of, and there is nothing more to expect; probably it is the height of art: a "dead end" *nec plus ultra*. Am I

really going to put the *Princesse de Clèves* on my list, or
rather the *Roman bourgeois?* Ah! why is Furetière not
Molière? Why is Javotte not Monsieur Jourdain!

Because there is no *Moll Flanders,* shall I now choose
Manon Lescaut? Perhaps. Warm blood runs through it.
However, I am uneasy about this book; it has too many
readers and some of the worst kind. I prefer not to like
it.

"When you read it you shed many a tear!"

"Exactly, that is why I am a little vexed with it. If it
had first appealed to my mind, I should be more willing
to let it touch my heart as well."

On the other hand, I do not hesitate a moment to lay
hold upon *Dominique.* So noble is the modesty of this
book that it seems almost indiscreet to speak of it. It is
not a sublime book, but a friendly one. It speaks so intimately that we seem to be talking to ourselves when we
read it, so intimately that we need no other friend.

Nothing is artificial in *Dominique.* Fromentin demonstrates that he is an artist, to be sure, but not especially
a man of letters; all the qualities of his pen are precisely
those of his mind and his heart.

What novel of Balzac do I prefer? How can one prefer
only *one* novel of Balzac? *La Comédie humaine* forms a
whole. To admire only a part of it is to be a poor ad-
mirer.

It is good to read Balzac before the age of twenty-five;
afterward it becomes too difficult. How much hodge-
podge one has to go through in order to find nourishment. Even then there is not always a reward, for as soon
as he has established his characters, their most sublime
remarks are foreseen; we have said everything when we
say that they are commonplace. I know. But it is impor-

tant to have read Balzac, all of Balzac. Some writers have thought they could dispense with this; later on, they were not quite able to understand just what indefinable trait was missing in them; we realize it for them.

I think I find *Cousine Bette* most profitable to reread; let us say that this is the book of Balzac I choose.

Next I choose *Madame Bovary* without comment. A discussion of Flaubert would get me involved; I shall keep it for later.

For a long time I loved Flaubert as a master, a friend, a brother; his correspondence was my bedside book. Ah! How carefully I read him when I was about twenty! There is not a sentence that I do not recognize today. Since that time, the most important development of my mind has been to dare judge the sentence.

Even today it is extremely painful for me to hear Flaubert criticized by anyone who did not first love him. Thus, I recently read an article on him that was almost odious to me; nevertheless, had it not been insulting, it would not have appeared too unjust to me. But it attacked only the form and seemed to fail to appreciate both the importance of Flaubert and the very basis of the question. Nietzsche, at least, was not mistaken as to the meaning of such a specious aberration; the violence with which he exposes it indicates a kind of lingering admiration, and his hatred is only the reverse of his esteem and love.

What will those who have already protested against *Madame Bovary* say when they hear me mention *Germinal?* Such a book cannot be omitted merely by stating that none of the praises that Stendhal deserved are applicable to Zola; nor can I be persuaded to find it less admirable. It is true that I am continually almost astonished that it is written in our language; however, I do not find it more easy to imagine it in any other language whatsoever. It is an annex to literature. It ought to be written in Volapük.

As it is, so this work exists; it asserts itself; it is masterly; it could not be written differently.

In this essay I have not been asked to indicate ten models. If I incline preferably toward these books, I am neither trying to recognize myself in them nor to adore my reflection in them. Some have blamed me for the eclecticism of my tastes and have called me a "dilettante" because I require only of myself the qualities that they demand only of others. They are working to reform public taste, they say; they do well, and I am grateful to them for preparing readers for me.

However, I perceive that still one book is missing from my list. As this last one, let us finish up with something new: for example, this one, and I blush at not yet knowing it: the *Marianne* of Marivaux.

TRANSLATED BY BLANCHE A. PRICE

Théophile Gautier

Gide was never altogether satisfied with the lecture he gave on Théophile Gautier at the Vieux-Colombier Theater in April 1914. Perhaps this explains why, instead of publishing it at the time in his own N.R.F., he held it over and allowed it to appear in November 1917 (when the N.R.F. had suspended publication for the duration of the war) in the first issue of Les Ecrits Nouveaux. *Yet, although he re-examined from time to time his harsh judgment of Gautier simply because it was at variance with the accepted opinion, he never could change his mind on this score.*

(FRAGMENT OF A LECTURE)
The glory of representing the Parnassian school falls mainly upon Théophile Gautier. I know that I am making an error in date, but I do so to simplify. Yes, I know that strictly speaking the Parnassian school was formed only a little later, but Gautier had already set an example for it and stated its theory. Sometimes it seems to me that Banville represents the Parnassian school just as nicely, with perhaps more naturalness, ease, diversion, than Gautier, but with less deliberation as well (and I congratulate him for this); however, it is precisely this continued deliberation brought to the exercise of his poetic functions that won Gautier both the gratitude of letters and that particular, special, almost royal position, which we may perhaps doubt that he deserves, but from which we will not oust him.

Yes, Théophile Gautier occupies an eminent position, and the greater our admiration for Baudelaire, the greater will be our astonishment to see the latter bow, nay, prostrate himself before Gautier and dedicate the *Fleurs du mal*

To the IMPECCABLE POET
To the perfect Magician of French Letters . . .
with feelings
of the deepest humility . . .

Elsewhere, in that long study which he wrote on the one whom he considered his master, he said: "Théophile Gautier is the writer par excellence because he is the slave of his duty, because he constantly obeys the necessities of his function, because a feeling for beauty is his destiny, because he has turned his duty into an obsession."

"For the superior writer, the inexpressible does not exist." Baudelaire quotes this statement by Gautier on several occasions and moreover, stresses it. The inexpressible does not exist; the poet must be able to express everything, and since Baudelaire does not tolerate the discovery of any deficiency in Gautier, he first attempts to cleanse him of that accusation of insensitivity that was beginning to be hurled at the master.

I quote Baudelaire: "First of all I wanted to prove that Théophile Gautier possessed, quite as well as if he had not been a perfect artist, that famous quality that the rubbernecks of criticism (I refer to ourselves) insist upon refusing him: feeling. How often, with what linguistic magic, he has expressed the most delicate shades of tenderness and melancholy."

I should like to take Baudelaire at his word, but unfortunately he quotes, and here is all he finds to quote, for he well knows that in spite of what he affirms, he

could leaf madly through all the volumes of the poet
without finding the slightest fresh emotion in them:

> *Mes cils te feront de l'ombre!*
> *Ensemble nous dormirons*
> *Sous mes cheveux, tente sombre.*
> *Fuyons! Fuyons!*
>
> *Sous le bonheur, mon cœur ploie!*
> *Si l'eau manque aux stations,*
> *Bois les larmes de ma joie!*
> *Fuyons! Fuyons!* •

"The inexpressible does not exist," says Gautier.

When we consider the distressing poverty of his reper-
tory, the aridity of his Parnassus, we begin to have
doubts as to whether this fine axiom does not simply
mean the denial of the existence of all that he cannot
express. And certainly, this unawareness, this decision
not to see anything but the exterior world, or rather,
perhaps, this blindness in respect to everything that is
not the exterior world, is the secret of his self-confidence,
of that peremptory tone which we find also in the Goncourts; just as in Vigny, whom it would be easy to contrast to him, we find the continuous awareness of the
inexpressible and the inability to express it, coupled
with the desire to do so, both of which remain the secret
of Vigny's anguish.

It would be unjust not to grant Théophile Gautier, in
the absence of depth, a certain suitability of form—
brilliance, sheen, clean contours—I should like to be

• My lashes will shade you
Together we shall sleep
Under the dark tent of my hair
  Oh! let us flee!

Happiness bows down my heart!
If there is no water when we pause,
Drink the tears of my joy!
  Oh! let us flee!

able to give him more praise. Alas! in the three volumes of poems that he has left us, there are very few poems in which we do not get caught up in every stanza by errors, poor style, incorrect vocabulary or syntax, platitudes, all of which, after all, we never or almost never encounter in Banville. This is already almost Mendès.

Once again I am not looking for the worst; on the contrary, I accept the choice of the admirers; but just try to reread *Ténèbres,* "that prodigious symphony," said Baudelaire, "which makes us think of Beethoven."

However, we read in Baudelaire: "Our neighbors say Shakespeare and Goethe in one breath! We can counter with Victor Hugo and Théophile Gautier." But we refuse to indulge in this game of parallels, of calamitous comparisons, modeled after the popular saying: leeks are the poor man's asparagus—a saying of which it is impossible to decide what it insults the most: the asparagus, the poor man, or the leek.

Yes, Gautier occupies an eminent position; it is a great pity that he fills it so poorly.

TRANSLATED BY BLANCHE A. PRICE

Prefaces

A friend of André Gide was able to collect in 1948 a whole volume of prefaces Gide had written throughout his career. Three of the best of them—those to Baudelaire, Stendhal, and Pushkin—had already been gathered together in Incidences in 1924.

The preface to Baudelaire's Fleurs du mal appeared originally in the Pelletan edition of the poems in 1917. Frequently Gide alluded to it as a more satisfactory writing than his lecture on Gautier, from which he borrowed certain elements for this preface.

To Stendhal's little-read novel Armance he wrote a stimulating preface for the edition of Stendhal's collected works brought out by Champion in 1925. The N.R.F. published it first in August 1921.

Prosper Mérimée had originally translated Pushkin's The Queen of Spades together with other stories by Pushkin and Gogol. It was that version which Gide revised with his Russian-born friend Jacques Schiffrin and prefaced in 1923 for the Pléiade Collection, which Schiffrin had created. Later the Gallimard firm took over the Pléiade library of French and foreign classics and made it famous.

PREFACE TO THE "FLEURS DU MAL"

One suspects that one of Baudelaire's most ingenious paradoxes was to have dedicated his *Fleurs du mal* to Théophile Gautier, to offer this cup, all overflowing with emotion, music, and thought, to the most dry, least musical, least meditative artisan that our literature has ever produced. Was he deluding himself? He was a critic with too lucid a vision not to be sensitive to the poverty of those *Emaux et camées,* which owed their reputation not to what they are but to what they claim to be. The *Fleurs du mal* are dedicated to what Gautier claimed to be: magician of French letters, pure artist, impeccable writer—and this was a way of saying: Do not be deceived: what I venerate is the art and not the thought, my poems will have merit not because of their movement, passion, or thought, but because of their form.

Form, that justification for the work of art, is what the public never perceives until later. Form is the secret of the work. Baudelaire never takes for granted that harmony of contours and sounds in which the art of the poet is displayed; he achieves it through sincerity; he conquers it; he imposes it. Like every unaccustomed harmony, it was shocking at first. For many long years, and I would be tempted to say: even until now, certain misleading appearances of this book have hidden its most radiant treasures, while, at the same time, it protected them. Certain gestures, certain harsh tones, certain subjects of the poems, and, as I think, some affectation, an amused satisfaction in being misunderstood, deluded his contemporaries and many of those who came

later. Without doubt, Baudelaire is the artist about
whom the most nonsense has been written, who has been
ignored the most unjustly. I know of certain manuals of
French literature of the nineteenth century in which he
is not even mentioned.

The fact that in the eyes of certain persons the figure
of Gautier has long appeared and still appears more important than that of Baudelaire is explained by the very
simple attitude (oversimple or simplified) of Gautier,
from which he did not for a moment swerve, thanks to
which he held on to that place in the limelight which he
had acquired right at the very first; it is also explained by
the cordial banality of his face, which suddenly opens
up when we encounter it and never means anything
more than what it first promised. Whereas we glimpsed
a disconcerting complexity in Baudelaire, a cabal of
strange contradictions, antagonisms almost absurd,
which could be taken for pretense, the more easily because he was capable of pretense as well.

I should not swear that Baudelaire, elsewhere so per-
spicacious, was not somewhat mistaken about his own
merit, about what constituted his value. He worked, not
always consciously, at that misunderstanding which isolated him from his period; he worked at it all the more
because this misunderstanding was already taking shape
in him. His private notes, published posthumously, are
painfully revealing in this respect; to be sure, Baudelaire
felt his essential originality, but he did not succeed in
defining it clearly to himself. As soon as this artist of
incomparable ability speaks of himself, he is astonish-
ingly awkward. Irreparably he lacks pride to the point
where he reckons incessantly with fools, either to astonish them, to shock them, or after all to inform them that
he absolutely does not reckon with them.

"This book has not been written for my wives, my
daughters, or my sisters," he says, speaking of the *Fleurs
du mal*. Why warn us? Why this sentence? Oh, simply

for the pleasure of affronting bourgeois morals with these words "my wives" slipped in, as if carelessly; he values them, however, since we find in his private journal: "This cannot shock my wives, my daughters, nor my sisters."

This ostentatious pretense, which came to shelter Baudelaire's fervor, antagonized certain readers, the more violently because some of his early admirers were most enthusiastic about this very pretense. He especially felt the need of taking cover from his admirers.

People thought they were completely rid of him when they buried these feints along with the romantic devices. He reappears, stripped of disguise, rejuvenated. He went about it in such a way that we understand him much better today than they did in his day. Now he quietly converses with each one of us. Certainly he begs and obtains from each reader a sort of connivance, almost a collaboration; in this way his power is proved.

"He was the first," says Laforgue, "to recount himself in the restrained mode of the confessional, without assuming an inspired air." In this respect he calls to mind Racine; Baudelaire's choice of words is perhaps more disquieting and of more subtle pretension; I claim that the sound of his voice is the same; instead of giving the greatest possible sonority to their inspiration, in the manner of Corneille or Hugo, each of them speaks in a whisper, with the result that we listen to them at length.

What a disquieting sincerity the kindred spirit, attentive to this discreet song, soon discovers! With Baudelaire, antithesis, born from personal contradictions, is no longer merely exterior and verbal, a technique as it is in Hugo; rather it is honest. It blossoms spontaneously in this catholic heart, which experiences no emotion without having the contours fade immediately, without having its opposite reflected like a shadow, or better, like a reflection in the duality of this heart. Thus everywhere in his verses, there is sorrow mingled with joy, confidence with doubt, gaiety with melancholy, and he seeks uneasily a measure of love in the horrible.

However, the anguish of Baudelaire is of a still more secret nature. At this point I seem to lose sight of his poetry: but where does one find the source and the prompting of so faithful a melody, if not in the soul of the poet?

We are often told that there is nothing new in man. Perhaps; but all that is in man has probably not been discovered. Yes, trembling, I convince myself that many discoveries are still to be made, and that the outlines of the psychology of the past, according to which we judge, think, and even act, have acted up to now, will soon appear more artificial and out of date than do the outlines of the chemistry of the past, now that radium has been discovered. If chemists have now come to the point of speaking to us of the decomposition of simple bodies, why should "we psychologists" not be tempted to envisage the decomposition of simple feelings? A simple way of considering feelings is what allows anyone to believe in simple feelings.

I shall not go so far as to say that Baudelaire felt as clearly as did Dostoevsky, for example, the existence—opposite to that force of cohesion which keeps the individual consistent with himself, through which, as Spinoza said, "the individual tends to persist in his being"—the existence of another force, centrifugal and disintegrating, through which the individual tends to be divided, dissociated, through which he tends to risk, gamble, and lose himself. But it is not without a shiver of recognition and terror that I read these several sentences from his private journal: "In a mature man, the impulse toward productive concentration must replace that toward wasting his forces." Or again: "Concerning the vaporization and the centralization of the self. Everything lies in this." Or: "In every man there are always two *simultaneous* [the whole interest of the sentence lies in this word] postulations: one toward God and the other toward Satan." Are these not traces of that infinitely precious radium in contact with which the old theories, laws, conventions, and the pretensions of the soul are all volatilized?

I shall not affirm that these fragments which I have just isolated are the only ones in his prose work; at least, it can be said that they have left a perceptible imprint on his entire poetic work.

And none of all this is sufficient to make of Baudelaire that incomparable artist whom we praise. Quite to the contrary, the admirable fact is, that in spite of all this, he has remained that artist. As Barbey d'Aurevilly said magnificently in that fine article which consoles us for the silence of Sainte-Beuve: "The artist has not been too defeated."

TRANSLATED BY BLANCHE A. PRICE

PREFACE TO "ARMANCE"

To speak properly of Stendhal, one would have to have something of his style. If we take his word for it, he almost always writes out of boredom; but so lively is his pleasure in doing so, that we never share his boredom, but only the pleasure that follows it. There is no struggle; he never says anything excepting when he wants to; that is, with the least effort. As others yield to idleness, he gives himself over to thought. When he is logical, he is naturally so because of a healthy mind; he does not claim to be logical, since he claims nothing; and he amuses us the most when he ceases to be logical, because then he is carried away by his passion and by that sensibility, in him more exquisite than reason, because logic is the property of all and sensibility is his alone, and because it is he, above all, whom we love in what he says. So much so that we are not vexed if he is mistaken and if we cannot adopt his tastes. But these he values, and I do not know which would astonish him more, if he were to return to earth today: the disrepute into which have fallen almost all the works of art that he extolled—operas, pictures, statues, poems—or the signal favor in which his own writings are held. I am well aware that he hoped to be read later; but could he foresee—and would he not have lost that natural tone, had he foreseen—that the slightest stroke of his pen would be sought out with a kind of meticulous devotion which Baudelaire alone was to share with him in our time, as also Baudelaire alone shared with him the very unjust rejection by his contemporaries; could he foresee, after all, that his work, devoid of artifice, of artificiality, would appeal to us today with such youthful grace among so many ruins; that Taine, who had extracted all the conscious theory from it, would not succeed in making us disgusted with it, that we would be able to find a completely different teaching in it, more secret, as if expurgated?

I am pleased to have been asked to speak specifically about *Armance*. Up to now this book has been somewhat neglected; unjustly so, in my opinion. Admiration is directed toward *Le Rouge et le noir, La Chartreuse, Lucien Leuwen* even, or toward the incomparable *Henri Brûlard,* for which, whenever I reread it, I feel that I would sacrifice all the rest. And yet I know certain writers, not among the least important, who retain a kind of predilection for *Armance*. But in the eyes of the common reader and even of Stendhalians, *Armance* has not yet fully recovered from the judgment of Sainte-Beuve:

"This novel, enigmatic in its basic premise, without truth in its detail, gives no promise of imagination and genius."

It must be confessed that the book is disconcerting. The plot unfolds not only among the characters, but especially between the author and the reader. I might almost be tempted to say that it makes game of the reader. If we read *Armance* superficially, at first we see only an idyl; if we persist in this interpretation, we sense vaguely that we are duped and we find this embarrassing. We need the explanation that I should be very bold in proposing, if I were not aided precisely by Stendhal himself: in a certain letter of his to Mérimée, we will find the key to *Armance,* the key to the enigma that the book poses for the reader. As long as the key word is lacking, the character of Octave, the hero of the novel, remains incomprehensible; once we have it, everything becomes clear; this hero, who is in love, is impotent.

Impotent: this is revealed in his gestures, his actions; but we could remain in doubt because the novel skillfully maintains the secret. On two occasions Octave is ready to reveal his secret to the woman whom we must call, in spite of everything, his mistress; but first his courage fails him, and rather than confess *that,* he uses another secret to feed the curiosity that he awakens, a shameful secret, but less ignominious in his eyes, an old transgression either imaginary or real; he "tells his friend that when he was young he had a passion for stealing." But we sense clearly that this is only a pretense, sufficient, however, to upset Armance and to disconcert the reader.

And later:

"Well," said Octave, stopping, turning toward her, and staring at her steadily, no longer as a lover, but so as to read her mind, "you will know everything; death would be less painful to me than what I must tell you, but I do love you much more than life. Must I swear to you, no longer as your lover (and at this moment his gaze was not that of a lover), but as a gentleman, as I would swear to your father, had the grace of heaven permitted him to live, do I need to swear to you that I love you, alone, in this world as I have never loved, as I shall never love? To be separated from you would be death for me, and a hundred times worse than death; but I have a hideous secret, which I have never confessed to anyone, and this secret will explain to you the peculiarities that are my fate."

However, he does not yet tell his secret; he finds it more expedient to write it. But the letter never reaches Armance; she will never know this secret—nor will the reader unless he has been able to guess it.

In addition to the explanatory letter to Mérimée, we have for our enlightenment a copy of *Armance,* annotated by Stendhal himself, in which, opposite this sentence: "Love her! I, a most unfortunate man!" we read this handwritten indication: "Try to make the reader guess the impotence, put here: 'And how could she love me?'"

And further along after the sentence: "He had a horror of this feeling [love]"; we find: "A thousand times in four years he had sworn to himself that he would never love. The obligation not to love was the foundation of his whole behavior and the great concern of his life."

Thus the impotence of Octave is never precisely mentioned; constantly implied, it provokes a certain attitude and certain gestures in the hero which are inexplicable unless we presuppose it. To make the reader guess this impotence is, we might say, the very subject of the book, and I know of no other that requires a more subtle collaboration of the reader; to tell the truth, not until we are informed and reread the book do we understand the full meaning of certain indications that we first take at face value. Take, for instance, this epigraph from Marlowe put at the beginning of the second chapter: "Melancholy mark'd him for her own, whose ambitious heart overates [sic] the happiness he cannot enjoy." • This is translated almost literally in the chapter that follows by this sentence: "A passionate imagination led him to overrate in his own mind the happiness he could not enjoy." If this exquisite sentence, which could just as well fit any human being of a somewhat romantic disposition, takes on a more concrete, more precise meaning when it is applied to Octave, we are given no indication of this in the beginning.•• Likewise, when Stendhal writes, speaking of Octave: "The only thing he lacked was an ordinary soul," we understand what he meant only later: if he had an ordinary soul, he would have been less tormented by this secret.

Stendhal knows perfectly well that we lack the explanation for which we are waiting during the whole course of the book; he knows he ought to give it to us; but, as he confesses in a note (26 May 1828): "I can find no way of saying this becomingly in the work; *rather in the preface.*" Of all of Stendhal's books, none other had greater need of a preface than this one; and if I seem to emphasize this a little too much, the words I have just quoted are my excuse.

• [Gide quotes the original English.]
•• "Victim of a profound melancholy, and especially without anyone in whom he could confide [Stendhal had first written and then crossed out: "of which none knew the secret"], Octave seemed to be a misanthrope before his time. As he could not anticipate a certain happiness that he imagined to himself as extreme, his imagination no longer saw any pleasure in life, nor anything that seemed to him to be worth the trouble of living." This we read in one of the marginal notes.

Thus in his first novel (and right away it is important to note that Stendhal was already forty-four years old in 1827 when he wrote it, and that this first novel is already his seventh work), Stendhal offers us a "case": the case of an impotent man; and what may seem paradoxical, an impotent man in love. On the contrary, is it possible that he found the theory of his master Cabanis paradoxical? "It is the seminal humor alone that . . ." a theory later adopted by De Gourmont, who also refuses to see anything in the feeling of love not dictated by this humor and not both aroused and satisfied by the act of procreation. The character of Octave is in direct contradiction to this truly elementary thesis. And since it becomes the feeling of love to find an opportunity for both recognition and exaggeration in obstacles and constraint, Stendhal seems to have wanted to show us that the strongest love rises up from the deepest frustration: of all the lovers in Stendhal, here is perhaps the most fervent one.

The obstacle is not exterior or moral; it is in his very constitution. Octave loves, and loves all the more passionately because he knows that he should not love, that he loves without hope, in spite of himself and the oath he swore to himself never to love, knowing very well that he can burn only with a completely mystic flame, and that, oh, shame! his flesh must remain deaf, not answering the call, knowing that he must disappoint his beloved.

To give this drama its fullest eloquence, Octave had to be endowed with the most exquisite scruples: for with a "common soul" Octave could have cheated—Stendhal notes this; and since everything in the character of his hero becomes clear after we learn his secret, we understand why Stendhal at this point stresses the "feeling of duty" which dominates all his thoughts. Octave consents to envisage marriage and love only in terms of all the obligations that they bring with them—obligations that he well knows he cannot fulfill. Now we understand why Octave first thought of becoming a priest, not through any religious vocation, but through cowardice, as if to conceal the reason for a compulsory celibacy under the rule. Finally we understand those pages, among the most mysterious and the most interesting in the book, which tell us of the bad company Octave keeps, at the time when he is most in love with Mademoiselle de Zohiloff; we understand that among women of easy morals, among those women, "the sight of whom is a defilement," he is seeking the possibility of experiences that may at last reassure him or confirm the cause of his despair.

So, therefore, the impotent man can be in love. Here Stendhal admits a possible distinction between the two elements that love usually unites. If one of the elements is lacking, the division is fatal; but think how much more astonishing it is when no lack is involved. I do not know that it can be better or more clearly established than it is in the admirable novel of Fielding, in which he makes Tom Jones, his hero, dally with the barmaids he meets on his way and shows that the more he is in love on the one hand, the more ribald he is on the other. "The delicacy of your sex," he says to Sophia, his virginal mistress, "cannot conceive the grossness of ours, nor how little one sort of amour has to do with the heart." • Here there is no longer a distinction, but a dissociation, a divergence. Fielding's whole novel seems to demonstrate this naïve divorce: it ends when pure love and carnal desire are reconciled in marriage.

Did not Victor Hugo himself, although he was a very mediocre psychologist, likewise say that Marius (in *Les*

• *Tom Jones,* Book XVIII, Chapter 12.

Misérables) would rather frequent women of ill repute than raise the hem of Cosette's skirt, even in thought? For, as Louise Labé wrote exquisitely in her *Débat de folie et d'amour* (Discourse III), "lubricity and glandular enthusiasm have nothing, or very little, in common with Love." This explains why then the impotent man is capable of a most fervent and tender love; more fervent even than that of ordinary lovers precisely because it is thwarted in its very essence. It is more constant, too, because it is granted no release that might, it is to be feared, make love subside—for if the satisfaction of desire can sometimes stimulate love, more often it exhausts it—and also because this is the kind of love over which time has no hold.

Stendhal had met this dissociation through his own experience. His amorous career, already lengthy (as we said, he was forty-four when he wrote *Armance*) offers us only rare examples of the fusion of the senses and the soul. Most often he appears either sentimental or cynical. When he recalls his mistresses in *Henri Brûlard,* we see him write the initials of thirteen names on the sand (and by an amorous lapse of attention he traces twice those of Angela Pietragrua) and then we hear him confess: "Most of these charming beings did not honor me with their favors, but they have literally filled my whole life. After them came my works." • And he adds: "As a matter of fact, I have had only six women whom I loved"; and if we want to count only his "successes," we are forced to reduce that number to four. It must be admitted that this is a very small number for someone who made pleasure the great affair of his life. This can be explained: for probably Stendhal was not very attractive,

---

• As were his preceding books, *Armance* was written to console himself and to distract himself from a sort of amorous despair, immediately after the abandonment of Madame Curial (that Clémentine whom he often called "Mento")—"despair in which I spent the first months of that fateful year" (1826), he tells us.

physically at least. He had no illusions about this. "Had I been happy," he wrote, "I would have been charming. Not because of my face and manners, certainly, but because of my heart, I could have been charming to a sensitive woman." But at that age when, filled with passion, it seems that he could have been most seductive, he experienced only rebuffs, so he confesses: "Therefore I spent without women the two or three years when my temperament was the most lively."

Not only did Stendhal know the dissociation of love and pleasure through his own experience, but he knew very well that an excess of love can go so far as to inhibit,• if not precisely desire, at least the physiological reflexes that enable us to satisfy it. In one of the final chapters of *De l'Amour,* after having noted this sentence of Montaigne: "This misfortune [the "fiasco"] is to be feared only in undertakings in which we find our being tense beyond measure with desire and respect. . . ." he adds, "if a grain of passion enters the heart, there enters also a grain of possible fiasco."

However, Octave's pride does not bear the idea of a fiasco; whether his impotence is incurable or temporary, he clearly foresees that if there is any woman in the world incapable of awakening his flesh, it is precisely the one whom he idolizes; whereas he can still hope to succeed with women of easy virtue.

Another consideration probably makes him keep to their society: he would rather have the reputation of a debauchee than to be thought incapable of being one. "The incredible scandal of your reputed conduct *is said to* have won for you an unfortunate notoriety among the most disreputable young people in Paris," says Armance to Octave, and the expression "is said to" is used only to indicate that she still has doubts; she expects a protest

• On 25 February 1828, he writes this note to Chapter 17 of *Armance:* "I reread this chapter, which seems true to me; and in order to write it, *it must have been felt.*"

from Octave, but Octave cannot utter a denial, and "noticing with delight that the voice of Armance was trembling" when she related the gossip she had heard about him, he finally says to her: "All they have told you is true but will no longer be so in the future. I shall not appear again in those places where your friend should never have been seen." He says this either because he is carried away by his love for Armance and fears hurting her; or because there is no further reason for his going there, having acquired both the confirmation of his impotence and the false reputation he wanted in order to hide the fact.

Thus, without stressing the nature of this impotence, Stendhal allows us to understand that there is no outward sign of it, that it is not, properly speaking, organic, and that it includes the exterior attributes of virility. For too often it is thought to be accompanied by a general effeminacy, to be visible in the features of a face that has remained beardless, to be heard in high-pitched voice. But in the mechanism of love, the gears are many; little good it does to have those of the body in perfect state if their functioning remains uncontrolled by those of the soul, if the shifting of the gears does not take place.

Of the few *"babylans"* (to use Stendhal's word) who have confided in me, the saddest case—which could indeed be that of Octave, and that is why I tell it at this point—seems to be that of a young man, perfectly normal in appearance and physiologically whole, but incapable of sensual pleasure. The only release allowed him came during his sleep, but he did not feel it and became conscious of it only upon awakening. For him, pleasure was a *terra ignota* of which he dreamed constantly, which he tried in vain to attain, and toward which the smug tales of travelers to that land attracted him. As he begged me to help him find some remedy to his anguish, I put him into the hands of a very expert little actress who, I think, could do nothing for him. It would have been necessary to begin earlier.

"But," you will say with Cabanis, "if you agree that Octave is physiologically whole and that the cause of his *babylanisme* is not to be sought in an organic insufficiency, but rather in the nonobedience of that organ to the incitement of desire, this means that you recognize, in spite of what you first stated, that the mysterious intoxication of the soul is still due to the seminal humor?" This I answer by saying that the cause of impotence can also reside in the very lack of desire; that, moreover, I have never thought of venturing to deny the action of the said humor on our being; that what it was important for me to note was only that the demands of this humor can be exercised independently of love, even when it first awakens love; that love can sometimes be emancipated from it and be the more exalted the less it tends toward carnal possession. There would be much more to say on this subject. . . .

The constant preoccupation of the impotent man is to hide his secret from the eyes of everyone. He is usually most skillful in doing so, and he succeeds all the more readily because men, on this point, are quick to allow themselves to be deluded; they take so much pleasure in imagining intrigues and hidden acts in every frequentation of man and woman, thus encouraging and flattering their own salacity, that it is always easier to make others believe that a woman is your mistress than to hide the fact if she really is. From all the above, it follows that the *babylans* are very hard to recognize and consequently much more numerous than one thinks.

However numerous the *babylans* may be, and even were they more so, the case of Octave is nonetheless *special*. And as soon as this word "special" is applied to matters of love, its narrow meaning shrinks even more; so much so that usually the public and the critics do not willingly allow the novelist the right of invading this retreat. The slightest anomaly that the hero manifests in his relations with woman excludes him, so it seems, from the common run of humanity, who alone have the right to interest us. From the literary point of view, he is foreclosed. And so I admire Stendhal's choice of such a subject for his first novel. However, in my opinion what attracts him in this case is not the *abnormal*, but rather the *particular*.

And this is what separates him from, even sets him opposite to, Marivaux, of whom I thought irresistibly when I reread *Armance*. Here we find the favorite theme of Marivaux's plays: love's surprise and the slow conquest of a heart that refuses to allow itself to love; and even the naïveté of the lover who becomes aware of his feelings only when they are revealed to him by a third person: "This unexpected word [of the Comtesse d'Aumale] revealed to Octave the true feelings of his heart. . . ." We find his delicacy, his subtlety, the same sort of "tender nobility," • sometimes almost his turn of mind. But I like this comparison only insomuch as it helps me sense more clearly an essential difference: whereas Marivaux (and this is what exasperates me in him) moves his heroes, who are depersonalized to the point of being abstract, through a land of delicate feelings whose map could serve anyone at all, the itinerary of Octave could be followed by no one but himself alone; the former proceeds from the general by way of deduction, and the latter works by induction; and if he seeks a general rule, he does so starting with a unique case, particular to the point of being an anomaly.••

• *Armance,* Chapter 8, p. 65.
•• I do not claim in the least that Stendhal was the first to think that each individual is more precious than the whole. We find this great psychological truth, which we had already learned in the New Testament, more or less formulated in Montaigne, Retz, Saint-Simon, Montesquieu, Rousseau (I am taking only French literature into consideration). But until Stendhal, and it could be said: until romanticism, more attention was paid to the study of man then of men. Molière

However clear this novel may seem to us at present—·
and I ought to have said again that of all the books of
Stendhal, I find this one the most delicate and the most
finely written—it nevertheless leaves us dissatisfied. Inasmuch as Stendhal tackled this difficult subject, we
should have liked to see him carry it through to the end;
but it seems that he loses courage at the last moment. He
draws away from the final question, probably the most
important; in the end, he skirts it and lets us wonder:
How would Armance have received Octave's confession?
That is just what we were waiting for. Faced with the
inadequacy of the man she loved, how would the love
of the beloved woman be transformed?

The letter to Mérimée gives us more information on
this point, and we see that although Stendhal eluded
this question in the book, it nonetheless preoccupied
him. This letter allows us to glimpse two possible solutions after the marriage—supposing that Octave does
not kill himself, the easiest way out, after all, and the
one that Stendhal first proposed; for he said: "The true
babylan must kill himself so as not to have the embarrassment of making a confession."

The first solution, that of the substitution of "the
handsome peasant" who, at the right moment, "in exchange for a sequin" would take the place of the hus-

---

portrays *types* rather than characters, as does La Bruyère most often,
in spite of the title of his work. Racine has a tendency to individualize
his heroes, but Corneille, on the other hand, and later on Voltaire,
generalize. In spite of his subtlety, La Rochefoucauld tries to propose
a sort of intimate canon to us—and the whole classic period does the
same—an image of the exemplary man, all of whose affective reactions,
and passions can, as it were, be codified. I am well aware that it would
not be difficult to find particular remarks in the little book of *Maximes,*
just as in the work of Stendhal many a statement of a general nature
could be found, but it is perhaps not imprudent to point out the domi-
nance of generalization in the former and of discrimination in the
latter—and to differentiate peoples, races and countries (as Montesquieu already urged us to do), if not always individuals.

band, seems to find some support in a singular sentence
of Fielding:

> That refined degree of Platonic affection which is abso-
> lutely detached from the flesh, and is, indeed, entirely and
> purely spiritual, is a gift confined to the female part of the
> creation; many of whom I have heard declare (and doubt-
> less with great truth), that they would, with the utmost
> readiness, resign a lover to a rival, when such resignation
> was proved to be necessary for the temporal interest of such
> lover. Hence, therefore, I conclude that this affection is in
> nature, though [Fielding adds] I cannot pretend to say I
> have ever seen an instance of it.•

Besides, I find it hard to believe that Armance, as
Stendhal describes her to us, would have accepted such
a substitution; no more so than to the second solution he
proposes: that of trickery, of makeshift. Shall I add that
I greatly distrust this letter to Mérimée? It seems to me
(I agree with many a Stendhalian on this point) that
Stendhal affects an excessive cynicism in it which he
deems to be of a nature to please his correspondent and
to win that certain consideration which his writings had
not seemed able to bring him up to that time.

There remains the solution of Saint Alexis: flight.
Please understand me. I am not claiming that the case
of Octave is like that of Alexis; I simply say that a mystical *babylan* would not have acted differently.

But why seek a solution? Life proposes to us a quan-
tity of situations which are clearly without solution and
which can only be untangled, at the end of long anxiety
and torment, by death. I imagine Octave wedded to
Armance; I imagine her first perplexed, then painfully
resigned (and here I do not mean just resignation in
love, but also the renunciation of maternity which fol-

• *Tom Jones*, Book XVI, Chapter 5.

lows and is probably even more permanently cruel for many women). I imagine Octave, less resigned than Armance, or rather, more deeply so, picturing to himself unceasingly all that he is depriving her of, and what is worse, depicting it to her. I imagine the vain attempts, the assurances of which love is prodigal, the doubts, then, assuming that their love has lasted, the slow purification of that love with the onset of age, the end, so dubiously attained, of which the boredom of other couples is but a parody.

But perhaps, without grieving too much, they will both acquire the wisdom of not exaggerating beyond measure the importance of what they are refused, and will convince themselves that the deepest love is not necessarily linked to the flesh. They will perhaps even come to the point of congratulating themselves that their love, pure of all carnal alliance, ignorant of the excessive ardor stirred up by the fumes of the senses, has escaped being seared, and that nature, which forbade them certain pleasures has allowed them, in compensation, to elude that Gehenna which follows pleasure: "to shun the heaven that leads men to this hell," • if Shakespeare is to be believed.

For I think of the terrible remark of Tolstoy which Gorky quotes to us: "Man survives earthquakes, epidemics, the horror of illness, and all the agonies of the spirit; but throughout all generations, the tragedy that has tormented him, still torments him, and will torment him the most is—and will be—the tragedy of the alcove." ••

TRANSLATED BY BLANCHE A. PRICE

• [In English in the original.]
• • *"Souvenirs sur Tolstoï,"* by Maxim Gorky (*Nouvelle Revue Française,* December 1920).

PREFACE TO "THE QUEEN OF SPADES"

French connoisseurs already know Pushkin's *The Queen of Spades* in Mérimée's translation. It might appear impertinent to offer now a new version, and I do not doubt that the earlier one will appear more elegant than this one, which has no merit other than its scrupulous exactness. That is its justification. A preoccupation with explaining and rounding off induced Mérimée to blunt somewhat the crystalline peaks of the tale. We have resisted adding anything to Pushkin's clean and spare style, with its slender grace, which hums like a taut string. When Pushkin writes: "Herman quivered like a tiger," Mérimée adds: ". . . lying in wait." When he has Lisaveta bend over a book, Mérimée says "gracefully." This charming writer thus marks his own manner, and if some criticize his dryness it is clear here that the criticism is ill-founded, or, at least, that only by comparison with the lush style of the writers of his period can Mérimée's style seem so unadorned to us. The clarity of Pushkin, on the other hand, chafes him, and nothing shows that better than a study of this translation. "Poets," Pushkin wrote, "often sin by neglect of simplicity and truth; they pursue all manner of external effects. The pursuit of form sweeps them toward exaggeration and bombast." He criticized in Hugo, whom he admired, an absence of simplicity. "Life is lacking in him," he wrote. "In other words, truth is absent."

The strangeness of most Russian writers, including the greatest among them, often baffles the French reader, and indeed, sometimes repels him; but I confess that it is the absence of strangeness in Pushkin that confounds me. Or at least what baffles me, is to see that Dostoevsky, that genius so prodigiously distant from us (despite all the secret affinities that some of us find in his profoundly human work) considered Pushkin as the most national of the Russian writers that preceded him. In vain would we seek here what we are accustomed to consider as characteristically Russian: disorder, penumbra, overabundance, disarray. In the majority of Pushkin's works, all is clarity, balance, harmony. No bitterness, no resigned pessimism; but a profound love, perhaps even somewhat primitive, of all the joys, all the delights of life, tempered always by the requirements of his cult of beauty.

Russian? Yes, doubtless; but if so we have formed a false notion of the Russians. Enamored of classical art from his early years, Pushkin translated Anacreon, Athenaeus, Xenophon, Catullus, Horace. He wrote in 1834: "Every cultivated European must have a sufficient and clear idea of the immortal works of antiquity." He admired also the great works of French and English literature. At thirty-two, he wrote to Chaadayev in French: "I shall employ with you the language of Europe; it is more familiar to me than our own." He imitated Chénier and Byron. He was always imitating and seemed to have no greater joy than that of losing himself and abandoning his personality. "Look at the scenes from *Faust,* from *The Avaricious Knight. . . .* Reread *Don Juan;* if there were no signature," says Dostoevsky, "you would never guess that it was not written by a Spaniard. In *The Feast During the Plague* you will hear the very genius of England."

What seems to Dostoevsky so profoundly Russian in the limpid genius of Pushkin is precisely that very universality, that singular faculty for losing himself to find himself in another. "European literature," he says, "offers us geniuses like Shakespeare, Cervantes, Schiller.

But show me, even one among them all, who possesses to the same degree as Pushkin the capacity for universal comprehension." And again: "Pushkin was the only one among the poets who succeeded in assuming the soul of other poets." But according to Dostoevsky it is to his profoundly Russian character that Pushkin owes his universality, for "the mission of each Russian is doubtless a universal mission. . . . To become truly a Russian," he adds, "to become completely Russian—means to feel oneself brother to all men."

The Queen of Spades, that brief masterpiece, offers us an excellent example of the admirable poetic qualities of Pushkin and his gift for self-effacement.

TRANSLATED BY JEFFREY J. CARRE

Upon Rereading "Les Plaisirs et les Jours" After the Death of Marcel Proust

Proust died in November 1922 at the age of fifty-one, and the following January Gide's N.R.F.—which had brought Proust into its select group by publishing fragments of his work as early as June and July 1914— brought out an issue of homage to the great writer. Among its numerous essays were Gide's thoughts on rereading Proust's first book, which can well be compared with his "Note to Angèle" of 1921, both of which properly belong in his Pretexts.

I never grow weary of wondering at the fact that the two writers of my generation whose glorious survival can be least rashly hoped for, so it seems to me—one a poet, the other a writer of prose—were almost completely unaware of each other, mutually incapable of understanding one another, and yet both had a fortune quite individual and at the same time very similar. I speak of Marcel Proust and Paul Valéry. At practically the same age and about the same time, each published his first writings, then remained silent for fifteen years. What a fine example they set our impatient age by showing what sudden glory can be attained by the artist who disdains success, and of what power an artist who learns to wait becomes capable.

When I reread *Les Plaisirs et les jours* today, the qualities of this delicate book, which appeared in 1896, seem so brilliant to me that I am astonished that we were not dazzled by them at once. Although in the beginning we were unable to see, today we have an experienced eye and now we perceive in the book all that we have since come to admire in the recent works of Marcel Proust. Yes, all that we admire in *Swann* or in *Guermantes* is already here, subtly, almost insidiously presented: the childish anticipation of the mother's good-night kiss; the intermittence of memory, the dulling of regret, the evocative power of place names, the perturbations of jealousy, the persuasive force of landscapes—even the Verdurin dinners, the snobbishness of the guests, the heavy vanity of the conversations—or a certain reflection especially dear to Marcel Proust, on which his thought will often feed—which I find indicated twice in this first book, the first time concerning that child, who feeling the constant need of comparing in despair the "imperfect perfection" of reality with the "absolute perfection" of his dream or his memory, is astonished and dies. Says Proust: "Each time he tried to find the accidental reason for his disappointment in the imperfection of circumstances." • And further on, in the "Critique of Hope in the Light of Love," "Like the alchemist who attributes each of his failures to an accidental cause, never the same twice, so do we, far from suspecting the existence of an incurable imperfection in the very essence of the present, accuse the malignity of particular circumstances." ••

Yes, all that will later blossom forth in splendor in his long novels is offered in its nascent state in this book, the fresh buds of those wide-open flowers—all that we

• *Les Plaisirs et les jours*, p. 184.
•• Ibid., p. 228.

shall admire later, unless what we admire is something other than that detail and abundance, the unusual profusion, the exaggeration and apparent multiplication of all that appears merely as promise or seed in this book. And not only all, or almost all the motifs that will be gleaned later from *Remembrance of Things Past* by this very research—but in addition even the announcement, almost the prediction of that future abundance; so much so that we seem to hear him speaking of his future work when we read: "In all that there were precise little details of sensuality, of tenderness in practically every circumstance of his life, and it was like a vast fresco that depicted his life without telling it, using the color of its passion alone in both a vague and particular way, with a great power of touching." •

Naturally I shall not go so far as to say that we find the subtle perfection of the pages of his maturity in these early writings—although among the twenty pages of his "Confession of a Young Girl" there are certain that in my opinion equal his very best, but I am astonished to find in these pages a type of preoccupation which Proust will entirely abandon later, alas—its nature is sufficiently indicated by this sentence from the *Imitation of Christ* which is pinned to it as an epigraph: "The desires of the senses drive us hither and yon, but when the hour has passed, what do we retain? Remorse of our conscience and dissipation of spirit." However, his unpublished work will probably hold many surprises for us. All that I can say is that of all the themes proposed in his first book, no other seems to me to be more deserving of Proust's full attention, no other which I hope more to find echoed in detail.

But there is something here even more strange and revealing: in the preface to *Pleasures and Days,* or to be more exact in his letter of dedication, dated 1894, we

• Ibid., p. 186.

read: "When I was a little child, the fate of no character in biblical stories seemed so miserable to me as that of Noah. This was because of the flood that kept him shut up in the Ark for forty days. Later I was often sick and for long days I, too, learned how to remain in the 'Ark.' Then I understood that Noah could never see the world so well as from the Ark, in spite of its being closed and of night's lying upon the earth." •

The life of Proust has filled this prophetic little sentence with a special emotion. For a long time illness had kept Proust shut up in the Ark and had tempted him or forced him into that completely nocturnal existence to which he finally became accustomed, against whose dark background the microscopic specimens furnished by his amazing memory stand out with such luminosity, and from which the din of the present moment no longer diverted him, except momentarily during his interminable leisure. At this point I shall not mention the anguish, the sufferings of his illness, nor the tactful impulses of a heart unceasingly filled with love—impulses that were amplified distinctly in the atmosphere, so mystically rarified, in which he had grown accustomed to living, amplified in such a way that each feeling, however slight, which would have been swept away by the daily life of anyone else, became an ingenious creation, serious, sensitive, painful—and this made of him a friend so marvelous, so demonstrative, that in comparison with him, one often felt caught up somewhat short, as if ashamed of a certain indigence of feeling. Further along in this preface he says: "Invalids feel closer to their souls." •• And in another place: "Life is a hard thing, squeezing us too tightly, perpetu-

• [The French text reads: "*Je compris alors que jamais Noé ne put si bien voir le monde que de l'arche, malgré qu'elle fût close et qu'il fît nuit sur la terre.*" (*Les Plaisirs et les jours,* p. vii.) Gide adds the following note: "What purist will dare blame Proust for his *malgré que?*"

•• *Les Plaisirs et les jours,* p. vii.

ally hurting our being. When we feel its bonds loosen for a moment, we can experience sweet moments of clear-sightedness." • The lucid genius of Proust already pervades this youthful sentence, and his future work will indeed be permeated with these "sweet moments of clear-sightedness." Beside this sentence I want to place another, which I read a little further along in the same book: "And who knows if our conscious immortality will be born from our wedding with death." ••

TRANSLATED BY BLANCHE A. PRICE

• Ibid., p. vii.
•• Ibid., p. 185.

Paul Valéry

Gide's close friendship with the great poet Valéry dates from 1890, when one was twenty and the other nineteen. It was Gide who brought Valéry back to literature after twenty years of almost complete silence by urging him to collect his early poems. Today their voluminous correspondence, extending from their first meeting until the poet's death in 1945, forms a capital document of modern literature.

The following essay originally appeared in an issue of homage which the Divan *devoted to Valéry in 1922. The "mysterious notebooks" to which Gide alludes toward the end of his essay are even now (as they appear in facsimile) revolutionizing our view of Paul Valéry.*

Through a natural development, all great poets eventually become critics. I pity those poets guided by instinct alone; for they seem incomplete to me. In the spiritual life of the former, infallibly there comes about a crisis that makes them want to reason out their art, to discover the obscure laws by virtue of which they have created, to draw from this study a series of precepts whose divine aim is infallibility in poetic creation.

BAUDELAIRE

I would speak of him more easily if I were not his friend. Friendship calls for modesty, and the expression of my admiration is somewhat constricted by my friendship. But only the expression, for an object need not be distant or comparatively unknown to me to appear admirable. I have known Paul Valéry for more than thirty years and I admire not just his work, but the whole man; however, since the work is accessible to everyone, I shall speak of the man, whom few know and who has been carefully concealed by his work.

There is no life more faithful; such as he was when we were twenty, such he has remained, going steadily forward in a single line without ever breaking off, retracting, or bending; he urges himself ever forward.

At that time (1891) he was living in Montpellier; that is where I first knew him. His motto was *"Ars non stagnat,"* but he was revolted by change that was not progress. His lucid mind discerned no greater enemy than vagueness. Just as he did not admit that the soul could exist without the body, so he did not allow feeling to enter his cosmos unless it assumed form; nothing was admitted that would not allow of measurement. He did not pardon an artist for proceeding haphazardly. "I admit nothing unless I understand it, and the word work is often synonymous with inspiration," he wrote me, and further: "For the tenth time I note that the most crass superstitions can coexist with talent to form the literati. Many a poet is as much a product of chance as the common herd." He claimed that every artist started with what he wanted to obtain, with the emotion of the reader or the spectator, and that the effect dictated its cause.

"Lascia la poesia e studia la mathematica," the Muse of Musset's *Nights* could have said to him, but he held in contempt the aeolian lyre of the poet of the *Nights* and rejected the Muse. To be sure, he found perfect mental satisfaction in the rigorous discipline of mathematics and his investigation led him preferably toward the science of numbers; but he claimed to apply this same discipline to poetry. Consciousness and lucidity

seemed to him to be the cardinal virtues of the artist. "Metrics is an algebra," he wrote to me in 1891, "that is, the science of the variations of a fixed rhythm according to certain values given to the signs of which it is composed. The line of verse is the equation, balanced when its solution comes out to equality, that is, symmetry." If the poetry he wanted included the most exquisite sensitivity, naturally that counselor of very bad verse, sentimentality, was excluded. "Sentimentality and pornography are twin sisters," he wrote to me at the same period. "I detest them." And exaggerating equally the importance of craft alone: "As for the mute *e*," I read a little further along in the same letter, "the only rule of poetry, the only touchstone, is the position of the mute letter."

Was it not precisely the method and the way of considering the work of art, poetry, painting, or music as a means toward a predetermined effect that he admired in his masters of that period, Leonardo da Vinci, Wagner, and "especially, always, powerless to tear myself away from that vertiginous and mathematical opium: Edgar Allan Poe"?• "What interests me is not the work but the recipe," he used to say at that time; and further: "I value only those works that can be remade." On the other hand, he had contempt for the irresolute effort of literature, "the flabby intumescence of the indefinite" (if I may be allowed to parody a well-known sentence of Chateaubriand), contempt for all that charms, deceives, lulls, puts to sleep, all that can be lengthened without surprise. (I was going to say: without effort, had I not remembered the hatred he felt for Flaubert, doubtless not so much for his *Salammbô* as for his statement: "I call beautiful that which exalts me vaguely." He valued the lucidity of Stendhal, his clear-cut line, his boredom

• Letter of 1891: "Poe is the only writer without sin. He was never mistaken."

with all that he could not use to create his pleasure, and his constant concern lest he be a dupe, lest he allow himself to be deluded.

However exquisite were the few poems that he took pleasure in composing at that time, he protested against the title of poet. "I beg of you not to call me Poet any more, great or minor. I am not a poet but the Gentleman who is bored. All moral, cubic, affirmative beauty turns me away from it. I care nothing about sentences and their rhythm and all that fairly predictable mechanical skill which does not entertain me. Expression alone wins me over." And soon he stopped writing poems completely.

In 1894 he came to Paris to live in rue Gay-Lussac in a little hotel room whose only piece of furniture, so it seems, was a big blackboard in front of which he spent hours seeking and finding the solution to difficult problems that he demonstrated to me at a dizzy speed when I went to see him. Like Leonardo da Vinci, he filled notebooks with sketches, formulas, and equations; there were as many figures and algebraic signs on the pages as words. His first collaborators in the reviews *La Conque* and *Le Centaure* were grieved to see him give up poetry and enter a path that to them seemed to lead only to powerless speculations. However, power was precisely what Valéry was seeking. Nothing seemed to temp him less than the success he could easily have obtained through an abundant production. His apparent renunciation concealed a higher ambition.

In 1893 he wrote me: "I wager that the error of many people concerning me is to suppose that in spite of everything I have literary interests in the back of my mind, to believe in short that through the restrictions I profess and my renunciation, I am tending toward some new genre." And in 1894: "I have always acted so as to make myself an individual who is potential. That is, I prefer a life of strategy to one of tactics. To have everything available without availing myself of it. What impressed me most of all was that nobody ever went to the very end." The only thing to do was to persevere. And for twenty-five years, Valéry was silent, working unceasingly.

Without jealousy he had seen his first companions become well-known, and they probably considered him one of those "literati" at whom he had once poked fun. He accepted being judged sterile, no longer showing the resources of his mind except in dazzling conversation. I know of no more disconcerting example of patience, disdain, and faith.

At the end of the war, whoever might have wanted to take stock of the intellectual resources of France would certainly not have dreamed of even mentioning the name Valéry. The poems of his youth were hardly remembered. Some knew this dreamer, this visionary, but they no longer expected any work by him, and deplored the vain use of such fine natural gifts.

Then, suddenly, that extraordinary blossoming about which we know. In two years appeared one after another *La Jeune Parque,* the *Odes,* the *Cimetière marin,* the *Serpent*—assuredly the most splendid poems our age can boast—and many pages of the richest prose, the most chaste and sonorous that we have been given to read in a long time.

It would be a grave error to think that Valéry put more than twenty years into writing them. He took all that time arming himself. Presently he felt ready, in full possession of himself and his method. After all, he claimed that this method was applicable not just to poetry. In no way did he consider the poems he gave us as a conclusion; they were a game, a sort of demonstration which he gave himself, an experiment, or better an experimentation. He even thought of collecting them under a common title *Exercises,* meaning by this word not a way of keeping in practice, but the setting into operation of a system, and I do not think that Leonardo thought of his paintings very differently.

It is not incumbent upon me to speak of this system. I want to share Valéry's conviction that his most important work lies still scattered through those mysterious notebooks in which he slowly elaborates it and which probably also call to mind those of Leonardo. But what would method or system, however excellent, be worth in creating a successful work of art without the special qualities of the person who puts it into operation? What I am the most pleased to find above all in the poems of Valéry, although they may offend him, is his tenderness. I remember that in the first days of our friendship, he used to quote to me a saying of Cervantes (I think): "How can a man be hidden?" At that time I did not seize the meaning of the saying very clearly. I awaited the work of Valéry to understand it.

TRANSLATED BY BLANCHE A. PRICE

Dada

Very few among the older writers looked upon the revolutionary artistic movement known as Dada with anything but horror. Consequently Gide's pages, which appeared in the April 1920 issue of the N.R.F., constituted the most impressive avuncular encouragement the young revolt received.

Founded in Zurich by Tristan Tzara in 1916 as a systematic negation of all intellectual and literary values, Dada shocked by its scandalous excesses. Gradually it fused with a more positive current represented by Aragon, Breton, and others, which became Surrealism. The short-lived Futurism founded by the Italian F. T. Marinetti in 1908 had likewise been a destructive move in modern letters.

In that languorous state in which man will be swept along by the course of events, he will have perhaps no other escape than that of a deluge that will plunge everything into ignorance again.
SÉNAC DE MEILHAN

The great misfortune for the inventor of Dada is that the movement he started upsets him and that he is himself crushed by his machine. This is a pity. I am told that he is a very young man. He is described as charming. (Marinetti likewise was irresistible.) I am told that

he is a foreigner—I can readily believe it; that he is a
Jew—I was on the point of saying so.

I am told that he does not use his real name, and I
should be inclined to believe that Dada likewise is but
a pseudonym.

Dada is the deluge, after which everything begins
anew.•

It behooves foreigners to set little store by our French
culture. Against them the legitimate heirs will protest,
not interested in weighing what others have to gain at
the expense of what they themselves have to lose. But
for a moment I want to take the point of view of those
others, granting them that perhaps, after all, what remains to be lost is not much, and even somewhat lost
already—not much in contrast to the whole horizon it
obstructs.

Yes, every form has become a formula and distills a
nameless boredom. Every common syntax is disgustingly
insipid. The best gratitude toward the art of yesterday
and in the face of accomplished masterpieces is not
attempting to imitate them. The perfect is what does
not need redoing; and setting the past before us is raising an obstacle to the future.

It is a serious mistake to assimilate Dada to Cubism.
It is possible to make this mistake; and I am not sure
that even certain half-Cubists do not do so . . . But

• Some will blame me for taking Dada too seriously. There are many
authors, among the most highly considered, whom I take much less
seriously than they are usually taken; but I have never regretted having
taken seriously the youngest tendencies and movements, especially
when they are anonymous. There is in youth much less determined
resolution than youth thinks, much more submission and unconscious
obedience; that is why I find so revealing these waves that lift it up
and float it along. Those who seem the leaders, in this case, are only
the first to be raised up by the wave, and the less apparent their particular reaction is, the better able they are to mark the heights and direction of the tide. I observe them assiduously, but what interests me
is the tide, not the bobbing corks.

Cubism aims to build. It is a school. Dada is a venture of negation.

And it would really not be worth while having fought for five years, having so often endured the death of others and seen everything questioned in order to sit down again at one's writing table and pick up the thread of the old discourse that had been interrupted. What! While our fields, our villages, our cathedrals suffered so much, our style alone should remain untouched! It is essential that the spirit not lag behind matter; it has a right to ruin. Dada will see to this.

Already the edifice of our language is too undermined for anyone to recommend that thought continue to take refuge in it. And before rebuilding it is essential to cast down what still seems solid, what makes a show of still standing. The words that the artifice of logic still lumps together must be separated, isolated. They must be forced to parade again before virgin eyes like the animals after the deluge, issuing one by one from the ark-dictionary, before any conjugation. And if, through some old and purely typographic convention, they are set end to end on a single line, take care to arrange them in a disorder in which they have no *reason* to follow one another—since, after all, it is at the antipoetic *reason* that you are railing.

And it is equally essential, perhaps even more so, after having separated words from one another—in the manner of typesetters who distribute the type before proceeding to new formations—it is essential to dissociate them from their history, from their past, which weighs them down with a dead weight. Each vocable-island on the page must present steep contours. It will be placed here (or there, just as well) like a pure tone; and not far away will vibrate other pure tones, but without any interrelationships so as to authorize no association of thoughts. Thus the word will be liberated from

all its preceding meaning, at least, and from all evoca-
tion of the past.

The trouble for every school is that possibility of exaggeration in which the disciple, more extremist than
the master, compromises the school. But such annoying
exaggeration is eluded by leaping suddenly to the extreme so that there is no way of going beyond. What an
advantage to have to protect oneself only on the right!
It was essential to invent what I hardly dare call a
method that would not only not contribute to producing but would even make the work of art impossible . . .

Indeed, the day the word "Dada" was discovered,
there remained nothing further to be done. Everything
written subsequently seemed to me somewhat watered
down. To be sure, there were still a few meritorious
efforts; but the intention was too obvious; indeed, at
times, a semblance of meaning, of wit. Nothing came up
to "Dada." Those two syllables had achieved the aim of
"sonorous inanity," an insignificant absolute. In that
single word "Dada" they expressed all at once everything they had to say *as a group;* and since there is no
way of going further in absurdity, they must now either
mark time, as the mediocre will continue to do, or else
escape.

I attended a Dada meeting. It took place at the Salon
des Indépendants. I hoped to have more fun and that
the Dadas would take more abundant advantage of the
public's artless amazement. A group of prim, formal,
stiff young men climbed onto the stage and, in chorus,
uttered insincere audacities . . . From the back of the
hall someone shouted: "What about gestures," and
everyone laughed, for it was clear that, for fear of compromising themselves, none of them dared move a
muscle.

In general I consider it not good to cling too much to
the past, or with too apprehensive a grasp. I believe that
each new need must create its new form. I believe,

finally, according to the wise word of the Gospel, that it is folly to try to pour "new wine into old bottles." Yet I hope that in this new barrel the best wine of youth will soon begin to feel somewhat confined.

TRANSLATED BY JUSTIN O'BRIEN

Portraits and Aphorisms

Every summer Gide used to reread Les Caractères et les mœurs de ce siècle *(The Characters and Manners of This Century)* by Jean de La Bruyère. *Although he did not consider that little collection of portraits and reflections as one of the greatest of French seventeenth-century works, he admired it for its simplicity and reasonableness. "So clear is the water in these basins," he wrote in his* Journals, *"that one must lean over them for some time to appreciate their depth." Remaining closer to concrete life than do Pascal and La Rochefoucauld, the moralist La Bruyère ridicules current abuses and judges without indulgence, but always in a highly personal manner according to his own changing moods. Probably it was his supple style, taking advantage of all the resources of rhetoric, that caused Gide to be "tormented" by the desire to re-do the* Caractères.

His own collection of Characters *first appeared in a limited edition in 1925 and was followed four years later by* An Unprejudiced Mind, *which offers a looser continuation of his reflections, somewhat closer to the* Journals. *In 1931 the two works were published together.*

CHARACTERS

The more numerous, the more diverse an artist's gifts, the harder it is for him to win public favor, or even public attention. For his gifts limit and temper one another, and the temperate is less apparent than the excessive. A particular artist seems very rich in a certain regard only because he is very poor in others.

In short, he who has but little to say finds no trouble in shouting it. Excess is often a sign of poverty, and true abundance involves a sort of "ponderation."

*

It is very rare that what is most commonly admired in masterpieces just happens to be what is most worthy of admiration. Lines such as "I should expect him to die!" or "He has no children!" or "Rodrigue, are you courageous?" may be compared to the big toe of Saint Peter's statue, which owes its high gloss to the kisses of the devout.

*

It would have been impossible to tell whether Jules suffered more when the columnist shared his opinion or, on the contrary, when he expressed an opinion at variance with Jules's. In the former case it seemed to him that he was being robbed of a possession and that, although he had never expressed it, that opinion belonged to him. In the latter case, it hurt him to think that if he had expressed that opinion he would have done so with such vigor and such unanswerable arguments that no one could have opposed it or at very least would then have been obliged to say: "Despite what M. Jules thinks . . ." or even "Contrary to M. Jules's ridiculous opinion . . ." so that at least he would have to have been quoted, taken into account. And as he had within him an unwritten article on almost every question of interest to our day (for the very habit he had contracted of never realizing or completing anything allowed his mind a greater diversity), he could not open a newspaper or magazine without feeling wronged.

*

The game the little girls are playing consists in seeing who will weep first. (Judith always won.) It was strictly forbidden to pinch oneself; one was supposed to "think of something sad." Judith thought of the tree that had been felled, from which boxes had been made and distributed to all the friends of the family.

*

Contact with life almost never produces simple reactions in me. Most often, when faced with any object (and I am not thinking only of material objects), the whole gamut rises to the surface. When, going through the Brévent Pass, I suddenly stood facing Mont Blanc, I heard twenty vague exclamations arise in me, a whole conversation:

"What a phenomenon!—Tremendous!—How beautiful it is!—15,781 feet!—A record!—(But only European.)—(Figures don't matter.)—It would look higher if it stood alone.—Yes, the range absorbs it.—Marcel would loathe it.—And how right he would be!—It's hideous!" And all this, not in succession, but all at once.

I always feel gathered within me a contradictory crowd. At times, I should like to ring the bell, put on my hat, and leave the meeting. What does *my* opinion matter to me?

*

Paying no attention to what might or might not interest others, Michel never found it hard to talk.

*

It was only at about thirty that Abel became resigned to his own mediocrity.

*

Frédéric. The utilitarian character, the practical aim of all his thoughts. His zeal in doing a service, at first deceptive, which he takes for generosity, is but a need to *obligate* others.

Frédéric always entertains the convictions, the ideas, the moral code that it is opportune for him to have.

Loathing of utopias and idols: Virtue, Justice, etc. He needs the relativist theories of Barrès to whitewash in his own eyes the concealing of an official record.

But a little later, he is the first to make use of those noble words. Frédéric hides his selfishness behind his paternal love like Wilfred who, upon refusing to subscribe to a collection, always spoke of his "daughters' dowry."

Frédéric takes care to identify his interests with those of France.

*

Michel used to exasperate Edouard by constantly repeating that in art it was above all essential to be sincere.

"What do you mean by sincerity?" Edouard finally
asked.

"Sincerity begins where imitation ends."

"How many artists think they are sincere the moment
they cease to be aware that they are imitating!"

*

"You would be strangely mistaken if you took me to
be lazy," said Maurice. "As others submit to a trade, I
make a profession of idleness. To be sure, I had an initial disposition just as an artist has natural gifts; but he
doesn't become a great artist unless he cultivates them.
For instance, if I let myself go, I could surrender to easy
satisfactions. I can readily adapt myself to the mediocre,
and to tell the truth, I assure you that during my military service I hardly suffered from the privations and
lack of comfort of which so many in the barracks com-
plained, though they were thicker skinned and less
sensitive than I.

"In my present insistence on high standards you will
see that there is less self-indulgence than resolve and
application. I do not let the Christian monopolize the
ideal of perfection. I have my own virtue, which I am
constantly cultivating and refining by teaching myself
not to tolerate in me or my surroundings anything but
the exquisite."

*

The worst suffering in love is probably not being deceived by the beloved but rather deceiving her oneself.

It is becoming aware that one has deceived her, disappointed her, that one is not the person she loved, the person one thought oneself to be when giving oneself to her; it is awakening as another in her arms. . . .

✳

Raymond hates that game warden, his stepfather, to the point of liking the blows bestowed by him. He enjoys the jibes of his half-brothers, whom he despises the more because he is weaker than they. He would like to be the more brutal the softer he is. A caress would make him swoon. He becomes aware of his sensuality upon seeing a pig bled (or a calf castrated). Despite his aristocratic instincts, even on the sidewalks of Paris or drawing-room carpets, he will remember having walked barefoot in warm mud. He liked the smell of sour apples and of manure. He liked to sleep in the barn and let the calves lick his legs.

✳

I tried to tell him (but he is still too young to understand what I didn't understand either at his age): pay attention only to the form; emotion will come spontaneously to inhabit it. A perfect dwelling always finds an inhabitant. The artist's business is to build the dwelling; as for the inhabitant, it is up to the reader to provide him.

✳

As Chopin did by sounds, one must let oneself be guided by words. The artist who complains that the language is stubborn is not a true artist. The true artist realizes that the stubborn element is the emotion, which must be adapted so that it doesn't block anything. It is never appropriate to let oneself be led by the emotion but rather by the line—for emotion distorts the line whereas the line never warps the emotion. Any artist who prefers his own emotion and sacrifices form to that preference succumbs to self-indulgence and contributes to the decadence of art.

✳

How, having set out for Tunis, can I awake this morning in Florence? Don't ask me to explain, for I don't understand myself.

This evening I am thinking of the desperate little girl who threw herself from the Ponte Vecchio *due anni fà.* She clung to the ledge for several minutes and a little beggar of the same age, that is, twelve or thirteen, who didn't know her but who had seen her climb over the parapet (it took place at noon on a holiday and no one could understand later the crowd's indifference or lack of attention) had grabbed her hand and was holding her back.

"No, no, let me go," the little girl said.

And, sobbing, the boy told how he had let go. Her skirt ballooning out kept her on the surface of the water for a time, then she sank. All day long, boats searched the Arno down to the weir. The body was not found until two days later.

✳

A banal music that nevertheless attracted me burst forth at that moment on the square. I hurried there. On a lighted bandstand sat the small orchestra blaring in brass. All around the bandstand, the night, lifted like a veil, dropped its folds beyond the motionless people gathered here by the music. Some of the nearer trees still caught the light on the tip of a branch; the rest sank into the night. Opposite the path by which I had come, another loftier, broader, darker path opened. I liked it for the silence filling it and I penetrated its mysterious depth.

My step slowed spontaneously as I got away from the sound and light and, as they decreased, I realized that the path's mystery consisted less of silence than of multiple whisperings.

*

Darius was talking of that sort of inhibition "that can be noted in the life of so many artists," he said. "And not the poorer ones but the best, the ones we admire the most. In most of them it is a sudden ceasing of production, a total or almost total ceasing that sometimes lasts ten years—just at that period of life which, it seems, ought to be the most fecund." (He gave examples.) "What happens then? I think that at that point in life when, before the decline sets in, there is a premonition of decline, the man of imagination, the artist, comes to wonder if what is about to escape him forever has not, after all, more reality than his dream, or rather if he has not sacrificed reality for a dream, if he has not agreed to a fool's bargain and accepted the shadow for the substance. Or else, if he doesn't tell himself anything like this, even for the sake of his art he needs to live more; in order to add substance to his art, he feels the need of plunging deeper into life.

"At times such an inhibition may become definitive. I think it very different in nature in such cases. It is a sort of paralysis, not of thought, but of the faculty of expression—I was about to say: of the pen—which attacks only the best. I add that to console myself. . . . At times I wonder whether I shall ever again produce anything. I remember Valentin. . . . For some time we thought his malady imaginary until a clever female doctor cured him. Only when he was cured was he able to tell us of his malady so as to be understood. 'Between the sensation and the reflex that was to follow,' he told me, 'an interval, a sort of gap opened. I had to do through reason everything I should have done through instinct. . . . Well, between my thought and my words I feel that gap widening, which doubt comes to fill up. There is no longer any spontaneity in my sentence. I no longer write a word, not even a single word, without willing it."

*

The village priest is lecturing little Louis. He blames him for being one of those rascals who think they know more than father and mother, than schoolmaster and village priest, for never praying the Good Lord. . . . Whereupon Louis interrupts him and calls him a liar.

"I do too pray your Good Lord, every night too! I pray him to send a zeppelin that will set fire to your church and to your damned parsonage too."

The village priest forgets himself to the point of slapping little Louis, and the child, screaming, swears that he will never again set foot in the church.

*

Old mother Dupuis has died; she leaves everything to Poldine, to the great indignation of Rosalie, the day worker who, while waxing the stairs, mutters until she can be heard upstairs.

"And then she'll have the clothespress and all full of linen! . . . And the whole set of china and then the coffee-service. . . . And then the two silverish candle sticks . . ."

This morning as I go up to work I encounter her:

"Well, Rosalie, poor old Mother Dupuis is dead."

"We were expecting it," she begins at once. "Asthma had undermined her. She breathed like a machine (she imitates her). I told her: 'Mother Dupuis, you shouldn't eat at night.' And then sometimes she would fall; she'd be found on the ground, her face a blank. I used to tell her: 'Mother Dupuis, you mustn't go out any more; you're running too great a risk with your sabots.' She couldn't lift her feet, you see. But I used to like seeing her. I'd go there often. She knew how to talk, you know. She remembered everything. She made everything come back to you. Old folks are interesting!"

✳

Edgar is reading Chekhov and exclaims: "How remote from us those Russians are!"

Nothing annoys me more than the conviction that the nationalists (and many others) nourish in the mass of French readers—that they are forever incapable of understanding foreign nationalities. Far from trying to bring out in them all that is human, despite the differences, and everything that suggests common bonds, they play up only the differences. This is so obvious that I should not bother to note it down here, but this morning the following reflection that seems to me rather new is added to it:

Are not the differences between nations singularly emphasized by the habits that lead each of us in his literature to exhibit this or that element of his nature that others are accustomed to hide or at least not to reveal in a state of nature? The same is true for costume, and through costume, for certain shifts in the sense of modesty.

The ancient Greeks had a habit and a need of displaying themselves naked, in a state of nature, but nothing seems less natural to us today. Achilles is not concerned with hiding his tears.

In every literature the first question to ask is: What of man is hidden?

(The question: What is revealed? is relatively less important.)

*

Let us leave to those who strive for influence and success to protest against injustice.

Who first spoke of Stendhal's insensitivity?

Insensitive people.

There is no prejudice that the work of art, in the last analysis, does not overcome.

*

I aim to give to those who read me strength, joy, courage, defiance, perspicacity—but I take care above all not to give them directions, for I feel that they can and must find them by themselves. I was about to say: in themselves. To develop simultaneously those two opposites: the critical spirit and energy. Generally among intelligent people are found nothing but paralytics and among men of action nothing but fools.

*

Oh, how embarrassing Freud is! And how readily we should have discovered his America without him! It strikes me that the thing I ought to be most grateful to him for is having accustomed readers to hear certain subjects handled without having to protest or to blush. Above all, he brings us daring, or, more exactly, he brushes aside a certain false and annoying modesty.

But how many ridiculous reflections in that idiot of genius!

✳

If it were as thwarted as the sexual appetite, mere appetite (hunger) would be the great supplier of Freudianism (just as thirst inspires the dreams of those who lack water as they cross the desert). In other words, certain forces owe their violence to a denial of outlet. This was known.

It is true that the sexual desire, when not directly satisfied, is capable of multiple hypocrisies—I mean of assuming the most diverse forms, as the other hunger never can. The point on which (if I were a doctor) my insistent investigations would bear is this: What happens when for social, moral, and other reasons the sexual function is obliged to leave the object of its desire in order to operate, when satisfaction of the flesh involves no satisfaction, no participation of the whole person—so that it is divided and a part of itself lags behind? . . . What remains of that division? What traces? What secret revenge is later taken by that part of the person which did not share in the banquet?

✳

They are much too anxious to know *my* thought; when writing, I am most often concerned only with theirs.

✳

The need to write novels is, it seems to me, not always very spontaneous in many young novelists of today. The supply tries to catch up with the demand. As for the desire to depict living characters, I believe it to be rather frequent. It exploits certain gifts of eye and pen. But the creation of new characters becomes a natural need only in those tormented by an imperious inner complexity and not satisfied by their own acts.

✳

It is very rash to assert that one would have thought as one did without having read certain writers who will later seem to have been your initiators. Yet it seems to me that had I not known Dostoevsky or Nietzsche or Freud or X or Z, I should have thought just as I did, and that I found in them rather an authorization than an awakening. Above all, they taught me to cease doubting myself, to cease fearing my thoughts, and to let those thoughts lead me to those lands that were not uninhabitable because after all *I found them already there.*

✳

The influences we never speak of; the strongest ones, it so happens, are the secret ones. That of women, of the public, of our juniors. It is possible to escape one or two of them, but it is very difficult, very rare, to escape all three. We let ourselves be influenced by a woman or by those whom we want to please, whose regard or esteem we want to win. The artist who is after success always lets himself be influenced by the public. Generally such an artist contributes nothing new, for the public acclaims only what it already knows, what it recognizes.

✳

Because I publish little, it is thought that I write slowly. The truth is that I go a long time without writing. The moment my brain is ready, my pen or pencil cannot go fast enough. I may perfectly well write in the train, in the subway, on the benches along the quays or on the boulevards, on a road-embankment. I have never had a "study."

When one sentence follows another, is born of the other, I feel an almost physical rapture as it swells into being. I believe that such artesian gushing forth is the result of a long unconscious preparation. Sometimes I subsequently retouch that first draft somewhat. Only the work of dovetailing and fitting together is occasionally quite painful and calls for a great concentration.

If my first drafts are occasionally marked up they are chiefly with cancellations.

✳

What is called "objectivity" today is easy for novelists devoid of inner landscape. I can state that I am interested, not in myself, but in the conflict of certain ideas of which my soul is the stage and in which I play the part less of an actor than of a spectator, a witness.

✳

In order to judge properly, one must get away somewhat from what one is judging, after having loved it. This is true of countries, of persons, and of oneself.

✳

Sleep never comes to me against a black background. It is always preceded by some vision, through which I escape from reality, so that I can truly say that I never go to sleep until I am dreaming.

✳

The book I am writing will not be good unless my first thought, my involuntary thought on awakening, is for it.

*

Never paint from nature;

Make one's preparations from nature;

But do not communicate those preparations to the reader.

Analysis must always precede synthesis; but between analysis and the work of art the difference is the same as between an anatomical drawing and a portrait. All the preparatory work must be absorbed, it must become invisible, though always present.

Just as "it is impossible to write well without skipping over intermediate ideas," as Montesquieu said, there is no work of art without short cuts.

*

"How is S. toward you?"

"He has been cold and hot in succession according to whether he thought me a royalist or a republican. As soon as he realized that I was neither, he became tepid. He grants me a certain value 'as an artist,' but considers me worthless 'as a thinker.' "

*

The Dadas, who know only too well how amusing it can be to displease, don't seem to have risen to the point of recognizing that it may be amusing to displease even them.

They are not satisfied that I wrote a book that suits them (*Les Caves*); I ought in addition not to write or have written anything but that.

Each of my books turns against the *enthusiasts* of the preceding one. This ought to teach them to applaud me only for the right reason, to take each of my books solely for what it is: a work of art.

*

Great offensive of M. in the *Revue Universelle*.
Those who attack me are not the ones I fear, but rather those who will defend me.

*

Certain days at certain moments, I completely lose the notion of reality. It seems to me that with the first misstep I shall slip over to the other side of the stage-set.

*

What they want is a criterion that will allow them not to need taste in order to judge; it is a recipe that will allow them to write masterpieces without effort, trouble, or genius.

*

It is not so much what you say in it that constitutes the value of a book as all you can't say in it—all you would like to say in it, which nourishes it secretly.

*

Fear of stumbling makes our mind cling to the banister of logic.
There is logic and then there is what eludes logic.
If my reason blames my heart for beating, I take the side of my heart.

There are those who reason and then there are those who let others reason. There are those who get along without living and then there are those who get along without being right.

In the chink of logic I become aware of myself.

O my dearest and most lovable thought, why should I try further to legitimize your birth? Did I not read this morning in Plutarch at the beginning of the biographies of Romulus and Theseus that those two great founders of cities, because they were "born secretly and of a clandestine union," were looked upon as sons of gods?

*

Every affirmation ends up in abnegation. Everything you renounce in yourself will take on life. Everything that strives to affirm itself negates itself; everything that renounces itself asserts itself.

Complete possession is proved only by giving. All you are unable to give possesses you. Without sacrifice there is no resurrection. Nothing blooms except through an offering. Whatever you aim to protect in you atrophies.

How do you know that the fruit is ripe? Simply because it leaves the branch.

*

Through renunciaton every virtue finds fulfillment. The very succulence of the fruit aims toward germination.

True eloquence foregoes eloquence. The individual never asserts himself more than when he forgets himself. Whoever thinks of himself stands in his own way. I never admire beauty so much as when it doesn't know it is beautiful.

The most stirring line is also the most resigned.

By forsaking His divinity, Christ really becomes God; and conversely by forsaking Himself in Christ, God creates Himself.

TRANSLATED BY JUSTIN O'BRIEN

AN UNPREJUDICED MIND

I

An unprejudiced mind (or one that has managed to get rid of its prejudices) is probably the rarest thing in the world; and it is to non-prejudice that I attach the greatest value.

Most often people seek in life occasions for persisting in their opinions rather than for educating themselves. Each of us looks for a justification in the event. The rest, which runs counter to that opinion, is overlooked. And the event is never so simple but that everyone can find confirmation of his convictions, even when they are most erroneous. It seems as if the mind enjoys nothing more than sinking deeper into error.

✻

"Tend toward Perfection."

Great minds tend toward banality. It is the noblest effort of individualism. But it implies a sort of modesty, which is so rare that it is scarcely found except in the greatest, or in beggars.

✻

Only a lack of imagination permits the pride of certain fools. True intelligence very readily conceives of

an intelligence superior to its own; and this is why truly
intelligent men are modest.

✳

The evenness of a flight, its steadiness, is a certain
relationship between the dimensions of the wing and
the weight of the body it supports. The whimsical gait
of certain weightless minds recalls the flight of those
broad-winged butterflies whose least flutter sweeps them
away, but without stirring the surrounding air.

✳

Keep art *on a human scale*. Proust's attention to
minute detail can divert the mind, and even more, instruct it; but I am unwilling to see in it more than a
preliminary work. Whoever limited himself to that
could not go on living; and indeed it was because he had
given up living that Proust himself was able to indulge
in it. Faced with that analysis, the public showed somewhat the same flabbergasted amazement it feels when
looking through the lens of a microscope: "What! is that
what's in my blood! . . . What's in the water I drink!
. . . in vinegar!" But it would be a great nuisance for
us to view the world always on such a scale; and furthermore, art cannot be satisfied with such a minute and
finicky approach to truth. Like life, art overrides it.
What interests and concerns me is an art that allows,
not new light on the infinite detail of the motives of
human conduct, but rather a deep stirring up and mix-
ing of that conduct.

✳

Imagination alone permits sympathy. A man is said
to be unfeeling when, incapable of imagining suffer-

ings he doesn't feel himself, he cannot sympathize with them.

∗

True kindness presupposes the faculty of imagining as one's own the sufferings and joy of others. Without imagination, there can be weakness, theoretical or practical philanthropy, but not true kindness.

∗

Who could deny that B. is intelligent?
But he is *self-satisfied*. And that excellent expression indicates that there is not much hope of seeing him ever acquire certain qualities of which he doesn't feel the need. He will be the last to notice that he lacks them.

∗

It is probably paradoxical to say that Racine would have changed Phèdre's character if the beauty of a line had required it. But it can be said fairly that the requirements of versification inspired, almost prompted, in Racine some of his most subtle, newest, and boldest observations, such as: *"Tremblante pour un fils que je n'osais trahir"* ("Trembling for a son I dared not betray"). The wonderfully elliptical "I dared not betray" whereby Phèdre, as if in spite of herself, implies that her love for Hippolyte has won out over her maternal feelings to the point of sacrificing them—that felicitous touch was obviously suggested to Racine by a certain rhythmic requirement and by the necessity of the verse.

∗

I should be inclined to appropriate La Bruyère's title as La Bruyère appropriated Theophrastus'—and the subject of his book and his way of handling it. Of

all the great works of the seventeenth century, it strikes
me that the *Caractères* is the only one that it would not
be impertinent to rewrite; I mean that it is perhaps not
too impertinent to attempt it. First of all, I must confess that my admiration for La Bruyère does not contain the same awe as my admiration for Bossuet, Molière, La Fontaine, or Corneille. Besides, he takes care to
warn us: he is depicting the men of his time, the manners of a century that is not ours. And man has probably not changed so much as our way of seeing him. So
that, at the very outset, the first sentence in his book
gives me pause: "We come too late," whereas I should
be inclined to write at the beginning of mine: "We
come too soon," for so much novelty swamps us.

✳

The beauties of La Bruyère are such that the intelligence always suffices to explain them. And he himself
is fully conscious of each of them. It is the result of
work. Not verbal, or mystical, or lyrical, or carnal, he
knows no intoxication; or at least he succumbs to none,
for whoever was never intoxicated is but a dryasdust,
and La Bruyère is not one.

✳

The book of *Caractères* is too reasonable to allow us
to discover in it much more than La Bruyère's contemporaries saw in it. No superlative suits him. With him
everything is moderate, even the love he inspires in us.
La Bruyère's moderation is exceptional in that no mediocrity of heart or mind motivates it, but rather a certain
fundamental honesty and a loathing for taking others in,
which is equaled only by a loathing for being taken in.
    La Bruyère depicts men as they are, but how they be-
come what they are he doesn't tell us, because it doesn't

interest him. No progress toward oneself. His characters are motionless. And that very immobility invites us to consign them today to the puppet-box. Not before examining them closely—for here I read in the portrait of Ménippe: "His vanity made him respectable, raised him above himself, made him become what he was not." And I am suddenly ashamed of what I wrote above. La Bruyère is so subtle—those remarks are perfect. They contain everything, even the admission that often the best in us springs from the worst in us.

*

"Writing a book is a craft." Of all La Bruyère's remarks, no other, unfortunately, has been better understood by men of letters; and today craftsmen have become so numerous that we often come to like a book because it has none of the craft on which they cast discredit.

*

Today hardly anyone dares state that he is good, that he is faithful, just, grateful; people only laugh. Whoever asserts too much that he is sincere makes people doubt of his sincerity. But all that is implied, and if it is doubted, the individual gets angry. La Bruyère writes: "No one dares say that his skin is soft, his teeth regular . . ." Of course not! Such things should be obvious. Wherefor people are silent as to their physical advantages; if there are other more hidden ones, certain self-satisfied fools have their way of boasting of them. Yet I see no reason that authorizes La Bruyère to conclude that the virtues of the heart are "considered as nothing" in comparison with the talents of the body.

✷

Jules Renard's *Journal:*
"It is not enough to be happy; in addition, it is essential that others should not be," he writes. I fear that there is more affectation of sincerity in this than true sincerity.

Many a remark of the most sensible kind: "The great error of justice is imagining that the accused always act logically."

✷

Jules Renard's *Journal.* Odd and painful impression of that life becoming progressively narrower. He cherishes his limitations, primps over his blind spots, cultivates his nearsightedness, spruces up his selfishness, and curls his baldness. From page to page can be observed —and therein lies the great interest of this diary—the progress of that emotional, and even intellectual, inhibition brought on by the demands of sincerity. Immediately after having exaggerated his admiration for Rostand's latest play, he writes:
"In Coquelin's dressing-room I tell Rostand: 'I should have been very happy if we could both have been decorated the same day. Since it is not possible, I assure you that I congratulate you without envy.'"
And he adds:
"That is not true; and as I write these lines, I begin to weep!" And farther on, after having expatiated on the quality of his envy, he backwaters: "Now, that is exaggerated. Ah, perhaps never has man spoken a single true word!" Instead of noting ingenuously that there

is no feeling so simple that it is not immediately complicated and distorted by introspection.

✳

There is no worse enemy of thought than the demon
of analogy.
"A freshly shaved field . . ."
What is more tiresome than that mania of certain
writers who cannot see an object without thinking at
once of another?

✳

Jules Renard's garden could do with a little watering.
His sentence always strangles the thought. He produces the right note, but always as a pizzicato.

✳

I am reading with rapture the new volume of Jules
Renard's *Journal* (1903 to 1907). Less shriveled up than
the preceding volume. At moments one comes on excellent, perfect touches, and sometimes even, oh surprise!
on a compassionate note.

✳

Church of Brou. Overloading: useless and cosmopoli-
tan luxury. Bought, imported art, come from a distance.
The marvel of Florence is that the art is born of the very
soil. The only really Christian art is that which, like
St. Francis, does not fear being wedded to poverty. This
rises far above art-as-ornament. Nothing is less Christian,
less spiritual than the ornamentation of Brou. Very beautiful, however, but profane. Preciosity begins with useless expense.

✱

I banish from my style bombast and prophecy, everything that hampers the progress of the thought, all ornament, all overloading: *"Que ces vains ornements, que ces voiles me pèsent"* ("How these empty ornaments and veils weigh upon me") . . . even to utter forgetfulness of any personal pretension.

✱

Inseparable from the deeper meaning, from the force and suasion of the thought, there is a certain swelling of the sentence—not redundancy, to be sure, but a depth of breath and life—a certain enamel, to which I am more sensitive than to all the rest.

✱

The soul's ambivalence of which we hear so much today has perhaps never been more powerfully expressed than in this line of Racine: *"Par quel trouble me vois-je emporté loin de moi"* ("By what perturbation am I swept outside myself").

✱

I read in Proust (*N.R.F.* for August): ". . . it was only out of her presence"—which I consider as a deplorable error; but I cannot consider as an error the use of *"réaliser"* in this sentence:

"Et d'ailleurs n'était-ce pas pour m'occuper d'eux que je vivrais loin de ceux qui se plaindraient de ne pas me voir, pour m'occuper d'eux plus à fond que je n'aurais pu le faire avec eux, pour chercher à les révéler à eux-mêmes, à les réaliser."

("And moreover was it not in order to tend to them that I lived far from those who would complain of not seeing me, in order to be more deeply concerned with them than I could have done in their presence, in order to strive to reveal them to themselves, to *realize* them.")

It seems as if Proust, by thus outlining the limits of the word, was careful to prepare an example for a future Littré.

To realize—to make real. Despite certain purists, I should dare to write: "Yes, I have gone into mourning, to be sure; but I do not realize this mourning in my heart."

✳

"Nothing is rarer than giving no importance to things that have none," Valéry writes. I don't really understand what he means. For each of us, things never have any more importance than what we give them. Literature and the fine arts, money, honors and decorations, human life, etc. We hold this or that of little account. One man attaches the greatest importance to what he has and would sacrifice the rest of the world to save his holdings. For another, nothing matters but what he covets because he hasn't it. The latter stakes everything on a future life; the former, on the present moment. The chips are down.

✳

I believe that in every circumstance I have been able to see rather clearly the most advantageous course I could follow, which is very rarely the one I did follow.

✳

At times it seems to me that I am living my life backward, and that at the approach of old age my real youth

will begin. My soul was born covered with wrinkles—
wrinkles that my ancestors and parents most assiduously put there and that I had the greatest trouble re-
moving, in some cases. I achieved this, not through
struggle, but by slowly and patiently playing a wily
game with myself. I achieved it only with the assent of
the gods.

✳

. . . for if, in *L'Immoraliste* once again, I revealed
great chunks of myself, I subsequently kept myself out
of my fiction so thoroughly that I can see how it may
have misled readers. And this was not the paradoxical
result of effort. I let myself be taken over so naturally
and fully that, for instance, I have never written anything with greater ease and rapture than Alissa's diary
and letters in *La Porte étroite* (*Strait Is the Gate*), so
comfortable and voluptuous was it for me to give her
the floor—yes, to give the floor to a less complex creature than I, who, for that very reason, had less trouble
expressing herself.

✳

I always was, I still am, bewildered in matters of
hierarchy and precedence, ever ready to step aside, to
yield, to apologize. And probably that natural inclination of mine was encouraged by the precepts of the
Gospel, which I used to take, which I still take, seriously and literally. They shaped my attitude to such a
degree that I can take nothing else seriously; that applause, decorations, honors are all but valueless to me;
that favors embarrass me, advantages disconcert me,
privileges humiliate me—as they must of necessity do
to all who hold as truths these words: "My kingdom is
not of this world. . . ." "[The] first shall be last" and

who practice this precept: "If any man . . . take away
thy coat, let him have thy cloke also."

＊

My lack of "manners" was unbelievable. Not that
my parents had brought me up badly; on the contrary,
I had received the best possible upbringing, and I don't
really know to what to attribute that lack of manners
which made me never feel completely at ease in a drawing-room or at a formal dinner. I would immediately
lose all naturalness and all native resources. Titles, in-
signia of rank, decorations made me dizzy; I could not
convince myself that the individual's value could be
recognized by his sleeve. At one and the same time I
took nothing seriously that called for reverence and was
so anxious to show reverence that I ran slap into every
rule, without rhyme or reason, ready for any self-effacement. At least that was noncommittal.

＊

My mind is, above all, inclined to organize. But my
heart suffers to leave anything outside.

And I understand only too well those who, not having the power to dominate, repulse, even before knowing them, the anarchical elements within them. But I,
convinced by experience and history that the most useful forces are those that appear the most dangerous at
first, and at the same time sure of my mind's authority,
I took care not to reject anything that I aimed to do-
mesticate because I felt sure of being able to get some
good from it.

The turbid elements of the mind will some day be
the best.

Whoever cannot tame lightning had better fear it.

*

There is not a single declaration of this type (profession of fidelity in the preface of my *Nourritures terrestres* [*Fruits of the Earth*]) that does not seem to me to ring a little false when I reread it a short time afterward.

What is the good of saying one was sincere when writing it? There is no character so simple that it does not involve complicated byways. The peculiarity that seems to win out is the one on which attention centers; the mere beholding eye already distorts and enlarges. One loses sight of the whole physiognomy, and a certain feature that one causes to dominate is perhaps not the dominant feature.

*

Because it has always been easier for me to choose and to reject in the name of someone else than in my own name, and because I always feel I am impoverishing myself when I limit myself, I am quite willing to have no well-defined existence if the individuals I create and draw from myself have one.

*

I often imagine such a preface for *L'Immoraliste, Les Faux-Monnayeurs* (*The Counterfeiters*), *La Symphonie pastorale*—one, above all, that would set forth what I mean by fictional objectivity, that would establish two sorts of novels, or at least two ways of looking at and depicting life (which in certain novels are joined).

The first, exterior and commonly called "objective,"
which begins by visualizing others' acts and events and
then explains and interprets them.

The second, which begins by paying attention to emotions and thoughts, creates events and characters most
likely to bring out those emotions, and runs the risk of
being powerless to depict anything that the author has
not first felt himself. The resources of the author, his
complexity, the antagonism of his too diverse possibilities, will permit the greatest diversity of his creations.
But everything derives from him. He is the only one to
vouch for the truth he reveals, and the only judge. The
heaven and hell of his characters is in him. It is not himself that he depicts, but he could have become what he
depicts if he had not become everything himself. Yes,
I could set forth all this. But haven't I already said it or
let it be sufficiently understood when speaking of Dostoevsky? What is the good of repeating? It is better to
say to the reader: read me more carefully; reread me;
and go on to something else.

One of the great rules of art: do not linger.

*

Nothing is accomplished if I have not truly been able
to become this character that I am creating, and to de-
personalize myself in him to the extent of being blamed
for never having managed to portray anyone but myself
—however different from one another may be Saül, Can-
daules, Alissa, Lafcadio, the minister of my *Symphonie
pastorale,* or La Pérouse or Armand. It is returning to
myself that embarrasses me, for, in truth, I no longer
really know *who* I am; or, if you prefer: I never am; I
am becoming.

✳

How well I should be if it were not for all these people shouting that I am ill!

They insist on seeing in *Les Faux-Monnayeurs* an abortive book. The same thing was said at first of Flaubert's *Education sentimentale* and of Dostoevsky's *Possessed*. (I remember that what made me read *The Possessed* and *The Brothers Karamazov* was the retreat of Melchior de Vogüé before these "apocalyptical and sinister books.") In ten or twenty years it will be recognized that what people now hold against my book are its rarest qualities.

✳

How much more flattering it is to see a critic, out of malice or spite, force himself to disparagement than, out of cliquishness, to indulgence.

✳

The finest virtues can become deformed with age. The precise mind becomes finicky; the thrifty man, miserly; the cautious man, timorous; the man of imagination, fanciful. Even perseverance ends up in a sort of stupidity. Just as, on the other hand, being too willing to understand too many opinions, too diverse ways of seeing, constancy is lost and the mind goes astray in a restless fickleness. If Maurras were not so deaf, perhaps he would not be so faithful; but it often happens that constancy precedes and involves a sort of deafness.

*

Whether I *believe* or *don't believe?*
What does it matter to you?
And what does it matter to me?
It is no more possible for me to adopt sincerely your
credo than to believe in the sun's rotation around the
earth. But, as a believer, I have known your spiritual
state. *Et ego* . . . I know that that monstrous idea,
planted in the core of our mind—the very limitation it
sets upon each of our thoughts—leads us to that emotional state of which the work of art can take advantage.
And what encourages one to think that art itself is essentially religious, what can make the *believer* believe
that art and creative power are dependent on faith, is
not only the increased eloquence the artist owes to his
faith, but also the increased receptivity on the part of
the believing auditor or spectator when faced with a
work of art of religious inspiration; it is the mystic com-
munion between artist and public, which only that common belief allows. One is in collusion. The sets are
already up, the instruments tuned, the tears ready.
Everyone feels that he belongs to the flock, to the family;
between the actor and himself (the author modestly
effaces himself), everyone feels a secret connivance.—
"That's my dish."

As for me, I want a work of art in which *nothing is
granted* in advance; before which everyone is free to
protest.

*

Nothing is more embarrassing than disciples. I have
done what I could to discourage them. I don't have

"office hours"; I don't acknowledge books that are sent to me, don't reply to letters or articles; I live far from Paris. And now I am blamed for having an influence. What can I do about it? I have always sought to encourage each in his own path and should not like to attract anyone to me.

✳

I owe much to my friends; but, all things considered, it strikes me that I owe even more to my enemies. The real person springs to life under a sting, even better than under a caress. The latter relaxes you, as Blake has said; the former braces you. In short, whenever I came to doubt myself, ready to read in praise rather a sign of others' affection than a certificate of value, the relentlessness of others in harming me and defacing my thought soon forced me to conclude in favor of its importance. I did not originally know I was so dangerous; but I am opposed, therefore I am.

✳

We call "happiness" a certain set of circumstances that makes joy possible.

But we call joy that state of mind and emotions that needs nothing to feel happy.

II

Much has been written of late (1922) about Flaubert, as to his style and whether or not he really wrote so well. When everyone talks, my only desire is to keep silent; only after everyone has ceased talking do I feel a desire to speak up. It did not seem to me (but perhaps I didn't read all the articles) that M. Souday, or M. Thibaudet, or M. X. said the most essential things; in any case I know that, despite the keen interest I had in reading them, I did not find complete satisfaction in any of their assertions,• and this is why I am now eager to enter the dance myself.

That Flaubert is not a great writer seems to me clear not only from the mediocrity of his youthful writings, as M. Thibaudet brought out very clearly, but also from his own declarations throughout his letters. He constantly returns to the subject: in comparison with a Montaigne, a Voltaire, a Cervantes, he feels like a schoolboy. Only by dint of hard work and of that patience that Buffon so speciously equated with genius did he make up for the gifts he lacked. Where born writers frolicked, he labors; from sentence to sentence his effort can be felt panting laboriously. Without going out of one's way, merely by opening Barbey d'Aurevilly's correspondence or *Memoranda,* for instance, what ease and what breadth at the same time! what tautness! what a variety of sentences, what abundance, what a happy choice of words, and what delight in the images, what sonority, what rhythm! How does it happen then that, despite this, Flaubert has so much importance for us? That he is for us, or at least was for us for so long, a companion, a master, whereas Barbey d'Aurevilly, despite such a noble bearing, has always seemed to us such a bad example, such a deplorable model? Isn't it because those gifts, which Barbey d'Aurevilly through pride and smugness used so badly, are essentially impossible to acquire, whereas the method and discipline to which Flaubert submitted are available to every one of us, even for different purposes?

No, I am not misjudging D'Aurevilly. There are not so many brilliant writers like him. At times he is amazing. But when he ceases to be amazing, he falls far below

---

• I should not have written these lines, nor probably even the following ones, if I had first read Léon Daudet's articles on Flaubert and on Barbey d'Aurevilly. In them he says excellently almost all I say here.

the mediocre. He is never willing to be natural. He is stilted. His best book is unspeakably pretentious. At one and the same time he scorns the reader and courts the reader, so that he simultaneously disdains to charm and constantly aims to amaze. His judgments are those of a simpleton. Nothing makes intelligent men more foolish than pride.

No infatuation in Flaubert. He constantly fears to be unequal to his task. He applies himself. He is never caught disregarding anything, and the wonderful remark of old Ingres (I think it is really Poussin's) "I have never neglected anything" finds constant application in his work. He is assiduous to the point of claiming (and perhaps not so paradoxically as one might first think) that inspiration consists in sitting down to one's worktable every day at the same time. He says that partly as a reaction against the romantic school, which thought that inspiration was inseparable from disorder. Many a scruple runs counter to his rapture and tempers it at once.

"But what of the work?" you will say. For in art results alone matter. Well, I must confess that, as for the works of Flaubert, I no longer admire them very much. It hurts me to write this, for it seems to me a sacrilege. Yes, I know, there is not one of his books that is not exemplary in appearance. In the *Tentation de Saint-Antoine* there are inexhaustibly sonorous groups of sentences. The *Education sentimentale* stands, despite him perhaps, as "the epic of mediocrity." And, to be sure, I could find it in me to praise each of the others. Yet it strikes me that if his entire work were to be put on one side of the scales, his letters alone on the other would weigh more. If I were allowed to save only one or the other, I should certainly take the latter.

The long article by Pierre Gilbert reprinted in *La Forêt des Cippes* angers me, for it seems to me indecent

to speak with so little respect of Flaubert; but, despite
my indignation, I am often obliged to agree with him.

*

The reasons that make those stars wane are perhaps
the very ones that linked them, according to Bourget,
to the generation preceding mine. For the moral dispositions of one generation are not at all the same as those
of the following generation. Bourget extolled the apostles of pessimism. And it is toward the constellation of
the Lion that we feel impelled today. Nothing can be
done about this; what we seek in our masters is not dis-
couragement. If Stendhal and Baudelaire still hold a
very high place in our firmament today, this is because
the rays emanating from their work have still other
virtues than those Bourget recognized in them. To tell
the truth, it is because, of the whole pleiad cited in the
Essais de psychologie, they alone are perfect artists, and
only perfect art is proof against aging.

*

The wise Sainte-Beuve denounces, I do not remember
where, that frequent intellectual failing of urging oneself by preference, and seeking invitations, in the direction in which one is most inclined by nature. And this
is what makes me so often deplore the fact that parents
should be given the care of children who already naïvely
resembles them and find in them the example and encouragement of their secret dispositions; so that, to tell
the truth, family upbringing rarely straightens them up
but simply helps them to bend in one way or another,
and the sons of set parents are even more set themselves,
bent over to the right or the left and often unable to
recover the vertical position without a revolt that is full

of risks. If I were not a lover of brevity, I should write a whole book on this subject, but one that would make people cry shame; for after all, out of some forty families I have been able to observe, I know hardly four in which the parents do not act in such a way that nothing would be more desirable for the child than to escape their influence. Some people are indignant at the alcoholic teaching his son to drink; but they, according to their lights, do not act differently.

*

Take care not to confuse art and manner. The manner of the Goncourts, which made them seem so "artistic" in their time, is the cause of their ruin today. They had delicate senses; but an insufficient intelligence made them go into ecstasies over the delicacy of their sensations and give importance to what should be subordinated. It is impossible to read a page by them on which that good opinion they have of themselves does not burst out from between the lines; they yield infallibly to that self-satisfaction which makes them think: "Ah! what artists we are! Ah! how crude other writers are!" Manner is always the indication, and it soon becomes the penalty, of a self-satisfaction. The most subtle, the strongest and deepest art—supreme art—is the one that does not at first allow itself to be recognized. True art doesn't give a rap for manner, which is but its caricature. And, just as "real eloquence doesn't give a rap for eloquence . . . ," etc.

*

The *charm* of poetry is often so subtle and depends on so little that it can be broken without changing the place of a single word.

These winged lines of Moréas sing in my memory; every inner shadow yields to their musical enchantment:

> *Je naquis au bord d'une mer dont la couleur passe*
> *En douceur le saphir oriental; des lys*
> *Y croissent dans le sable; ah! n'est-ce*
> *Ta pâle face des lys de la mer natale?* •

Without changing a word, were I to imagine them for a moment printed in the following way:

> *Je naquis au bord d'une mer*
> *Dont la couleur*
> *Passe en douceur*
> *Le saphir oriental*
> *Des lys y croissent dans le sable*
> *Ah n'est-ce ta face pâle*
> *Les lys de la mer natale*

the charm is immediately broken. And had we originally seen them printed this way, they would have seemed to us most ordinary, and none of us, however musical he was, would have imagined their native rhythm, which lifts them up and divests them of all weight.

✳

Valéry grants too little value to Hugo's *Contemplations* and to all poems in which a certain sentimental interest seems likely to compromise in his eyes the verbal purity and formal splendor. Certain poems of the *Contemplations* are in no way inferior to the poem for

---

• I was born beside a sea whose hue
Outdoes the Oriental saphire; lilies
Grow there in the sand; Ah! are you
The pale face, the lilies of my native strand?

Gautier's tomb that Valéry sets above all the others. I am well aware that what he thinks I admire in them is just that sentimentality that bothers him. In fact, it might compromise the beauty of the verse were it not for Hugo's extraordinary mastery; but from the sole point of view of technique, can anything more *clever* (and I am using this word [*habile*] to please Valéry) be cited than *"Paroles sur la dune"* ("Words Spoken on the Dune"); could there be found in all Hugo's work a more extraordinary use of the mute *e* than in the third line of the next to last stanza:

> *Comme le souvenir est voisin du remords*
> *Comme à pleurer tout nous ramène!*
> *Et que je te sens froide en te touchant, ô Mort . . .*●

Those three uses of mute *e* in succession (*"Et que je te . . ."*) after the two beautiful lines preceding, confer a funereal mystery on the word *"froide"* that follows them; those three mute steps are, indeed, a measured progress toward the tomb.●●

And in the first stanzas of the same poem (one of those by Hugo that I am most inclined to call to mind), what a masterful use of *"que"*—considered by some as annoying and such as to weigh down the sentences un-

---

● How close memory is to remorse
    How all leads to tears!
  And how cold you are to touch, O Death.
●● The same incantatory effect is found in Baudelaire's

> *A quiconque a perdu ce qui ne se retrouve*
> *Jamais, jamais.*

(To whoever has lost what can never,
Never be recaptured.)

bearably, whereas all the great writers of the seventeenth century, Bossuet in particular, knew so well how to use it.

Maintenant que *mon temps décroît comme un flambeau*
Que *mes tâches sont terminées*
Maintenant que *voici* que *je touche au tombeau.*•

Is there anything more majestic, more noble?

✳

A quarrel has quite recently been picked with Hugo about the first line of *Oceano Nox:* "*Oh! combien de marins, combien de capitaines*" ("Oh, how many sailors and how many captains"). A ridiculous quarrel. Hugo doesn't seem to suspect, it is said, that navy captains are sailors too, that the word "*marin*" embraces both enlisted men and captains. And as evidence there are cited certain lines of Tristan Corbière that supposedly rectify matters. Obviously, it could never have been Hugo's intention to oppose sailors and captains; the meaning of the line is: "Oh! how many sailors, and, among them, even captains." The word "*capitaines*" was essential for the rhyme, not only to rhyme with "*lointaines*," but the sonority of those two words was such that better ones, more evocative of a daring undertaking, could not be imagined; the word "*capitaine*" applying likewise to the army, it had to be preceded here by the word "*marin*" to indicate clearly the navy. Etc. . . .

A pedants' quarrel.

• Now that my time is waning like a candle
That my tasks are over
Now that I am approaching the tomb.

✳

Poetic crushing of thought in Baudelaire:

. . . cœur meurtri comme une pêche.
. . . . .
Va cueillir des remords dans la fête servile.●

(I don't much like *"servile."*)
That is: adulterated pleasures such that memory of
them will soon take on the color of remorse. *"Comme le
souvenir est voisin du remords,"* said Hugo in a beautiful line.

Nothing could be less poetic than an explication of
this type, than (even if merely implied, even when unconscious) the logico-moral apparatus that relates the
concepts evoked by this fragment of a sentence. Less
poetic by far than the other example, where there are
not abstract concepts but rather sensations and emotions linked by the words "bruised heart" and "peach."
A peach is not necessarily bruised, but particularly
likely to be. It is not yet bruised; it will be so. An example of poetic futurition even better than Chénier's *"l'épi
naissant mûrit"* ("the budding ear ripens") quoted by
all the manuals.

III

Might not waste be the characteristic of our era? I
wonder not so much at its dreadful consumption of systems, ethics, principles, and aesthetics as I wonder at the

---

●. . . heart bruised like a peach.
. . . .
Go gather remorse in servile gaiety.

fact that they should all be so badly consumed. The marrowbone is thrown into the garbage after the meat on it has been barely nibbled. Merely by being a rag-picker one could get the reputation of an inventor.

*

> Who but I knows what Ariadne is!
> NIETZSCHE

Thus it is that, in order not to be bothered by them, we have relegated the Greek myths to the attic, whence some poet occasionally takes them out only to clothe some thought too decrepit to go about naked. For me those fables are alive. I am very little concerned to know how they came into being, and I am willing to leave to philologists the shadowy past in which their origins are lost. I am willing to leave to historians of literature the use that the classic age and the romantics made of them. What matters to me is the way in which they touch us and what they have to say to us. Everything that comes down to us from Greece is so divinely and humanly nat-ural that every age has been able to draw sustenance from it and yet for the following generation it is all full of substance, new, and rich in meaning.

I claim to query the Greek fable in a new way and tell you that its psychological meaning is intact. That is the meaning that matters to us and that it behooves our era to bring out.

What keeps that psychological meaning from being apparent to you is that you have inherited from past generations the habit of underestimating the initiative of the demigods and heroes. With the gods it is quite different; I believe they must be granted the least possible, and for a very good reason. But as for the heroes— no, I cannot believe it was by chance or through forgetfulness that Theseus did not change the sail of the ship bringing him back from Crete. You recall that he had gone there to brave the Minotaur. His old father, Aegeus, without much hope, awaited the ship's return every day, from morning to evening, seated on a lofty promontory. And it had been agreed that if the son returned a conqueror, the ship would bear a red sail; and if he were defeated, a black sail like the mourning-sail it bore upon leaving. And the fable relates that, Theseus having *forgotten* to change the sail, his father in despair threw himself into the sea, so that on his return Theseus found but a crown. It is a very childish tale.

And I am almost on the point of admitting that Orpheus, annoyed to be followed by Eurydice, turned back in her direction, aware of his homicidal glance (see Jean-Jacques Rousseau's letter to Madame de Francœil). I recall too well that Plato accused Orpheus of cowardice for having contrived to go down to the underworld alive. I confess that I never fully understood Plato's accusation, and all I retain of it is this: that Plato did not like music. He refused musicians a place in his Republic, and when he tells us that Orpheus was cowardly, he adds: ". . . like the musician he was." Yet it is true that there was nothing of the hero about Orpheus. In Theseus, on the other hand, everything seems to me heroic; if he was cynical also, I leave it to others to be indignant about this. If he, the companion of his faithful Pirithoüs, goes down to the underworld, it is to rape Proserpina. What tempts him is the defiance: defiance of rules, of nature, of ethics, of laws. The only son he has is born of the chaste Amazon. Ariadne clings to him; he clings to Ariadne's sister. It is impossible for me to imagine him as being afraid, and when he advances in the labyrinth, it is Ariadne, not he, who fears he may get lost. The thread she attaches to his hand bothers him, and at the first stop he breaks it. I fancy him at the court of Minos, anxious to know what sort of unmentionable monster the Minotaur may be, whether he is as frightful as all that or perhaps charming? He carries off at one time the two daughters of the future judge of the underworld; by one he is loved and he loves the other, the younger one, who will prefer his son to him. In all his exploits there is something more than bold, something frenzied, abominable, and ferocious. Nothing philanthropic and kind in the manner of the good Hercules.

I query him too. He is a demigod. And if as such he is more glorious, if he is immortal, he is under compulsion and like all the earthly children of Zeus, subject to fatal laws. However there is this element that distinguishes him from all the other children of Zeus: he is moral. He is the first virtuous hero. A single and amazing exception in the whole Greek fable. But, as in the whole Greek fable I know nothing that is not motivated and justified, I seek the explanation for this exceptional character. And I wonder if any specialist in mythology has ever noticed this (but I have not found this elucidation anywhere): Alcmene, Hercules' mother, remained virtuous even when she received Jupiter into her arms, for Jupiter had to borrow the appearance of her husband to seduce her. Her conjugal fidelity was taken by surprise, and adultery hid in the guise of duty. When, later on, Hercules hesitates at the crossroads between vice and virtue, his mother's blood chooses for him. I have already said all this somewhere.

"Heredity, the only god whose real name we know,"

said Wilde. Even though they didn't name him, the
Greeks too knew him well.

✱

The books I have read on this subject have stood in
my way; I mean the books that theorize. I am not saying that they taught me nothing, but rather very little,
for most of them have set out to reduce to the same
common denominator extremely complex data that, I
confess, interest me because of their very complexity.
One of them sees in each of the Greek myths the image
of the sun and of the great Uranian phenomena; every
higher impulse, every soaring, every crescendo is the
dawn, and every decline, the evening twilight; every
combat becomes a struggle between light and darkness,
and according to whether the solar hero wins or loses,
it is said to be a morning-myth or an evening-myth;
from time to time the myth will be called lunar; at
times the seasons will be involved. Thus means are
found to explain everything, there being no fewer resources in the ingenuity of scholars than in the sky's
suggestions.• And, thanks to these explanations, the
myths become at one and the same time completely
clear and totally uninteresting. Another school (at the
moment I am writing this I believe it is the most recent)
recognizes in every great myth the monstrous growth
and exaggeration of a local custom; and that school derives from another, which went to a great effort to un-
ravel the tangle of superstitions which formed *mythology,* seeking hither and yon the origin of each of the

---

• See notes on the *Dionysiaca* of Nonnus, p. 42 (Canto XI, note 15)
regarding Ampelos: "Here, I confess, M. Creuzer seems subject to the
contemplative mania of Dupuis; and it is utterly *impossible for me to
find the slightest influence of the stars and a sidereal legend* in this
simple story of Ampelos," the Comte de Marcellus writes.

threads that the lore of very diverse peoples twined around the sensitive spindle of Greece.

That they are right I am not questioning; but this does not explain either the fortune of those myths through the arts or how, without distorting them in any way, until after the Alexandrian period they managed to satisfy the most harmonious civilization that humanity ever attempted. If they owe that concurrent harmony to that very civilization, and if each of them can be compared to a vase that each philosopher and poet slowly took care to fill, it is when the vase is full that I enjoy lifting it to my lips. It is up to the philologist to instruct me of the myth's origin; I wish to grasp it only when its meaning overflows it.

Scholars in our day are ready to demolish the finest monuments of the Forum in order to unearth the *cloaca maxima*.

May it be possible to prefer to the study of origins, to the contemplation of the seed and the egg, that of full adult beauty.

There is a point of development just before decadence sets in, when the anagenetic forces still dominate the catagenetic forces; a moment later, the inner thrust having disappeared, the form alone will remain and liberate itself; we fall into Alexandrinism; then every myth becomes fable and a pretext for ornamentation; the flower has become flourish.

✳

Probably it is not a negligible lesson to note that the ancients, and particularly the Greeks, who nevertheless knew what it means to live properly—and by "properly" I mean: living in such a way as to leave us an example of the highest virtues—that the Greeks, I say, acted definitely according to the dictates of their inclination, of their passion whether good or bad, of their virtue, of their pride or their fancy. But they never had to deliberate at length to find which of several resolutions the reason would consider preferable, as we constantly do today—eager as we are to choose the best of all possibilities, that is to say, the most advantageous for God, for others, for the public weal, for ourselves (according to our degree of virtue).

And even if, on occasion, those Greeks came to deplore the consequences of this or that deed, such regrets did not bear upon the act itself and involved neither repentance nor remorse; it never seemed to them that they could have acted otherwise. With the sole exception of Hercules, no demigod or hero of antiquity hesitates or weighs things in the balance. Each of them acts according to the prompting of his deepest nature; and don't you think that the word that best suits all their wonderful deeds, the most virtuous as well as the worst, is the word "thoughtless"? •

Don't you think that this is the appropriate way to act, and that the thoughtless act has a great chance of also being the wisest, for we know only too well that, the more the reason tries to intervene in action, the more we are kept from acting? For the immediate or remote consequences of the least of our acts are infinite; for acting according to the weight of the greater number of motives is not acting in a very sincere way. Most often instinct is a better guide than reason.

*

What an absurd thing, that fear of the self in literature: fear of talking of oneself, of being interested in

• The wonderful figure of Ulysses does not fit what I am stating here; there is so much common sense and wile in him that he is almost antiheroic, for, as Montaigne says, "nothing noble is done without chance."

oneself, of showing oneself. (Flaubert's need of mortification made him invent that false, that deplorable virtue.)

Pascal blames the talk of self in Montaigne, seeing in it a ridiculous itching, but is never so great as when he himself yields to it, despite himself. Were he to write: "Christ shed his blood for mankind," his words would strike us without force. As soon as the "I" intervenes, all springs into life, and when that God comes and addresses him personally: "I shed this drop of blood for thee." This particular drop for thee, Blaise Pascal . . . At once each of us feels included in this adorable use of "thee."

*

The great difference between Christianity and paganism: •

Zeus crucifies Prometheus.

God offers his Son to be crucified by men. He is "in collusion"!

I really believe that is the central point, and the most important.

*

Greece—where one could change gods without thereby changing religions—did not aim to set up before men a sort of moral canon, as she did a physical canon.

A shifting equilibrium of virtues.

• I had originally written: "the great superiority of Christianity over paganism"; but is it correct to see superiority in this?

*

And if, in the bottom of Pandora's box Christianity were to be found, my word! I should not be too surprised.

*

Kingdom of God. Eternal life. Life in the eternity of the moment.

. . . *nunc, in tempore hoc* (Mark 10:29)

even now.

. . . *et nunc est* (John 4:23; 5:25).

No, vainly you search the Scriptures to find the promise and assurance of another life.

"Search the scriptures; for in them ye think ye have eternal life: and they are they which testify of me. And ye will not come to me, that ye might have life" (John 5:39-40).

"The kingdom of God cometh not with observation: Neither shall they say, Lo here! or, lo there! for, behold, the kingdom of God is within you" (Luke 17:20-1).•

*

"But," G. told me soon after his conversion, "it is a serious error, and a particularly Protestant error, to

• [Gide gives this passage from Luke in the King James translation.]

believe that the word of God is found only in the Gospels. God has never ceased speaking since the creation of the world, and the revelation is uninterrupted. I listen to God in the Gospels, but it is just as much His voice that I hear in the latest encyclical. . . ."

How pleasant it is, in contrast, to reread the *Mémorial de Pascal:* "Forgetfulness of the world and of all, except God. *He is found only through the means taught by the Gospels."*

And farther on:

"Jesus Christ . . . May I never be separated from Him. *He is preserved only through the means taught by the Gospels."*

What is the strange story of the three lines in which a "confessor" is mentioned—lines that don't figure in the autograph manuscript of the Bibliothèque Nationale and are perhaps not by Pascal?

Such as it is, the Gospel is enough for me. As soon as I face it again, everything again becomes luminous for me. Man's explanation only darkens it.

✳

Whereas other religions managed to form nations in their image, why this bankruptcy, this inadequacy? Is it not surprising that solely Christian nations were able to create the civilization most remote from the precepts of the Gospel, most opposed to any form of Christian life?

But when I seek Christ, I find the priest; and behind the priest, Saint Paul.

✳

I take the Gospels as they come to us and leave to exegetes the problem of determining whether or not certain lines, in which I see already an attempt at interpretation, were added subsequently: "But this spake he of the Spirit, which they that believe on him should receive: *for the Holy Ghost was not yet given;*• because that Jesus was not yet glorified" (John 7:39).

nondum enim erat Spiritus datus.

But, moreover, after Pentecost the Apostle had no further reason to put divine felicity in the future.

"But will you not be led to look upon hell also as immanent, so to speak, and already finding in present life the immediate realization of its horror?"

"I grant that every lucid sinner can have an immediate and total foretaste of hell. And isn't this already hell: knowing the place of rest, knowing the way to it and the door, and being barred from entering? Feeling the light of love darkening, the envelope of flesh thickening, that flesh constantly growing heavier and oneself ever becoming more attached to it? Stagnation is always spoken of in connection with hell and this absence of progress is made the last degree of the horrible. But there is worse: there is the slow progress in estrangement as there is progress in the union of love. It is not sudden darkness, but a progressive dimming. Hell—just like paradise—is within us. Milton expresses this wonderfully in this line, when he makes Satan himself say:

Which way I flie is Hell; my self am Hell;
(*Paradise Lost*, IV, 75.)••

• [The emphasis is Gide's.]
•• [Gide quotes the original English.]

*

But what happens? Simply that Christ himself has been made responsible for . . .

. . . which springs only from you. Simply that, wishing to repudiate this that is false, we find ourselves led to reject at the same time that which is just; to reject at the same time Him who is just. It is a cross of lies to which you have so solidly nailed Him that the wood cannot be removed without tearing the flesh.

"But," you say, "that Christ could not stand alone. Henceforth He needs that backing, that brace . . ."

"If your love is strong enough to allow Him to live again, He will be able to leave that cross."

*

Gospel. Through and through a work of life, a work of joy. (See John 8:51.)

It is because "they shall be comforted" that Christ says "blessed are they that mourn." He weeps but once Himself: when faced with death. His first miracle is to increase *joy*. His first word is *"Blessed."*

But he wants a joy that even the poorest can achieve —and even a joy that only poverty can give.

Take the words of Christ literally.

People try to cheat with Him like Sapphira.

When He says: "sell all that thou hast," this is not an image, nor is it a command. It is a secret *of happiness*. The *kingdom of God* is just that—a *state of joy* that only *poverty* can give.

Worry ceases at the same time as the feeling of individual possession, of individual limitation.

"Take no thought for your life, what ye shall eat, or what ye shall drink; nor yet for your body, what ye shall put on," etc.

"It is easier for a camel to go through the eye of a needle, than for a rich man to enter into the kingdom of God."

When intelligent people pride themselves on not understanding, it is quite natural that they should succeed better than fools. The camel has been discussed, the eye has been discussed, the needle has been discussed, and people have above all discussed to find out to what degree the rich man could or could not approach the kingdom of God. Yet what is more luminous than the word of the Gospel? It should be clear to the blindest that for "a camel to go through the eye of a needle" is the Oriental equivalent of "jumping over the moon" or some other image of which the utter absurdity tends to exaggerate the *impossible*.

It simply means: it is *impossible*, forever impossible, and among impossible things there is none more completely impossible than this: a rich man in the kingdom of God. The kingdom of God is formed of the surrender of riches.

Nothing is heavier, more important than this: necessity of option between the temporal and the spiritual. The possession of *the other world* is based on the renunciation of this world.

✳

Consequently, even the Gospel according to Mark, the oldest, had already felt the influence of Paul. It is essential above all to explain that influence.

Certainly Christ and his disciples on their way to Jerusalem were marching toward triumph—Christ with the certainty of his divine vocation. There was, in the eyes of the world at least, complete failure. This is the first thing that it was important to save. It was essential to work for the justification of the cross, of the torment, of the ignominy to which that career seemed to lead. It was essential to show that that end had been foreseen, show that it was necessary to the accomplishment of the Scriptures and likewise to the salvation of humanity. And that Christ died *because* of sinners, or *for* sinners; the distinction was mystically so delicate that it was easy to pass from one to the other and that a happy confusion grew up in favor of Saint Paul's preaching. People ceased to see Christ anywhere save on the cross; the cross became the indispensable symbol. It was the mark of ignominy that it was important to glorify most. Only thus could appear as triumphant, in spite of everything, the work of the one who called himself the Son of God.

That was indispensable in the beginning; for the official recognition and propagation of the doctrine.

But, after all, that ignominious end, though it became indispensable to the dogma, was in no wise a part of the very teaching of Christ. It was, on the contrary, its check, or rather the supreme obstacle over which the lesson of happiness (see the words spoken on the cross) was likewise to triumph.

No matter: once that doctrine had mastered minds and hearts—that is to say, when people felt they had a right to seek out Christ before the torment, and in the fullness of his *joy*—it was too late; the cross had overcome Christ himself; it was Christ crucified that people continued to see and to teach.

And thus it is that that religion came to plunge the world into gloom.

✳

"In order to speak in this tendentious way you are very careful to forget the texts of the Gospel in which, well before the crucifixion, Jesus speaks of his cross and says that, without taking up one's cross, one must not try to follow him."

"That is true. That is why I did not give out this page at first. But if it is proven to me that those texts are apocryphal and interpolated—does not the tacit admission of the need that was felt for them reinforce what I am saying?

TRANSLATED BY JUSTIN O'BRIEN

Index